ZEE EDGELL was born and grew up in Belize City, Belize. One of her first jobs in the early 1960s was as a reporter on the *Daily Gleaner* in Kingston, Jamaica. From 1966–1968 she taught at St Catherine Academy and worked as the editor of a small newspaper in Belize City. She has lived in Jamaica, Britain, Afghanistan, Nigeria, Bangladesh and Somalia. In the early 1980s she returned to Belize to teach and served as the Director of the Women's Bureau in the Government of Belize (1981–82) and later as the Director of the Department of Women's Affairs (1986–87). Zee lectured at the University College of Belize from 1988–1989, and was a Visiting Writer in the Department of English at Old Dominion University, Norfolk, Virginia in the USA in 1993. She is currently an Associate Professor in the Department of English at Kent State University in Ohio, USA.

Beka Lamb (Heinemann, 1982) was awarded the 1982 Fawcett Society Book Prize. Edgell's short story, 'My Uncle Theophilus', won the Canute A. Brodhurst Prize for short fiction and was published in *The Caribbean Writer* in 1999. She has also had published *In Times Like These* (Heinemann, 1991), *The Festival of San Joaquin* (Heinemann, 1997) and *Time and the River* (Heinemann, 2007). In 2007 Zee received an MBE from the Queen for her services to literature and to the community.

ZEE EDGELL

BEKA LAMB

Orders: please contact Bookpoint Ltd, 130 Park Drive, Milton Park, Abingdon,
Oxon OX14 4SE. Telephone (44) 01235 827720. Fax: (44) 01235 400454.
Email education@bookpoint.co.uk Lines are open from 9 a.m. to 5 p.m.,
Monday to Saturday, with a 24-hour message answering service.
You can also order through our website:
www.hoddereducation.com

Text © Zee Edgell 1982
Study notes © Evelyn O'Callaghan 1986

First published 1982
Study notes first published 1986
Second edition with study notes published 2007

20 19 18 17
IMP 10 9 8 7 6 5 4 3

British Library Cataloguing in Publication Data
is available from the British Library on request.

ISBN 978 0 435988 46 3

All rights reserved. No part of this publication may be reproduced
in any form or by any means (including photocopying or storing it in
any medium by electronic means and whether or not transiently or
incidentally to some other use of this publication) without the written
permission of the copyright owner, except in accordance with the
provisions of the Copyright, Designs and Patents Act 1988 or under
the terms of a licence issued by the Copyright Licensing Agency,
Saffron House, 6–10 Kirby Street, London EC1N 8TS (www.cla.co.uk).
Applications for the copyright owner's written permission should be
addressed to the publisher.

Cover illustration by Ian Pollock
Cover design and typesetting by Sara Rafferty

Printed and bound by CPI Group (UK) Ltd, Croydon, CR0 4YY

For permission to use two lines from 'Land of the Gods' by
Dr Selwyn Walford Young, the publishers gratefully acknowledge
Miss Rita Young and Mrs Jean Campbell

To my family

CHAPTER 1

On a warm November day Beka Lamb won an essay contest at St. Cecilia's Academy, situated not far from the front gate of His Majesty's Prison on Milpa Lane. It seemed to her family that overnight Beka changed from what her mother called a 'flat-rate Belize creole' into a person with 'high mind'.

'Befo' time,' her Gran remarked towards nightfall, 'Beka would never have won that contest.'

It was not a subject openly debated amongst the politicians at Battlefield Park — a small, sandy meeting ground near the centre of town. At home, however, Beka had been cautioned over and over that the prizes would go to bakras, panias or expatriates.

'But things can change fi true,' her Gran said, slapping at a mosquito.

The front verandah was in its evening gloom, and the honeyed scent of flowering stephanotis, thickly woven into the warping latticework, reminded Beka of the wreaths at her greatgranny's funeral. The vine half-screened the verandah from excessive sunlight during the daytime, and at night, provided a private place from which to observe passersby. Beka fingered the seed pod that dropped like a green mango from the glossy leafed vine. Her Gran continued,

'And long befo' time, you wouldn't *be* at no convent school.'

On the far side of the street below, Miss Eila limped her way to the waterside, a slop bucket heavy in her right hand. As she drew abreast the Lamb yard, she called,

'Any out tonight, Miss Ivy?' Beka was grateful for a slight breeze that carried the bucket's stench away from the house.

'One or two, Eila,' Beka's Gran called across, brushing at her ankles with a cloth she used as a fly whisk. Steadying the swing, she got up and leaned on folded arms over the railing,

'The boys went into prison this morning, Eila! Going to the meeting tonight?'

'Shurest thing, Miss Ivy,' Eila said, turning into the lumber yard opposite on her way to the creek.

The People's Independence Party, formed nearly two years before, was bringing many political changes to the small colony. And Beka's grandmother, an early member of the party, felt she deserved some credit for the shift Beka was making from the washing bowl underneath the house bottom to books in a classroom overlooking the Caribbean Sea.

Miss Ivy wasn't completely at ease with the shift. But whenever her daughter-in-law, Lilla, had troubles with her eyes, Miss Ivy washed and ironed the family's clothes so that Beka could study. At those times, however, she seldom failed to comment that at fourteen, Beka's age, she had long been accustomed to handling a bowl and iron alone, and do some cooking as well.

'Gran?' Beka said, lifting her head off her knees. 'What woulda happen to me before time?'

Miss Ivy glanced over to the corner of the verandah where Beka sat on the floor twisting the seed pod around and around. Beka had been asking that same question since she was ten years old, and Miss Ivy always tried to explain the present to Beka with stories about the past. But Lilla had told Miss Ivy during their last big quarrel to please stop filling Beka's head with old-time story. Lilla said it would make Beka thin-skinned and afraid to try. Miss Ivy picked the square of laundered flour sacking off the swing, and with it began a slow flap, flapping against her legs.

'Eh, Gran?'

'If you turn that pod around one mo' time, Beka Lamb, it will pop right off the vine!'

'But Granny Ivy . . .'

'Eila coming back,' Miss Ivy said.

In the sawmill yard across the street, Beka watched Miss Eila's rinsed-out enamel pail glinting in the abruptness of complete nightfall. Dousing her flashlight, Miss Eila crossed the street, and paused by the picket fence. Miss Eila had lost most of her front teeth. Beka couldn't see her face clearly in the dark, but the two teeth she had remaining on either side of her gum space gleamed white like the posts that supported Government House gate.

'Flies really bad at waterside, Miss Ivy,' she said, brushing her frock tail against her legs.

'Sawdust in that swamp by the creekside would help with these flies,' Miss Ivy replied. 'And I suppose the Comp'ny will wait for more accident befo' that latrine bridge gets fixed.'

There was no sound from Miss Eila for a while. In the quiet before Friday night began, Beka heard the insistent grumblings of frogs, and the nervous continuous shrilling of every cricket in the high grass of the swamp opposite. Miss Eila's flashlight licked against the bucket handle.

'But look how Toycie gone – eh Miss Ivy? December comin' will make it four months.'

'Too soon to stop the grievin', Eila, but time to start.' Miss Ivy said.

'My sister will never forgive me, you know Miss I. She only lent Toycie to me.'

'You gave of your best to Toycie for fourteen years, Eila, ever since Toycie was three, so your sister can hardly grieve more than you.'

Beka slapped at a mosquito whining around her face, and Miss Eila called a little louder,

'That you up there, Beka pet?'

'Yes, Mam.'

'I hear you pass first term, Beka.' Miss Eila said.

'Yes, Mam.'

'She win that contest too, you know, Eila,' Miss Ivy interjected.

'Tell me ears now! Keep it up, pet. Toycie woulda win the music prize.'

'There was no music contest, Eila,' Miss Ivy said, 'and whatever happened to that guitar?'

'It's still there in the house, Miss Ivy. I cover it with some crocus bag.'

'You should sell it in these hard times.'

'Maybe I'll do just that, Miss Ivy. I eat soso rice and beans Sunday to Sunday since devaluation.'

'Eila,' Miss Ivy said as if reminded of something, 'come early so we can get a seat near the rostrum this time.'

'Shure thing, Miss Ivy,' Eila said picking up her bucket.

As Miss Eila began moving off down the street towards her

house, Miss Ivy called laughingly after her,

'And don't forget your stool, Eila!'

'Gran!' Beka exclaimed, scandalized.

'Well, she never even bring a box to sit upon the last time she was at Battlefield,' her Gran retorted in anger. 'Can't you take a little joke nowadays?'

'Eila must be getting over Toycie if she's going to the meeting tonight,' Miss Ivy said after a while. 'You coming too, Beka?'

'Not tonight, Gran,' Beka answered.

Miss Ivy got out of the swing, settled her bosom, and without saying another word to her grand-daughter, limped on fat, varicose-veined legs into the house.

Beka went over to the swing and sat down. Street lights came on illuminating the wire baskets of lavender bush-orchids her mother strung at intervals high along the front wall of the house. It wasn't quite seven o'clock, but a few shopkeepers on the corner opened their doors and windows spreading rectangles of light onto Cashew Street where it became Manatee Lane. Outside Gordillo's Grocery and Dry Goods, the Salvation Army captain and three women were setting up a drum. A man in a white suit and Panama hat peddled lottery to a scrawny creole woman standing in the mud-caked drain. A customer in Chico's Saloon and Bar punched the juke box. Street boys lounging near the doorway broke into song and dance, punctuating the American pop tune with sharp claps as they moved sideways together in a straggly chorus line. The Salvation Army drum began to boom boom boompety, boom. Tambourines jangled.

Loud laughter came from down the street. A dancing boy with a deep manish tone shouted,

'Soldier taffee!'

Beka pulled the swing against the verandah railing and peered over. National Vellor was coming down the street pretending to ignore the hisses, boos and mimicry of the boys playing men outside Chico's Saloon and Bar. A purple velvet dress flopped around her ankles. She swung along on gold, high heeled sling backs, and the silver sequins on her bag winked on and off. Beka went quickly over to the bushy end of the stephanotis vine where she couldn't be seen from the street. She felt ashamed of herself. Vellor had tried hard to save Toycie, but Lilla had said, only the night before,

'If I catch you conversing with that half-crazy coolie woman once more, Beka Lamb, I'll report you to your father!'

Her mother watched her of late, Beka felt, like a john crow eyeing dead crab.

Vellor clacked by in a stink of Kus Kus perfume. Her straight black hair was swept to the side in a sweep, and the rhinestones of her comb glittered. She didn't so much as glance up at the house. Beka wondered if Vellor had a date in town with one of the British soldiers stationed at Airport Camp, nine miles from Belize.

Miss Ivy came out of the house, a three-legged stool tucked under one arm.

'That Jamaican lawyer might talk at the meeting tonight, Beka.'
'About what, Gran?'

"Bout why he couldn't save Pritchad and Gladsen from going to jail. Why don't you put on your shoes and come? There's no school tomorrow.'

'Not tonight, Gran.' Beka said, 'I just feel tired.'

'All right then, but try not to fret too much, especially on a day like today. I'll wait for Eila outside the gate.'

'Bye, Gran,' Beka said as Miss Ivy grunted her way down the front steps.

Beka yawned and stretched out full length on the verandah floor. No wake had been held for Toycie, not even one night's worth. Miss Eila had explained to her Gran that times were too hard to hold a proper nine nights for Toycie, especially as Miss Eila didn't belong to a lodge or a syndicate. Miss Ivy offered to pay for the food, but Miss Eila's refusal had been strong.

'Toycie would not have want me to put misself in Poor House over wake, thank you all the same, Miss Ivy,' she'd said.

Beka felt that a wake should have been held for Toycie, at least a remembrance in the privacy of Beka's own heart. Through the space between the railing and the floor, Beka could see Toycie's house down the street. Miss Eila was padlocking the door before coming to meet Granny Ivy who was clearing her throat impatiently as she waited at the gate.

Beka hesitated. It was only today, with a small success of her own, and the panic and fright subsiding, that she dared pause for breath. She turned her head consciously in her mind, expecting to take one quick look before continuing a flight she had begun. But the past surprised her, the pain wasn't so bad anymore! She stayed longer, turned fully around, caught glimpses of sun shafts, the glint of the sea, a slight brown-skinned figure with crinkly hair made a bird's nest by the wind, running along the hot sand path at Fisherman's Town ...

'I'm so sleepy now, Toycie gial,' Beka muttered to herself, 'so sleepy and tired, but I'll keep a wake for you when I wake, I swear by jumby's block.'

CHAPTER 2

In her dream, barefooted old men, trousers rolled to their knees, were chaining off the bridge approaches, in front and behind her, to prevent people, trucks, cars, mules, carts and bicycles from delaying the five o'clock swinging of the bridge. Beka rushed along the aisle nearest the market desperate to reach Northside before the bridge swung to the middle of the creek to give waiting sailboats a passage from the sea to the creek. She screamed above the uproar,

'I'm coming! Please wait 'pon me, sa!'

It was too late. The bridge, shuddering beneath her feet, began turning slowly away from the shore. Back and forth along the narrow aisle she ran, stopping again and again to shout and beat on the high iron wall separating the main traffic line from the pedestrian aisle. But the rattle and creak of machinery, and the noise from both sides of the creek, prevented the operators behind the wall from hearing her voice.

Laughing uproariously, the crowd pressed against the barriers, pointing elongated fingers to where she now stood exhausted, clinging to the railing. She felt shrunken except for her head which had grown to the size of a large calabash. Bicycle bells rang continuously. The chain attendant shouted directions she couldn't hear. Drivers honked their horns, short beeps and then longer blasts like the sawmill whistle. Sailors standing on the decks of their boats stretched muscled brown arms upwards, calling,

'Jump, nigger gial, jump! We'll ketch you!'

Beka stared at the laughing faces below her, and at the whiskered catfishes nibbling at the filth floating on the surface of the water. Without warning, the bridge canted downwards propelling Beka into the waters and excrement of Haulover Creek . . .

The tapping of the adding machine woke her up. The shops were shuttered and barred for the night. It was after nine o'clock. A rain breeze was rising, and her heart thumped in her chest like a pestle pounding plaintains. Slowly she got to her feet and stumbled into the house. The polished pinewood floor felt cool underfoot. Bill Lamb was at his desk under the attic stairs in the dining room. A tin of coffee anchored a stack of waybills on the table behind him. Beka leaned against the table rubbing one dusty foot against the other, watching her father tap out a long row of numbers. Finally she asked,

'Importing coffee from Guatemala now, Dad?'

'What do you mean by "now"? Belize has always traded with the Republics around here,' Bill Lamb answered, turning to peer at Beka over the top of his rimless glasses.

'But you said that since Guatemala wants to take over Belize, it was dangerous to have contact with them.'

'When did you hear me say such a thing?'

'That time you and Granny Ivy quarrelled about P.I.P. maybe getting money from Guatemala to help start the party.'

'There's an alligator under my bed! I said, bad as it is, the British brand of colonialism isn't the worst we could have. Our politicians are new to politics, and they'd better watch which countries they accept aid from including Guatemala. I didn't say a word about trading.'

'Can they take us over?'

'Who, Beka?'

'The Guatemantecans!'

'Britain and Guatemala signed that treaty, Beka. It's not really our quarrel, but how should I know? Look what happened to India after the last world war! Look at the mess in the Caribbean! After all that how can a few people here matter that much?'

'What happened in those places, Dad?'

'I am busy tonight, Beka. Several ships came in yesterday. Why don't you go to bed — it's late.'

'I just woke up, Daddy!' Beka said sitting down on a chair.

In the brief sketch of the colony Beka had studied at school, there was a drawing of two black men, bare to the waist, standing on either side of the spreading branches of a mahogany tree. One held an axe, the other, a saw. Beka had been told in history class, the year she failed first form, that the Latin words beneath the picture meant: 'Under the shade we flourish.'

Beka, who had never seen a mahogany tree in her life, examined the laughing senorita decorating the label of the coffee tin. The Lamb family was black, but it was not one of those that flourished under the shade of a mahogany tree. Beka couldn't think of many families that did nowadays except maybe shareholders of the British Lumber Company, who still owned much of the forests where the mahogany grew. Her family seemed to be doing all right, though, under Blanco's Import Commission Agency. People depended on condensed milk imported from abroad, as well as flour, rice, beans and many other basic commodities needed to sustain life. Moreover, Beka's Dad was too impatient a man, he said, to subject himself to the uncertainties of the mahogany tree scattered fewer than ten to an acre out in the bush.

'May I have some?' Beka asked.

'Some of what, Beka?'

'Dis here cawfee.'

'At this time of night? Gial, what is wrong with you of late?'

Her father's bloodshot eyes glared round at her. The electric light above his desk make his forehead shine. The workers at the bond shed near the sea called him 'Wild Bill' behind his back. But Granny Ivy said unless Daddy Bill got wild, the workers at the shed would let the boxes pile high in the warehouses, and then Daddy Bill would be in trouble. Of course, Granny Ivy always added, wages everywhere were so low, you couldn't blame them for stretching out the work or dropping a box now and then and splitting the goods amongst themselves, especially at Christmas time.

As if remembering that Beka had redeemed herself earlier that day, his eyes softened as he said,

'All right, Beka, one spoonful.'

Jumping up, Beka went into the kitchen and removed a pottery mug from a high shelf her mother reserved for the promotional gift items her Dad brought home from work. 'Drink Scotch Whisky' was fired in blue glaze across the front of the big mug. She filled it with water from the thermos, sweetening the scalding water with a generous amount of condensed milk from a tin in the grocery safe. Stirring the milk and water, Beka returned to the dining room. *The Bulletin* lay on the table next to the coffee tin. The headlines read: PRITCHAD, GLADSEN IMPRISONED TODAY MEETING AT BATTLEFIELD TONIGHT. Restlessly, Beka flipped through the four pages. She was beginning to regret not going to the meeting with her Granny Ivy.

The door leading to the other part of the house was closed against the noise of the adding machine. She turned the knob. Her small brothers were asleep on cots drawn close together under a large square mosquito net. Passing them quietly, she tiptoed into her parents' room. Lilla lay on her stomach, peering through the blinds. Beka knew that her mother was worrying about her rose plants, and hoping it would rain once more before the dry season began. Two years earlier, all her bushes dried up in the drought. Miss Ivy and Lilla exchanged words because Granny Ivy felt that Lilla had no business 'going on so bad over rose bush when people out district watching corn and yams shrivel under the sun.'

When the rains finally came that drought year, Beka's Dad tried to persuade Lilla to concentrate on bougainvillea, crotons, and hibiscus. Plants like these grew easily and luxuriantly in the yard, but Lilla kept those trimmed back, and continued to struggle year after year in her attempt to cultivate roses like those she saw in magazines which arrived in the colony three months late from England.

'How are your eyes, Ma?' Beka whispered from the doorway. A small fan rattled as it whirled from left to right on the bedside table.

'Not too bad, Beka, and the headache is gone.'

'Do you want your headcloth wet with more bay rum?' Beka asked, going further into the room.

'All right.'

Beka took a green pint bottle off the table, sat on the edge of her Dad's bed, and began saturating the cloth her mother passed to her. The rummy smell burned Beka's nostrils making her eyes water. Lilla raised herself up on the pillow and Beka retied the cloth firmly around her head.

'Shall I switch off the fan? It's cooling down.'

'No, leave it on. And, Beka?'

'Yes, Mama?'

'Can you manage to pass the other two terms?'

'I'll try, but this last one was very hard.'

'Things won't always be as bad as it's been for you these last months. If you manage to finish school, your education will help you to reach a clearing.'

'Then what do I do?'

'There are more opportunities nowadays, man.'

'You think so, Mama?'

'I hope so, Beka.'

'I'll try then,' Beka said. 'Night, Ma.'

'Night, Beka pet. Leave the verandah door unlocked for your Gran but fasten the shutters upstairs — it will rain.'

In the dining-room once more, Beka quickly shovelled three heaped teaspoons of coffee into her mug of milky water and called,

'Night, Dad,' as she started to climb the stairs to the attic floor she shared with her Gran.

CHAPTER 3

Beka found the place in the middle of her bed where the spring sagged. She sat there, legs crossed, stirring her coffee, gazing through the open window, enjoying the rain breeze tumbling over her, filling her ears like water, releasing the tensions which had built up within her during the heat, humidity and excitement of the day. Overhead, pyramiding clouds blue-blacked the sky. In neighbouring yeads, the feather-shaped branches of coconut trees shivered and soughed in the rising wind. Tomorrow, young emerald green nuts with brown scalloped caps would be scattered upon the ground, and children would collect the treasures in tin cans to play at market beneath the trees.

At times like these, Beka was glad that her home was one of those built high enough so that she could look for some distance over the rusty zinc rooftops of the town. Many of the weathered wooden houses, built fairly closely together, tilted slightly as often as not, on top pinewood posts of varying heights. In the streets, by night and by day, vendors sold, according to the season, peanuts, peppered oranges, craboos, roasted pumpkin seeds, and coconut sweets under lamp-posts that also seemed at times to lean. For a while, after heavy rainstorms, water flooded streets and yards at least to the ankles.

A severe hurricane early in the twentieth century, and several smaller storms since that time had helped to give parts of the town the appearance of a temporary camp. But this was misleading, for Belizeans loved their town which lay below the level of the sea and only through force of circumstances, moved to other parts of the country. It was a town, not unlike small towns everywhere perhaps, where each person, within his neighbourhood, was an individual with well known characteristics. Anonymity, though not unheard of, was rare. Indeed, a Belizean without a known legend was the most talked about character of all.

It was a relatively tolerant town where at least six races with their roots in other districts of the country, in Africa, the West Indies, Central America, Europe, North America, Asia, and other places, lived in a kind of harmony. In three centuries, miscegenation, like logwood, had produced all shades of black and brown, not grey or purple or violet, but certainly there were a few people in town known as red ibos. Creole regarded as a language to be proud of by most people in the country, served as a means of communication amongst the races. Still, in the town and in the country, as people will do everywhere, each race held varying degrees of prejudice concerning the others.

The town didn't demand too much of its citizens, except that in good fortune they be not boastful, not proud, and above all, not critical in any unsympathetic way of the town and country. Then in bad times, whether individuals forsook the common reality, murdered or went bankrupt, Belizeans generally rallied around to assist in whatever ways they could. The townspeople rewarded those citizens perceived as truly loyal, with a devoted tolerance that lasted for generations.

The inhabitants of the other five districts of the country, and those living on some of the offshore islands, seemed to feel more or less about their towns and villages as the Belizeans felt about Belize, the main town. In times of danger, it was a tradition for all races to present a united front.

Beka moved nearer the barred window, her nightgown ballooning about her. A nurse, going on night duty at the Belize Hospital, struggled on her bicycle against the wind, a starched white cap in one hand. It was Nurse Palacio. She, too, had tried to save Toycie.

When Toycie was alive, the girls used to take Beka's brothers, Chuku and Zandy, for walks nearly every Sunday evening. They titivated in their respective houses for hours after lunch, meeting on the streets after the heat of the sun had abated, in ballerina length dresses of swishy waterwave taffeta and tulle, a little shorter and a little less elaborate than those evening gowns worn by women of the community to live band dances held on a Saturday night. Sunday evening was a time when Belizeans promenaded through the streets in their finest clothes, visited friends and relatives, or went, later in the evening, to one of Mr Blanco's cinemas to see an American film. Many, dressed more modestly, sat on front verandahs after the afternoon nap, to observe and comment upon the passing parade. Beka always had strict instructions from her mother not to take the boys to 'anybody's house'. They were to walk with them 'out front'.

Three streets fronted the sea. Beka and Toycie often dawdled outside Toycie's gate trying to decide which street they would choose for their walk that evening. They took it in turns.

Toycie most often chose Fort George where the wealthier elements of the community lived. There they would wheel the big pram up and down the streets of the neighbourhood where many expatriates lived, admiring the quiet and lovely houses and gardens, stopping for a while opposite the Fort George Hotel, where Toycie's boyfriend, Emilio Villanueva, worked some Sundays as a substitute waiter. They would pause self-consciously by the sea-wall, craning their necks as they tried to catch glimpses of Emilio carrying trays of whiskies and rum punches to visitors from overseas who were sitting or standing on the verandah overlooking the swimming pool and the sea.

Sometimes, waiting for Emilio to come off duty and walk home with them, Beka and Toycie lay on the grass at the base of the lighthouse, towering above Baron Bliss' grave, allowing the boys to run loose with other children in the overgrown grass of the small park opposite. They never failed to make up stories about why the crippled British Baron had left his entire fortune to the country. The girls thought he was very lucky to be buried on a knoll overlooking the sea rather than in a swampy hole at Lord's Ridge cemetery. Waves crashed against huge rocks at that point of land. Boats sailed home, flotilla-like from the coral islands, and the girls could speculate on the cargo of foreign vessels, which had been guided by local pilots through the natural channels of the barrier reef that bracketed the coast from Ambergris Caye, in the north, to the Sapodilla Cayes, in the south.

Beka preferred Southern Foreshore on Southside. On those Sundays, the girls walked slowly down Cashew Street as far as the post office, crossing the swing bridge on the fire station side. If the boys were sitting quietly in the pram, they stopped in the pedestrian aisle, facing the rear of the market, looking over the railing at idle sailing dories from which fishermen, early on weekday mornings, delivered loggerhead turtles, barracudas, king fish, and red-tailed snappers to bidding stall-keepers. On Southside they meandered down Regent Street for a while, made a left turn at Scots Kirk, opposite Battlefield Park, and continued past the courthouse. Then they were again by the sea.

Beka and her brothers enjoyed watching sailors on the unpainted sandboats shovelling island sand and conch shells onto the street. Chuku and Zandy clambered up and down the damp hills getting sand in their socks and their hair. Beka sat usually on the wall, her feet dangling above the sea, listening to the clink of shells and the comments of the sailors, as she gazed across the water at the activity of the boats around Custom House Wharf not too far from Baron Bliss' Lighthouse. But the fishy smell of shells would bore Toycie after a while, and they continued their stroll, allowing the boys a few minutes to jump up and down the stone steps of the Legislative Council on the other side of the courthouse.

Because it was Beka's Sunday, and if the door was open in preparation for some function, the little group would tiptoe into the Bliss Institute, along Southern Foreshore, where the library was located. In the Institute they would look at neatly-spaced Maya artefacts in glass cases, puzzling over the amazing items displayed there, or the girls would hold up the boys simultaneously so they could peer up onto the empty stage of the auditorium. Then they sat on a front row of chairs, gazing straight ahead, pretending to be most important persons watching a play. Although the library itself was always closed on Sunday, Toycie would 'mind' Chuku and Zandy while Beka ran quietly upstairs to look through the glass doors at the books stacked neatly on the shelves. If it wasn't too late, they continued along Southern Foreshore to Government House to see the royal poinciana trees blooming in flamboyant orange-red sprays against green leaves, and to wonder at the sprawling two-storied white mansion, where no one ever seemed to sit on the wide verandahs circling the house. A helmeted black policeman, on duty on the gravelled semi-circular driveway, walked up and down, ignoring the girls and their charges lingering at the closed gates. Across the street from Government House, and islanded by more green lawns, was the Anglican cathedral, built a century and a half ago with bricks imported from England.

The Barracks, beside the sea on Northside, they seldom chose to visit at all. The girls didn't like to pass the 'crazy house' and see men and women peering out onto the street, shouting and screaming obscenities. It was along that street, too, that the poor house and the tuberculosis huts were situated, and although the small houses were set very far back from the street, Beka and Toycie felt sure they could catch 'it' just passing by.

There were two clubs much further down on Barracks Street, one for creoles, local black people, and the other one for bakras, local white people and expatriates. The pania club for Spanish-speaking people overlooked the creek in the centre of town, a short distance from the swing bridge.

If Beka's Dad was on the verandah of the creole club treating his civil service ballies to whiskies, he would be certain to say something to Beka about being 'that side' with her brothers. So they stuck mainly to Fort George, Southern Foreshore and their byways.

It was always a bit of an anticlimax for the girls when they were returning home for tea before the street lights came on. Few real Belize people, rich, in-between, or poor, lived on the streets they had just left. But after the exhilaration of the sea air, in which they had constructed their world of fantasy, and the seemingly miraculous order of the neighbourhoods fronting the sea, the core of the town always seemed staler, dirtier, noisier and altogether much less pleasant than the lovely areas they had just left.

They clothes-pinned their noses tightly crossing the bridge over the stinking canal bordering Holy Redeemer Cathedral, built from wood, on Cashew Street, and they were always silent, except when scolding the boys or squashing them down in the big pram. And Toycie would vow as they reached Beka's gate,

'One of these days, Beka Lamb, I am going to live right da seafront, hurricane or no hurricane.'

And Beka would reply,

'Me too, gial. It only nice out da side,' in a quiet voice.

The rain crashed down at last. Beka wondered if her Gran was sheltering under Sodie's store front. Nurse Palacio should be at the hospital by now. Beka hoped she'd reached Female Ward before the storm broke.

Once when Beka's mother had gone to Merida to see an eye doctor, Beka was in the kitchen helping her Granny Ivy fry conch fritters for tea. Her Gran was frying and Beka was grinding.

'Gran,' Beka said, 'Why didn't Mama just go see Dr Lyban at the Belize Hospital?'

'He went back, Beka,' her Gran had replied, stabbing at a

fritter.

'Went back to where?'

'Where he studied — England.'

'But he is from Belize, Gran.'

'I know. But nothin' lasts here, Beka,' her Gran answered. Her eyes looked funny. 'Tings bruk down.'

'Ah wonder why?' Beka asked, bringing the conch and minced habanero peppers to the stove.

Her Gran leaned the fork carefully against the frying pan, pushed the window over the back stairs, and propped it open with a long pole. Then she said,

'I don't know why, Beka. But one time, when I was a young girl like you, a circus came to town. I can't remember where it was from, and don't ask me what happened to it afta. The circus had a fluffy polar bear — a ting Belize people never see befo'. It died up at Barracks Green, Beka. The ice factory broke down the second day the circus was here.'

Beka's Granny Ivy was crying. Her apron tail was over her face, and she said again and again,

'It died, Beka, it died.'

The conch fritters had burned.

Rain was blowing in sheets onto Beka's bed. Hooking the shutters, she got out of bed to check her Gran's windows in the eastern part of the attic. They were tightly shuttered. Beka pulled the glass-paned windows down to prevent the rain from spitting through the blinds. Water rushed along in the gutters below the roof. She curled up in the barrel-shaped rocking chair beside her Granny Ivy's bed, neatly spread with her dream books, *King Tut* and *Aunt Sally,* protruding from beneath her pillow. The day had been long and exciting but the nap earlier in the evening had refreshed her, as had the rain. She decided to sit there until her Gran returned from Battlefield Park and try to remember everything that had happened to her from April past, when she had failed first form, until today. She rubbed her finger into the deep gash on the mahogany rocker where Chuku had tried to saw off the arm with Granny Ivy's meat saw.

'That is the only way, Toycie gial,' she muttered to herself, 'I can continue keeping my wake for you.'

CHAPTER 4

What Beka recognized in herself as 'change' began, as far as she could remember, the day she decided to stop lying. Things were getting almost beyond her control. She sat on the top step of the back porch that April Friday, seven months earlier, eating crayfish foot left over from tea and contemplating her latest, worst lie. The sun was going down, and a cool breeze from the Caribbean, several streets away, blew now and then reminding her that it was 'Caye Time' once again.

Popping the last scrap of fish into her mouth, she tossed the shells between the railings and watched as they fell amongst the red bells and green crotons, dappled yellow, growing in the dry earth alongside the bottom of the stairs. Her parents had sat at the table finishing tea when Beka told them she had been promoted to second form. Without looking up from the report card he held between thumb and forefinger, Bill Lamb said, 'It says here that anyone failing more than three subjects at the end of the school year must repeat the class. You failed four subjects, Beka.'

The brown mulatto crust on her mother's cheek bones became extremely dark against the paleness of her skin. She said to Beka, perched on a chair opposite,

'Answer your father, girl.'

'I pass in truth, Daddy!' Beka almost shouted. 'Sister Virgil read my name off a list.'

'Well, all I can say is that Sister Virgil must be helping you out, which for her is unusual. You are a lucky girl. Excuse me.'

The chair scraped against the wooden floor as he pushed himself away from the mahogany table. Stalking into the living room, he sat down in his easy chair, and snapped on the radio that stood on a high cabinet alongside one wall, and the radio announcer said,

'This is the British Honduras Broadcasting Service.'

Lilla put her cup slowly down on the wet saucer, and with the forefinger of her right hand drew beads of sweat off her forehead. Beka opened her mouth, but before she could speak, her mother said quietly,

'Clear the table and wash the dishes now if you are finished, Beka. Your Gran and the boys ate before you came home from school. Change your uniform first.'

Lying was one of the things about Beka that her parents detested most. When they discovered the truth about this latest one, her Dad was going to shout and holler, and definitely beat her till she couldn't stand up. She looked up at the blue sky and rosy clouds. Maybe there'll be a hurricane this year, she thought hopefully. If one came, the school records would all 'wash way' and then her parents would never know she'd failed.

'Let's see,' she murmured. 'How does that rhyme go again? June, too soon; July, stand by; August, come it must; September, remember; October, all over.' A hurricane couldn't come in time to rescue her then. School reopened in June. In any case, Sister Virgil, the American principal, would remember every girl that failed.

Beka shuddered at the thought of the leather belt her Dad wore. Sometimes Bill Lamb would come home from work, the tensions of the work day raging within him, and Lilla, filled with the frustrations of her own day, would sit down to tell him of Beka's insolence, her laziness, and her ingratitude. The story invariably concluded with Lilla saying,

'And the worst thing of all, Bill, is that she lied to me. I could see she hadn't swept the attic properly. Why did she lie to me?'

Because he was in a hurry at those times to have his tea before going for an hour's relaxation at the club, Bill Lamb would say impatiently,

'I don't want to hear a word from you, Beka. Get upstairs. I am going to put an end to this once and for all.'

His felt hat askew on his head, Bill Lamb would follow Beka upstairs stamping his feet with emphasis. On the landing, Beka would begin to scream at the top of her voice before the belt touched her skin,

'No, Daddy! No, Daddy!'

Between lashes, Bill Lamb paused to ask,

'Do you know why I am beating you?'

'No, Daddy,' Beka would reply.

'Not because of the thing you did, but because you lied!'

On one such occasion, the buckle end of the belt escaped accidentally from Bill Lamb's clenched fist and cut Beka on the left corner of her mouth. The next day at school, Beka told anyone who asked that she'd fallen down the back steps and cut her face on the concrete slab at the foot of the wooden stairs.

When her Dad returned from the club that night, he came up to Beka's bedside in the attic where Lilla was rubbing Beka's head and saying,

'It was all my fault, Bill. I can't understand why I complain so much to you about Beka. She had such a pretty smile, Bill, such a pretty smile. That was the nicest thing about her face.'

Looking down at Beka's lip, Bill Lamb said,

'She still has a pretty smile. Smile, Beka! Show your mother what a pretty smile you still have.'

Beka smiled as naturally as she could manage, because her parents always seemed to suffer for such a long time after Beka herself had forgotten the beating, and it was a rare child in the community that didn't get a whipping now, then, or more often.

Turning to go downstairs again, Bill Lamb said,

'Don't worry, pet. Your Gran will rub it with cocoa fat when it heals and then it won't scar.' But although Granny Ivy rubbed it every night for a long time with cocoa fat, the scar browned over but remained visible, and Beka eventually gave up all hope that it would completely disappear.

After that, Lilla tried to keep her annoyance at Beka's shortcomings mostly to herself. She didn't talk much about them to Granny Ivy either, for Granny Ivy nearly always 'took up' for Beka. Beka wondered if her Dad would be able to help himself from beating her when he found out about this latest, most provoking lie.

At those times when Beka's behaviour forced Lilla to complain, Beka's Dad resorted to calling her names. He couldn't understand how a girl with enough food to eat, decent clothes to wear, and a roof over her head could be such a trial. Beka didn't know which she disliked most, the beatings or the name calling. The worst and most hurtful name of all was when her Dad called her 'phoney'. Liar and thief were bad, but those words didn't really worry her. She knew she would never reach His Majesty's Prison where Uncle Curo, Granny Ivy's second son worked as a warder. In any case, she had long ago stopped taking money from her

Dad's pants pocket to buy panades and 'cut-o-brute' from the vendors who set up shop outside the school playground at recess. And she was definitely through with lying as from today. But the word 'phoney' peppered her insides good and hot.

On the outside, she probably looked phoney in truth. Twice a month she sat in Miss Doodie's kitchen, which smelled of stale fried beans and burnt rice, to have her hair hotcombed. Her Dad had been against straightening her hair from the start.

'I don't want Beka using hot irons on her hair, Lilla,' Bill Lamb said. 'None of the women on my side of the family hotcomb their hair. What's wrong with it anyway?'

'Clearing the tangles out of Beka's hair takes nearly an hour every morning, Bill. That's one of the reasons she's so often late for school. This way Beka can take care of it herself. Anyway it's only the style.'

'Style! If you're not careful, she's going to grow up ashamed of herself and her people.'

'Bill, if Beka grows up ashamed of herself, or her people, the hair straightening won't be the main cause of it.'

'Go ahead, do what you want. I have no say in this family. I only provide the money!'

Lilla looked at her husband, and Bill Lamb rattled his paper and began reading aloud to them as they started stacking dishes, about the decision of the Workers' Union to support the People's Independence Party with funds.

But the lying was the thing that made her seem the most fake to her Dad. That, and perhaps the way she gave herself airs.

'I don't know who you are imitating,' Bill Lamb would sometimes say on a Sunday evening. 'We are a humble family. Wash that lipstick off before you leave this house! Your mouth looks like a red bell.'

Beka didn't feel in the least bit humble. She felt all right most of the time, and her family wasn't all that humble compared to other families on Cashew Street. She looked at the house, set about three feet from the street side the way most Belizeans' houses were built. The house was a decent size, painted white with green blinds, shut now against the mosquitoes and sand-flies that often came out for a while in the evenings. In fact, the Lambs and the Hartleys were two of the few black families on

Cashew Street that had much of anything at all. Most of the other prosperous families on Cashew Street were mestizos who owned shops or other businesses. But Beka knew that her Dad didn't mean a Good House and enough food to eat. He meant humble in the sense that the Lamb family was in a different class from the Blancos and the Hartleys. Bill Lamb was struggling to progress in the business world of the town, but he was quite satisfied to remain in the class where he was comfortable. He had no use for what he called artificiality and sham.

The green shutters of the back window jerked open and Chuku said,

'Beka! Mama wants to know when you are going to wash the tea things.'

'Inmediatamente, niño,' Beka answered, not moving.

'Show off!' Chuku snapped the shutters and returned noisily to the front verandah where Lilla sat with three-year-old Zandy and Granny Ivy watching the passersby.

Beka pulled dark brown knees up under her chin. The setting sun was throwing a tinselly gold light on the neighbourhood houses and yards all around, making everything seem much softer and prettier than it looked at midday, although it couldn't do anything extra for the lush redness of her bougainvillea vine that arched over the back fence to waterfall into Miss Boysie's yard. Miss Boysie didn't like that one bit. She said all that bloody bougainvillea was taking up space in her yard, harboured flies, and was breaking down the fence besides.

The cooling wind, and the fright of what lay before her, made Beka shiver in her thin cotton blouse. She looked down at herself. One of her breasts was growing but the other one remained flat. Dr Clark, a West Indian doctor resident in the town, had said that the right one would soon catch up with the left. Beka really hoped he was right.

Suppose when her Dad found out, he said she couldn't go back to school. It would be the washing bowl underneath the house bottom for her then and no mistake. How could she be a politician if she had to stand around a bowl and barrel all day long? Last summer holidays, her mother had been sick, and the family had not gone out to St. George's Caye. Granny Ivy quarrelled with the maid Daddy Bill hired the very first day. Beka did the washing. She remembered the mosquitoes in the swampy yard buzzing around her face and arms, biting her ankles even with long pants and rubber boots on, as she tried to hang out the clothes. Then there had been the white clothes to boil in the big lard pan. She struggled to light the fire with pine wood brought from Abrero's across the street, but the stink from the outside latrine was so unbearable, she kept having to run to the open space between the house and the vat to take fresh breaths.

'Aie, ya yie!' Beka groaned.

Chilly, she sprang up and went into the darkening kitchen. Switching on the light, she began scraping the shells from the plates piled on the counter through the back window and into the yard below. From the window, she could see the street through the branches of Mr Ulric's custard-apple tree. A woman struggled by holding an aluminium bucket filled with water on her head. She carried another full one in her free hand. Beka turned on the tap and let just enough water run into the basin. She didn't want the vat to dry up before the rainy season came for sure, otherwise, she would have to carry buckets of water every day from the public pipe round the corner. The voices of her brothers sounded subdued from the front verandah where they sat with Granny Ivy. The latch on the bathroom door snapped back loudly making Beka jump. Her mother came into the kitchen with an empty kettle in her hand.

Banging it down on the stove she said,

'Beka, how many times I tell you not to throw scraps into the yard? It's a low down thing to do. That's why I put Sodie's expensive garbage pail on that back porch!'

Beka began to cry. She couldn't help it, although crying was something Lilla detested and rarely did herself that anybody could see. She used to tell Beka when she was little and had hurt her knees in the yard,

'Stop that crying, Beka. Get tough. Be strong like London with all those bombs falling. Our boys aren't crying over there, they're fighting so we can be free.'

'Who help them when they are hurt?' Beka would ask, brushing the sand off her knees, and Lilla would say,

'Don't you remember Miss Nadine and Miss Dotsy went too? They are doing the nursing.' And with the wet sheet her mother was hanging on the line flapping a pleasant coolness against her face, Beka listened again to the story of Miss Darweather's boy whose plane got shot down over the sea, far away in a place called Europe.

But this time, although Beka's tears were coming out in ugly gulps, Lilla held her against soft breasts that seemed too big for her small frame and said,

'You failed, no true, Beka?'

'Yes, Mama, I fail, I fail.'

'I know you failed, Beka. I could tell from your face. Your Dad knows too.'

'Do you think Daddy will send me back, Mama?'

'It's too soon to think about that now, Beka. You'd better go and tell him first. I wish I could find a way to help you stop lying, my daughter.'

CHAPTER 5

Beka left her mother standing in the kitchen and walked into the dining room, and on into the hall. She stood at one corner of the archway that separated the dining room from the living room, watching her father, his eyes closed, stretched out in the cane chair, his feet on her mother's centre table.

She hugged the archway post. A radio announcer was saying,

'The commissioners, under the chairmanship of Mr S.D.Hartley, have recommended in the proposed new constitution that universal adult suffrage be introduced in the colony. All prospective voters will be required to take a literacy test . . .'

'Daddy, ah fail,' Beka said.

Bill Lamb opened tired eyes and looked up at her. Beka scratched at a spot on the pale lemon paint of the post. She couldn't stand to look at the pain in his face, at the sadness that went back to the years she didn't understand.

Turning down the radio, Bill Lamb said,

'What are we going to do, Beka? You are growing wild like that bougainvillea that's breaking down Miss Boysie's fence. All flash and no substance.'

'I am sorry I failed, Daddy.'

His mouth twisted into a grimace.

'Sorry? For me or for you?'

'I don't know, Daddy.'

'Let me tell you something, Beka. I never wanted you to go to high school. How you passed the entrance examination to St Cecilia's I'll never understand. Your mother gave me a lot of excuses and reasons why you were developing so late. None of them made any sense to me because we gave you a better start than anyone in this family on both sides ever got. I told Lilla that you've never shown much interest in your studies since abc class. One of these days, I want you to take a good look up and down this street. The money you wasted could feed a poor family for six months.'

'Daddy . . .'

'Do you know why I didn't go to the club this evening?' Bill Lamb interrupted 'I was waiting for something like this. But I think I will dress and go out now before I lose my senses and beat you.'

He slipped on his creaky leather sandals and started towards the bathroom.

'Daddy,' Beka said taking a few steps behind him. 'May I try again, Daddy, please? I promise I'll pass. I'll come first, if you let me go back.'

He paused in the small passage between the kitchen and the bathroom. A disbelieving smile started in his eyes making the dimples in his cheeks show briefly.

'Aie, Miss Beka. I wonder if it's too late to do anything with you? Nobody at home here ever asked you to come first. We would have been satisfied with a pass!'

'Eh, Daddy, may I go back?' Beka asked.

'I'll think about it while you are all at the caye, Beka. When I make my decision, I'll let you know.'

'Daddy?'

'Yes, Beka?' He sounded so tired.

'Toycie wants to know . . . excuse me, Daddy, but . . . Toycie wants to know if she can still go to the caye with us if I go.'

'My instinct tells me I should cancel this whole trip, Beka, but it wouldn't be fair to your mother or the boys and Toycie is always a help to your mother. I'll write a note to Miss Eila and leave it on the desk. Did Toycie pass?'

'Yes, Daddy.'

Bill Lamb went into the bathroom and closed the door.

The next morning Beka woke up to find Chuku standing by her bedside. He shook her shoulder again,

'Beka, Beka, Dad cutting down your tree!'

'Which tree?' Beka asked wishing she didn't have to get up ever again in her life.

'Your tree, Beka! The one you plant next to Miss Boysie's fence!'

Beka stumbled out of bed and ran to the back window overlooking the yard. Her father, dressed for work in a white shirt and khaki pants, had nearly finished cutting down the vine. She rushed downstairs, through the kitchen and down the back stairs.

'No, Daddy, no!' But the last trunk of the vine was already on the ground.

'Why you cut it down, Daddy?' Beka asked, picking up a large branch and trying to stick it into the ground. She felt as if somebody had put a watermelon inside her chest.

'It was breaking down the fence, Beka,' her Dad said sheathing his machete and walking towards the house.

Beka let the branch in her hand fall. She stood there in her nightdress looking down at the magenta leaves of the bougainvillea vine sprawled in a crude circle all over the grass. Screwing up his little round face, Chuku stooped over the branches saying,

'It's easy to plant again, Beka.'

'I am never going to plant another thing!' Beka shouted.

'No vex with *me*, Beka!' Chuku retorted.

'I am not vexed with you, Chuks,' Beka said, rubbing her palm against the comforting roughness of his hair. 'I am vexed with me. Let's drink tea.'

Later in the morning, a coolie man with hair to his shoulders came to the house with a mule and cart. Beka and the boys watched from the front stairs as he tied the prickly branches into wilting bunches before piling them onto his cart, to carry them to a dump on the edge of town. She played at playing marbles with Chuku and Zandy for a while, but when a neighbour boy peered through the fence palings, she let him through the gate, and went upstairs to attack the attic.

Saturday, pay day for many families, was the biggest marketing, house-cleaning, and cooking day of the week. Women and girls, whether they lived in a 'good house' or a 'dawg-siddown' scrubbed, dusted, polished and cooked in order that they might do as they pleased Saturday night and Sunday afternoon, satisfied that their duty, as best as could be managed with what was available, had been done.

Lunch on a Saturday was mostly crushed avocado or potted meat sandwiches, with perhaps pounded calves' liver fried with lots of onions and creole bread for six o'clock tea. But the intense activity, and the smells of what was to come on Sunday noon, assuaged the need for bigger meals. In the houses of even the poorest, at the very least red kidney beans and bits of salty pigtails stewed on outdoor fire hearths waiting for the addition of raw rice, assiduously picked over for stones, and washed several times until the water ran clear. And in the houses of those that could better afford it, chickens, pork, or beef roasted in ovens; great pots of grey-black relleno soup thickened on stoves with a dozen hard-boiled eggs per pot bobbing up and down like dumplings, and the corn mills of the town ground busily in preparation for the mounds of tortillas that would be needed the following day. Seafood and groundfood were rarely cooked on Sundays: fish, crayfish, conch, yams, cocoa, sweet potatoes, breadfruit and the like were everyday fare.

Beka cleaned the attic with feverish energy; here was a way to start, a way to show her family that she could be different. She didn't skip an inch of the floor, either when sweeping or polishing, nor did she push old newspapers or dirty clothes under the beds. Not once did she stop to leaf through the months-old *Jamaica Gleaners* piled on Granny Ivy's low-topped press, and she scrubbed the attic stairs as if her brush could bore through wood. When she got up from her knees, her arms were sore, but she didn't leave the bucket of dirty water on the stairs for Chuku or Zandy to knock over by accident, nor did she leave the tin of expensive wax open for them to smear all over the walls. It was only a small beginning, but Beka felt she had handled the job like a woman and in Belize, to be able to work like a woman was an honourable thing. But that day, nobody climbed the attic stairs to inspect her work, and even though the cupboard door in the kitchen bumped against Lilla's leg, she seemed not to notice that Beka was putting the wax and cloth carefully to the rear of the cupboard.

While she carried buckets of rainwater from the vat downstairs to fill the deep aluminium pan upstairs, Granny Ivy continued to wield the long-handled broom through the bedrooms, swishing out the dusty corners, and swiping under the beds to bring out the week's accumulation of dead roaches, mosquitoes and houseflies. Every time she reached a window, she shoved it outward against the walls with such force that Beka felt the vibration go through her lungs. Her Gran's face was made up like a squall, but her eyes held a look of puzzled disappointment.

Pouring the final bucketful into the pan, Beka stood for a minute before removing her dirty clothes. For most of her life, the members of her family had surrounded her tightly, like sepals around a bud. But today that security had fallen away, and for a while she felt very lonely. She needed to talk with someone outside her immediate family, but the one other adult she could trust, Lilla's own grandmother, was beyond everyone's reach. Great Grandmother Straker was ill, and had been for a long time. Daddy Bill told Lilla, in Beka's presence, that the old lady's mind had finally gone.

Great Grandmother Straker was over eighty, but in the days when she was younger and stronger, she used to come around to spend the day whenever she could. Greatgran Straker had raised two daughters, and when her second daughter died giving birth to Lilla, she raised Lilla, too, mostly on her own; and although that was not an uncommon thing for a woman in the creole community, it had not been easy. Once, Greatgran had told Beka that no matter how many people there are around, nobody could sleep for another, and so she had better learn to deal with the loneliness of bedtime. To help her get to sleep, Greatgran would give her an album with old time photographs. There were no names under the pictures, but in the midst of replaiting her hair to go home to her first daughter's house, Greatgran Straker would sometimes stop, and pointing with her big toothed tortoise-shell comb say,

'There's your Daddy in short pants. From the time I met him till now, he's always been like a son to me.'

'Tell me about it again.'

'Well,' she would say beginning to scrape the comb through her bushy, grey hair, 'Your Dad used to deliver goods over by Yarborough where we were living at the time. Mr Blanco had just come up from Orange Walk and started his business. One day I was outside a shop where he was hauling a sack of flour through the door all by himself. Couldn't have been more than fourteen. I grabbed one end, and we pulled it into the shop together. He took off his straw hat and said,

'Thank you, Mislady.'

'Was that after the great hurricane?'

'Yes, that was maybe some years after. I remember because we were very depressed. Things had broken down. My gentleman couldn't get work cutting wood because nobody overseas was buying much, even what we had to sell. And the Governor at the time was really mean. The boss of the British Lumber Company was living at Government House, and all the big merchants and so on were mostly foreign, and paid bad wages and were in league. We didn't go for the sweet rice the government finally decided to give to our poor people. And some men had to break stones in the big sun-hot for five cents a day.'

'Was that when your gentleman got the job at Sodie's?'

'Yes, that store was owned by foreigners too. He managed to get a messenger's job, and what did he do but go and lose it. That's what caused the final split between us. He carried a placard in the unemployment brigade march because he wasn't satisfied with his pay, and so he lost what little work he had.'

'Wasn't that a good thing — him joining the brigade?'

'I am not saying it was a bad thing he did, but we lost the job, and we needed food, and we were trying to rebuild the house!'

'What did your gentleman do then?'

'For a while he travelled around the country following the

leaders of the unemployed brigade but finally the Governor with all the powers he had, clamped down on them, and the brigade broke down. So you see, Beka, your Dad was lucky to get a job at Blanco's during that time to help support your Granny Ivy and your Uncle Curo who was still in school then.' And often they would continue right through the album, and Beka would fall asleep not knowing Greatgran Straker had 'downed' her net and gone.

'You in that water trying to bleach white or what, Beka?' Granny Ivy was banging on the bathroom door with the broom handle.

'No! Just coming, Granny Ivy.'

'Well, hurry up. Your mother is finished with the list!'

After she was dressed, and had emptied the bath pan, Beka took the note for Miss Eila off her Dad's desk, and went into the kitchen. Lilla's eyes, the colour of sparkly river water tumbling over smooth brown stones, examined Beka as they might her rose bushes, wondering what to try next to improve the quality of the blooms. Wiping a droplet of sweat off her broad nose, she only said,

'Don't stay long, Beka. Tell Mr Gordillo to send the groceries early, and if Toycie is going, tell her to get here by seven, Monday morning.'

'All right, Mama,' Beka replied, taking the pieces of paper and the money for last week's groceries. Saturday afternoons used to be such special times for Beka before yesterday. There were so many interesting things to see and do as she went about her errands, particularly if she was sent over the big bridge to Augusto Quan's, or to the Jerusalem Fancy Store on Albert Street, the main business sector of the town. She always had a feeling of adventure on Saturday afternoons for she never knew whether her errands would take her to Mesopotamia, where an old school friend of her mother's lived, whether she was going to Greatgran Straker's to deliver bread, or whether her errands would confine her to Cashew Street. On the Saturdays her errands took her over the big bridge, she invariably ended the afternoon by going to the library where the sea breezes entering the circular room from vents beneath the shelves, swirled around her legs and puffed out her dress as she selected a book. She had enjoyed Saturday afternoon only the week before, but it seemed so far away, as though it had all happened when she was four like Chuku.

Cleaning the attic so thoroughly had not reduced the watermelon in Beka's chest, and she was beginning to understand that atonement required more now than dusting and polishing, and she had to find a way to atone. She needed to do that more than anything. Usually, even if the family was going to the island for a single day, she would be racketing around the house singing about 'The battle of old St George's Caye' or about 'A land where palm trees whisper', until her screechy voice would jangle Granny Ivy's nerves and Beka would be put to grating coconuts. When the bit she was grating reached about an inch square, Beka popped it into her mouth for she was always afraid of cutting her fingers on the grater's sharp teeth. Her Gran could grate a piece of coconut until it was the size of a fingernail.

The atmosphere of the house this caye time was different. There was no shouting of instructions back and forth; Daddy Bill did not pop in at the back door with a box; no belly laughs as Granny Ivy and Lilla exchanged the latest town gossip. The 'spunks' had gone out of the whole thing, and Beka knew that she was to blame.

Beka was not generally a sulky girl. Her relatives, in town and out of the district, always said that you saw Beka's teeth coming before any other part of her. Today, she felt as if she had lockjaw, and could hardly talk, much less smile. And worst of all, a new feeling for her, she dreaded going into the street. In the town, gossip spread with the rapidity of a pine ridge fire with gale force winds behind it. The whole town must know by now that she'd failed. She went down the back steps so reluctantly that her mother pushed her head around the kitchen door and called,

'Hook your sampata, and hurry up!'

Beka buckled her right sandal, raced down the stairs and right through Chuku's marble game. His friend from across the street sucked his teeth in irritation, and Zandy said,

'You broke up the ring, Beka!'

'Sorry, sorry,' Beka muttered, stooping to retrace the circle in the dust with the forefinger of her free hand.

'Want a spin, Beka?' Chuku called.

'No,' she replied, stopping to bolt the gate carefully behind her before stepping into Cashew Street.

CHAPTER 6

A masked man was pedalling his bicycle cart towards the shops at the corner of Cashew Street where it became Manatee Lane. His progress was slow because the square cart was piled high with heavy sacks of flour from the warehouses of Blanco's Import Commission Agency. The flour powdered the air around the cart giving white masks to little barefooted boys prancing alongside yelling,

'Unhood yourself, maskman! Mek we see your face!' But the man concentrated on pushing one pedal forward, then the other, gazing straight ahead of him. He was used to rude boys taunting him, and probably did not hear. Adults and children alike were mesmerized each time they saw this man, who on the street wore a black oilskin hood in heat and in cool, in dry and in wet, never taking it off when anyone could see. The hood covered even his neck. He wore gloves, a long sleeved shirt, long pants, and rubber boots. All one could get was a glimpse of dark eyes sheltering behind a small rectangle of heavy plastic.

Of the many stories about him that circulated amongst the children of the town, one said that in his youth, Maskman had been a handsome 'sweet boy' who, during a sojourn in Stann Creek, a coastal town south of Belize, compromised the daughter of a Carib man who had befriended him. Maskman could not marry the girl, though he loved her, without losing face in the creole community, whose members seldom married among the Caribs, although these two groups shared, in varying degrees, a common African ancestry.

One night, so it was said, a group of Carib people, in painted masks, entered the house where 'sweet boy' lay alseep in his hammock. Each person touched his face and neck obeahing him so that these parts of his body became dotted with white speckles, leaving the rest of his body black. In pain now herself, Beka could no longer bear to stop and gaze at the man. She kept her eyes averted as she hurried along to Toycie's house.

Toycie's house was not a 'dawg-siddown' or lean-to, but it nearly could have been. What saved it was Miss Eila's industry. The house, darkened grey by many years of rain, stood on several thick posts about two feet off the ground, just high enough, most of the time, to prevent muddy water from sweeping through the floor boards during the years when rain fell for several days in a row. Miss Eila's parlour was separated from the bedroom by a frame partition over which was stretched and tacked cotton material printed with gay, bright flowers. Carefully set out on the green linoleum in front of the partition was a mahogany settee, a table and two chairs. The parlour-set looked new because it had been re-finished very carefully by Miss Eila and Toycie in time for Christmas the year before.

In front of a window facing the street, 'to block out interfering eyes', Miss Eila had put her glass case in which were displayed her Christmas tumblers, mugs, plates, and other treasures like Toycie's report cards, certificates and prizes from abc class to the present day. A grocery safe and a small pinewood dining table with four stools underneath, stood on that side of the room also.

Miss Eila cooked in three or four black iron pots on a waist-high four-legged firehearth set under a zinc roof at the back of the house, and she washed clothes in a dug-out wooden bowl under a wide-branched cashew tree, not too far from the outside latrine. There was no vat in the yard, only three kerosene drums under the gutters of the rusting zinc roof to catch rainwater for drinking. Two other drums held creek water near Miss Eila's washing bowl. When Miss Eila and Toycie ran out of drinking water during the months of dry, they carried buckets at night or early morning from Beka's yard. The Lambs always had free bottles of cashew wine on Christmas Eve night. Toycie was scrubbing the two front steps of the house when Beka reached the gate.

'O Toycie, Toycie O, I bring the note,' Beka called.

Dropping her brush, and flinging the dirty cloth into the bucket, Toycie ran across a series of planks, put down for easier passage during the wet weather, leading from the steps to the gate where Beka stood waiting.

'We are still going? We are still going, Beka?' she asked in uncertain excitement. The waves in Toycie's hair, parted in the middle, rippled back into a rough bun at the nape of her neck; and the concern in her eyes as she looked at Beka made them coal black against her skin, the colour of cinnamon.

'I was sure Mr Bill would cancel the whole thing, and I didn't dare drop by . . . you tell them yet, Beka Lamb?'

'Ahahangh,' Beka answered making a guttural sound in her throat.

'What happen?'

'Nobody is talking much, and Daddy cut down the bougainvillea bush.'

'For what?'

'It was breaking down Miss Boysie's fence, but it was to punish me somehow or other.'

'Because you fail?'

'Not that so much, though he's sad about that too.'

'Then for what?'

'I told them I passed early on, then later that I fail.'

'You are lying, Beka!'

Beka looked at Toycie's frightened, incredulous face and said right into it,

'I swear by Jumby's block!'

Toycie clapped her hand to her forehead,

'Why you lie on top of failing, Beka?'

'I don't know *why* Toycie, but it wasn't for fun.'

Toycie latched and unlatched the gate, and Beka kept biting pieces off her mother's grocery list. The people walking back and forth on the street with market baskets and shopping bags all seemed to be talking out loud, and cyclists in a hurry were making a terrific din with their bells. Beka was preparing to move off when Toycie said,

'Come on in, Beka. I learnt another part of that tune, and Aunt

Eila made fresh coconut tableta.'

'Not today, Toycie,' Beka said quietly. 'Can Miss Eila spare you for the trip?'

'Aunt Eila so happy I pass, she'd let me go to the moon. One more year, Beka, one more year, then maybe I'll get a good job and Aunt Eila won't work so hard anymore. Maybe we'll save enough money to buy a property near Baron Bliss lighthouse!' Toycie laughed at this insane ambition, and Beka had to smile because beginning typists only received ten dollars a week, if that.

'Come in for a minute, Beka. I got a note from Emilio. He went to the caye with his grandfather as soon as St Anthony's closed last week. We'll see him there!'

Beka stood for a while looking at Toycie's slender fingers gripping the top of the gate. Toycie was seventeen, but despite the difference in their ages, a close friendship had grown up between them, not only because there was an exchange of goods and services between the Lambs and Qualos, but because Toycie remembered what it was like to be fourteen, and Beka had the ability to pretend seventeen. The girls switched backwards and forwards in time as fancy or necessity dictated. Also, Toycie and Beka were different on the street where economic necessity forced many creole girls to leave school after elementary education to help at home, work in shops and stores as salesladies or take jobs as domestic servants in the houses of those who could afford such help.

Seeing the unusually serious and wistful expression in Beka's dark brown eyes, and the droopy hang to her lips, Toycie's face closed in, and she said as humbly as she could manage,

'It's a case of full belly telling empty belly to take heart, no true, Beka?'

The blood was beginning to boil in Beka's face, and how was she to cry on the big, open street? She looked down at her sandals and noted with surprise that she was scuffing mud off the drain and her toenails were all dirty. Toycie tried again,

'It's only two months before school starts, then you must really put your mind and heart to it. If Sister Virgil could give you sixty-nine for arithmetic, it was mean not to give you seventy.'

'I fooled around instead of doing my work.'

'How did you manage to fail religion?'

'It's that trouble I had with Father Nunez.'

'The first thing you better learn, Beka Lamb, is to keep your tongue between your teeth.'

'I wish, Toycie! But how? My mouth naturally big. Anyhow, I may not go back. Daddy won't let me know for a whole week.'

'We'll be at caye then!'

The shocked and agitated expression on Toycie's face was getting on Beka's nerves and she was sure she was going to cry so she said,

'Let me go with the list now, Toycie. Get to our house seven Monday.'

'Hurry up then Beks. Aunt Eila will cook for Mr Bill so tell Miss Lilla not to hire anybody.'

'All right, that will relieve Mama. She hasn't gotten anyone yet.'

'No walk tomorrow, right?'

'Right. See you Monday now, Toycie,'

'Ba bye, Beka.'

Going to Toycie's house to talk while she scrubbed and washed or to listen as she practised guitar chords, had been one of Beka's Saturday afternoon treats. Beka used to take music lessons herself once upon a time and Lilla had hoped she would take to it. But the music teacher would leave Beka in a front room repeating scales over and over again, emerging from the kitchen once or twice during the half-hour lesson, reeking of tea and cheese, to correct Beka's fingering. Beka started playing hookey — going to the park or the library — and the lessons stopped.

Toycie's guitar was a beautiful, highly glossed instrument that Mrs Leigh, an English woman, had given Toycie when Mr Leigh finished his tour of duty in the colony's civil service. Miss Eila had been the Leighs' housekeeper, and sometimes Toycie used to babysit for the Leighs if they went to a party at Government House or to anything special like that. The evening she received the guitar, Toycie brought it over to Beka's house, and together they sat on Beka's bed stroking and admiring the look, feel and sound of the instrument. Toycie was beginning to show Beka how to hold the guitar, and how to press the fingertips of one hand down on the strings, when all of a sudden Beka peered through the hole in the guitar and exclaimed,

'Toycie! It says, "Made in Spain".'

'Could-a-never!' Toycie exclaimed in turn, but her surprised tone did not altogether convince Beka. Together they peered through the hole, heads bumping.

'You're right, Beka, but why you always bring politics into everything?'

'It's not me that's bringing it in, Toycie! Guatemala claims Belize from Britain through rights inherited from Spain, and Spain got rights from the Pope, and who are we going to get rights from?'

'All right, Beka, all right!'

'Beka had a feeling that Toycie had seen the label before, but still her face had a crushed, disappointed look. The guitar was the most beautiful and only expensive thing Toycie owned, and Beka knew Toycie wanted her to like and appreciate it, even though Beka often claimed she didn't like music at all.

'Whe fu do, Toycie gial?' Beka asked in a conciliatory way.

'I can sell it and ask Mr Bill to buy me another one when he goes to Chetumal on business. Mexico say they have rights too, but they aren't going on bad.'

'You can't sell it!' Beka said fervently. 'It's too nice. Besides, you've worked for it and you're used to it and a new one won't be the same.' She went to the pinewood table in the centre of the attic where she did her homework, and began sharpening a long pencil with a razor blade.

'What's that for, Beka?'

'Well, we can change it.'

'Change what?'

'We can scratch out "Espana" and write in the name of any country we want.'

'That's the idea, Beka!' Toycie exclaimed reprieved. 'Give me the lead.' Grabbing the pencil from Beka, she poked it very carefully through the hole and scratched out the word "Spain".

'We don't have to write a name on the label,' Beka said.

'That's true, but if we put a name, we can pretend to forget what was there. We'd feel better, what do you say?'

'All right,' Beka agreed. 'What shall we put?'

They sat on the bed thinking for a while. Beka knew that there was no point in mentioning America, because apart from anything else, Toycie would think about her mother up there in Brooklyn every time she saw the guitar.

'How about England?' Toycie asked, getting a little impatient. 'After all, Mrs Leigh comes from there.'

'So does Governor Radison!' Beka shot back. 'And look how he is treating Granny Ivy's party leaders.' But Beka was uneasy. She had once heard her father say to Granny Ivy at the dining table,

'We can't sit down and keep rehashing what people did to us in the past, Ma, or use those injustices as any kind of complete excuse for our present situation. Every people have some kind of grievance. Fighting for our rights is a natural thing, but things don't often go according to rights, and rights have to be maintained one way or another. My main worry is, will we be able to hold onto our rights once we get them? Only the good-will of the world will help us do that in our present situation.'

Beka picked up the guitar off the bed and laid it gently on Toycie's lap.

'There's no need to put anything,' she said again.

'Shure there is,' Toycie answered, 'And I am going to put Belize!'

'I doubt if we make guitars like this one here, Toycie.'

'One day we might.' Toycie said determinedly, poking the pencil through the hole to scrawl 'Belize' on the label. She played three successive chords swiftly on the guitar, and tapping it lightly, shouted,

'Olé!'

Shortly after that Miss Eila asked Daddy Bill to ask Mrs Villanueva, a typist at Blanco's, to give Toycie weekly guitar lessons. And that was how Toycie met Emilio Villanueva.

CHAPTER 7

Men, women and children, of all colours, shapes and sizes, stood two deep at the three counters in Gordillo's Grocery and Dry Goods Store gossiping, laughing, banging coins on the counter, and complaining aloud at the length of time it was taking to get service. The smell of kerosene, onions, cheese and briny pigtails made the shop stink. Beka squeezed her way between shoppers, sacks of flour and rice, barrels and drums, until she reached a counter at the rear of the shop where Mr Gordillo stood slapping lard onto a piece of blottery paper on a creaky scale descending from a chain attached to the ceiling. Standing on tiptoe, she pushed her arm over the top of a display case, waving the list to attract his attention. An item on the long strip of paper caught her eye, and she pulled her arm down to have a closer look. It was printed quite clearly: one thick exercise book, fifty cents. Beka, who had a number of half-used school blanks at home, was puzzled by her mother's need to purchase another one. Beside her at the counter, a large mestizo woman, a cast in her left eye and a braid to her waist, was disagreeing with one of Mr Gordillo's salesladies about the total cost of two tins of evaporated milk, one pound of black beans, and five balls of ricardo spice. Beka pushed her arm up again, and called above their voices, arguing in a mixture of Spanish and Creole,

'Mr Gordo, Mr Gordo, I only bring the list.' Mr Gordillo was a mestizo man from Orange Walk, a district north of Belize, whose family, many years before, had crossed the border from Mexico during a Maya Indian uprising there against anyone of European blood. Mr Gordillo had neither wife nor children, and people whispered strange things about him because he lived alone at the top of his shop. Mr Gordillo was friendly with nearly everyone, but there were certain neighbourhood boys and girls in whom he took a special interest. He had never been anything but polite and nice to Beka, and Granny Ivy said people were only jealous because Mr Gordillo came up from Orange Walk, worst hit during the depression, with only the shirt on his back, and now he was getting rich. 'He'd be a lot richer,' Daddy Bill had added, 'if he didn't give so much credit to some of the same ones grating his back.'

Mr Gordillo, straight black hair falling over his forehead and touching the top of his gold rimmed glasses, pushed the upper part of his body through the narrow space between the two showcases and said,

'Tardes, Beka,' smiling expectantly at her just as if it weren't the busiest day of the week in his shop. He glanced at the list and said,

'Do you need anything now, Beka?'

'Not this very minute, Mr. Gordo, but Mama needs everything early today because we're preparing to go to the caye on Monday. Last week's money is in this envelope.'

He shoved the bulky envelope into his apron pocket, and passed Beka a fresh honey bun out of the case where he displayed creole bread, meat pies and sweets that he bought from women who sold baked goods for a living on the street. Beka wasn't hungry so she put it in her skirt pocket to share with Chuku and Zandy.

As Beka was inching around to go, Mr Gordillo touched her shoulder with one hairy hand and asked,

'Did you pass, Beka?' Beka shook her head, and began rubbing a variegated knot in the pinewood around the display case immediately in front of her.

'One creole bread, Gordillo!' A big, black man in a sweaty undershirt was waving a green dollar bill over Beka's head, and the stench emanating from his underarms reminded Beka of over-ripe guavas. She recognized him as one of the gamblers in the camp behind Abrero's wood shop. Mr Gordillo's face had gone red, and Beka knew it wasn't because the man was shouting. He adjusted the thick lensed glasses on his hooked nose and said,

'I offered a special mass at the Cathedral, Beka, and every night for one week, the beads. You had much trouble, corazón, I realize, but your papacita and mamacita are struggling so hard. You are lucky to have both of them living with you, helping you, trying to protect you.'

Beka didn't lift her eyes and she didn't answer. It was hot in the shop. Heat gave her prickly heat which raised up in watery pimples, and she was beginning to itch all over. The day was never going to end. How she hated hot weather! Ignoring the customers calling for attention, Mr Gordillo selected a small bar of imported chocolate from the case opposite Beka and offered it to her. On the label was a red-faced girl, about Beka's age, wearing a starched, pointed hat that flared out at the sides into wings. A pail of milk hung on either end of the long pole balanced on the girl's shoulders, and in the distance was a range of jagged mountains covered with snow.

'No, thank you, Mr Gordillo,' Beka said, 'not after the mass and rosaries, and everything, but thank you all the same.'

Shoving as politely as she could, Beka escaped the shop and ran all the way home. On the back porch she slipped off sticky, dusty sandals before entering the kitchen. The stitch in her side ached.

Granny Ivy stood 'swingeing' a chicken over the kerosene stove, picking out the tiniest feathers with one hand as she turned the chicken with the other. The smell of burnt feathers made Beka want to vomit. Her mother pounded dough on the counter nearest the sink. Beka went into the dining room, and up two stairs to sit on the large platform leading to the attic stairs. A cool breeze blew through the window reviving her, but she sat there drained, unappreciative of the freshly cleaned house, the smell of wax, the red bells in a bowl on the table.

The year before, Beka had come home for lunch, sweaty and hungry. An old half-bakra man was seated at the table, an empty whisky glass at his elbow. Lilla said to her,

'Beka, this is your grandfather.'

Beka's stomach turned puppalicks. She wanted to lambaste the man who, she felt, had no right to be seated in their home. Mumbling 'Good afternoon', she turned to set her books on the archway shelf. That was when she noticed the roses in an earthenware bowl, decorated with Maya motifs, her mother had bought from a Mexican trader at Cinderella Plaza. Beka's mother seldom cut the few really good roses that bloomed every once in a while. The man touched the roses with a tanned forefinger and said,

'Your mother liked these, too, Lilla. Times were different back then, girl.'

Her mother said,

'I understand you're married now, Pa?'

'Not formally, you understand, but I live with a Maya lady out in the bush. My, but you're doing well here, Lilla,' he continued, looking around. 'This is a fine house, and cool! Bill says he's saving to build another one. Personally, I think he would be wiser to invest abroad.'

'He's got faith in this country, Pa.'

'Well, he's a better man than me. I would be afraid to invest another cent until I knew what was going to happen here.'

'Why do you stay then, Pa?'

'Well, I've had bad luck like my father did before me, lost all my money, and the mahogany works is all I know. But one of these days, if I get a pile together, I'd like to go to England to see the place where my father was born.'

'He never married your mother either, so why do you want to go there?'

'It's just a feeling I have for the place, Lilla. I can't explain it.'

A tense frown was gathering around Lilla's eyes, and Beka left them and walked through the kitchen to the back steps. She sat there watching a coconut branch scrape the vat top until she heard the creak of the front gate. Lunch was late, and Beka returned to school that afternoon long after the sawmill whistle blew at one.

The voices of her mother and grandmother were rising in the kitchen and Granny Ivy was saying,

'And I told Boysie that I give that bougainvillea stump six weeks to shoot, and if it don't, I personally will plant two more beside it, and they will grow as high as they please, and we'll see who will make me cut them down.'

Lilla was saying under Granny Ivy's voice,

'Beka's bush meant as much to me as to you, Miss Ivy. It's the first thing she planted that took root, but all the same, the fence *was* leaning into Boysie's yard. I wish you hadn't said anything to Boysie. People around here are already beginning to resent us, if I could only find a little peace and happiness at least inside our yard, then I could manage better.'

'Peace and happiness!' Miss Ivy was laughing an ugly laugh that hurt Beka's ear. She jumped off the platform and went to stand at the kitchen door. There was a hurt look on Lilla's face, and seeing it, Granny Ivy said, in a much softened voice,

'Those things only visit in spells, Lilla, best to accept it. I have lived these sixty odd years, and I haven't yet met anyone at peace or happy, I don't even know what happiness means. Far as I can make out, it's like love, there when you need it less, gone when you need it more. Hope is the one reliable thing I know.'

'You're probably right at that, Miss Ivy. I hope Bill will let us move one of these days especially now that we are thinking of trying to put in a septic tank and toilet. It's hard to have nice things amongst people that don't. Even though we plan, and save, and work so hard, people don't understand, they think we are lucky, or did something bad to get them, they don't understand the generations of sacrifice and humiliation it took to get even the little we have.'

'Bill will agree to it one of these days. More and more shops are coming up on this street and he can't nap good after lunch. But it'll take him a while. He's trying to progress but at the same time, he wants the goodwill of the people he came from. He's a good man that way.'

'You think so, Miss Ivy?'

'Shure, I think so, and I know many people around here that think we are all right. And those that don't, well, we creoles have a habit of watching for other people's lives to break down, then we laugh. But we are not laughing at the people, we are laughing at something we recognize. If we cried every time somebody's life fall apart, this country would be called the one true valley of tears. You do the same thing at times, Lilla, like all of us, only you don't notice.'

Lilla rubbed her hands together over the enamel basin so that her rings clinked, and little rolls of flour fell over the sides onto the scrubbed counter. The kerosene bottle feeding the stove gurgled, and Miss Ivy switched off the stove with thick, unringed, work roughened fingers.

'You always mean the best, Miss Ivy. It's taken me years to understand that. Let me go downstairs now and see what there is for the cemetery tomorrow. Come and help me, Beka.' Miss Ivy didn't reply. Her plump back in a loose house dress was bent over the chicken to more carefully inspect the singed skin in the darkening light, and the pale brown flesh of her bare arms sagged against her body.

Downstairs, Beka trailed her mother around the yard with a full bucket of water and two tin cans. Chuku and Zandy were already hard at work, pulling out grass and weeds from under the rose bushes planted in the bottom halves of twelve kerosene drums cut off at the middle. The soil in the yard was too poor for roses so, every now and then, Lilla bought richer soil from a man who filled his dory with it miles further up the creek and then paddled back to sell it to gardeners in the town. While Lilla tended the roses and maidenhair ferns, Beka dashed water at the bushy crotons, at the oleander, and at the red hibiscus flowers with their tongues hanging out, even though Lilla had told her, time and again, that they didn't need all that much water.

Tomorrow, Sunday, Lilla would come downstairs to cut whatever nice flowers she could find in the yard. There were two small graves at Lord's Ridge that needed some attention, and many Sunday mornings, excepting when it rained, Lilla and Bill took bouquets to place upon them and stayed at the cemetery to pull out the high grass that grew quickly around the stones. Beka didn't remember the girl that died when she was four, but she remembered her four year old brother who had died when she was eleven. Her brother became sick one day and was buried in the late evening of the next. Dr Clark said the malaria fever had gone to his brain. The dry was coming now, and the sprays from Beka's bougainvillea vine would be missed.

CHAPTER 8

In Beka's mind, of late, a tidal-like wave was always there, and she lived in constant tension between the drawing back of the water, and the violence of its crashing against the shore. And when it crashed, the sound in her brain was the squawking of pelicans, and she was always afraid. And Toycie saw, and she understood, and Toycie was calling to her across the shimmering water. Feeling corned, by the hot sun and salty sea, Beka struggled to her feet, and saw Toycie as if through the rough fishing net upon which she had lain. The net left octagonal shapes on her legs and she felt drunk from sunshine, the ever blowing wind, and the noisy turbulence within her. Toycie was calling again, quieting the monotonous squawking, and her voice was vibrant, and Beka's head cleared,

'You've got to practise, Beka! Climb up on that post and begin!'

Beka's voice trembled as she replied,

'Suppose I fall down, Toycie Qualo? This water only deep.'

'You'll never reach Battlefield Park if you're so *fraida*. Get up on the post. Use the skiff rope!'

'Coward man ke-e-e-ep sound bone,' Beka droned, but she left the safe front porch of the rectangular swimming crawl, built of mangrove trunks lashed tightly together, to teeter cautiously along one of its narrow wooden ledges, towards a thick post near the flat, zinc-roofed stage of the crawl where Toycie stood.

Nigger Gial the Blanco's skiff was moored to the post with a thick rope. Grabbing a dángling end, Beka hoisted herself up. Green long guards and yellow tailed grunts, flicked around the tangles of brown seaweed in the turquoise water below. A strong wind washed over Beka. Squinting her eyes, she looked out towards the blue. Foam surged, and resurged over the reefs but the boat bringing her father for his weekend visit to the island was still nowhere on the horizon.

'All right now, Beka,' Toycie was saying, in a business-like way, waving her arms about. 'Do just like the politicians at Battlefield Park. I am the crowd. I will sing the opening song, and when I am done, you give the speech, all right?'

'All right then, Toycie, but sing quickly because if I fall down off this post, you'll see my moaning ghost walking under thundery clouds, I swear!'

Toycie hooted, and tossing her hair backwards, held up the hand in which she held the imaginary song sheet. She cleared her throat several times before beginning to sing in a rich contralto,

'Oh land of the Gods, by the Carib Sea, our manhood we

pledge to thy liberte-e-e.'

As Toycie sang, Beka squeezed brown feet tightly together and looked towards the island fringed with white shell sand. The left strap of her orange swimsuit was slipping off her shoulder but she didn't dare adjust it. She caught a glimpse of Granny Ivy disappearing with a straw basket in the direction of Fisherman's Town. 'Fried snappers for tea,' she thought. Toycie was singing the last lines,

'Keep watch with the angels, the stars and the mo-o-n, for freedom comes tomorrow noon.'

Beka unfurled her arms toward the island thick with coconut palms and mangrove trees. Several wooden houses were scattered across its centre. One of the larger two-storied ones, directly opposite the long pier leading to the crawl, belonged to the Blancos. Around the bend to the right was Fisherman's Town, where Emilio's grandfather lived, and a long way to the left was the old cemetery where some of the first settlers of the country were buried. Two hundred or more years before, to escape the insect life, disease, heat and swamps of the mainland, British settlers and their African slaves had established residence on the island, returning to the mainland in the dry seasons to cut and ship logwood, later mahogany, to buyers in Europe. The island had been larger then, but hurricanes had blown away large chunks of land, and now from a distance, it seemed to be nothing more than a small length of sand spiralling in the hugeness of the sea.

'We are waiting, Beka!' Toycie called. Beka's head tilted slightly in a bow to the island, and to Toycie sitting about a foot below her, on the edge of the crawl, trailing her toes in the water.

'Good people of Belize,' Beka began in a high falsetto. 'It gives me great pleasure to be here with you all this evening . . .'

Toycie was cracking up with laughter. The wind blew crinkly hair across her face, and sent spit flying from her mouth.

'Beka, gial, you sound exactly like Lady Radison!' She howled again, and said in a choking voice,

'If you talk like that at Battlefield, people will boo you, even your Granny Ivy!'

'Well, there's very little wrong with her ladyship's accent, my pet,' Beka said, mimicing her mother's voice, and as Toycie leaned back on the wide wooden slats howling again, Beka began inching her way to the stage of the pier. Not a good swimmer, she was relieved to be off the post, and didn't mind Toycie's laughter. A huge bank of clouds began to move across the late afternoon sun, and the air was suddenly chilly. Jumping off the narrow ledge, she looked towards Fisherman's Town.

'I think I see Milio coming already, Toycie!' Toycie glanced swiftly towards the island and both girls looked for a minute at the lean figure walking along the beach, his white shirt puffing in the breeze.

'Let him come then,' Toycie said, in attempted nonchalance.

'Did you two quarrel, Toycie?'

'Not quarrel exactly, but he's beginning to act funny.'

The girls sat huddled together under a large, fraying, striped towel, their backs resting against the small changing room. Far out in the purpling blue, the foam continued to break without rest over the reefs. Somewhere out there in 1798, the battle of St. George's caye had been fought. A few British masters assisted by black slaves had beaten back a fleet of Spanish man-o-wars, and this event was celebrated throughout the colony on September Tenth each year. Granny Ivy said that Belize people liked to remember the battle, because it was one of the few things attempted in the country that hadn't broken down. The slavery part, what was known of it, Granny Ivy often commented, many liked to pretend hardly ever existed.

'Do you think the boat will come after all today, Toycie? It's getting so late.'

'It can still come,' Toycie replied distractedly, and Beka understood that Toycie was feeling unusually nervous about Emilio's regular evening visit. Emilio fished for the greater part of the day with his grandfather, and so Toycie saw him mostly in the afternoons and in the evening, until just before darkness when the girls were expected to be inside the house. But some nights, Toycie slipped out of the house when she thought everyone was asleep, and she wouldn't return until after midnight. Beka knew, and often lay awake wondering whether to tell on Toycie or what else to do.

'You think Milio will marry you when you graduate, Toycie?'

'He said so,' Toycie replied, standing up and wrapping the towel into a skirt around her waist.

'Panias scarcely ever marry creole like we, Toycie.'

'It's nobody's business but my own,' Toycie said, beginning to hum a popular West Indian calypso.

The humming annoyed Beka. She knew what Toycie was like when it came to talking about Emilio but she was afraid for her friend. Granny Ivy said that Toycie was trying to raise her colour, and would wind up with a baby instead of a diploma, if she wasn't careful. Beka didn't get on very well with Emilio, and only spoke to him when she absolutely had to do so. He made fun of her swimming, and would sometimes duck her in the water, laughing with his head thrown back when she surfaced spluttering. Sometimes, Milio took them fishing in *Nigger Gial* beyond the crawl where the sea was quite rough. Beka would often ask to be put ashore because she felt seasick which annoyed Toycie and made Emilio say, only half-amused,

'A big Belize gial like you and you can't even take a little salt water!'

He would shy the oar at her, making the boat rock even more. Emilio had come between the girls so often that week that Beka was beginning to feel displaced in Toycie's affections.

Emilio Sanchez Villanueva was a real 'cayebwoy' who loved the sea, and all the activities connected with it. He was seventeen, like Toycie, and could swim better than all the boys in his age group, and some out of it. He enjoyed a kind of celebrity at Fisherman's Town because he could dive for a long time, and was always sure to bring up a big conch. Emilio could scale and gut fish as well and as fast as his grandfather. His hair was prematurely greying, and the Maya Indian blood was more pronounced in his complexion than the Spanish, of which he seemed more proud.

The Villanuevas didn't belong to St. George's Caye. Emilio was born at Ambergris Caye near the Mexican border, and lived there until he was fourteen. After he passed the entrance examination to St. Anthony's Jesuit College, his parents sold their caye property to finance Emilio's education in Belize, where the whole family, except his paternal grandfather now lived. Emilio's father got a job as a salesman at Blanco's, and a year or so later, his mother started working there as an invoice typist. Whenever Mrs Villañueva was visited by her caye friends, she always said the Agency's name in full. It sounded impressive, and her friends were always impressed because the whole country knew that Mr Blanco worked his employees hard, but he always gave some consideration to their welfare. Grandfather Villanueva had been allowed to live for as long as he wished on Mr Blanco's small property in Fisherman's Town.

Emilio had nearly reached the pier. His shirt was open in front and tied in a knot at his waist. His faded pants were rolled to the knees. Toycie said to Beka still leaning against the changing room.

'I'll just go with Milio for a little walk, Beka. Wait for me by the dory on shore, all right?'

'Don't go, Toycie gial,' Beka said. 'Let's wait for the boat a little longer.'

'I must go, Beka!'

'You'll wind up with a baby if you're not careful, Toycie Qualo!'

'Shut your pound of liver lip, Beka Lamb!' Toycie shouted. 'At least I passed into fourth form even if I *am* thinking about boys.' She began to run towards Emilio who was coming towards them along the pier.

'Toycie, Toycie, wait 'pon me!' Beka called beginning to run after Toycie. But Toycie and Emilio had jumped off the pier and were beginning to walk quickly along the sand path in the direction of the old cemetery. Beka stopped her chase breathless, beside a small storage crawl used for storing live seafood. At the bottom, a conch sucked into the sand, while another was on its back exposing the deep pink pearliness of its shell. A big crayfish clawed at the mangrove posts, fraying the cloth-like bark, as it tried to gain the open sea. Near her bare feet, on the pier, were tiny silver sprats cut into pieces of bait, alongside thread and safety pins Chuku and Zandy had been using earlier in the afternoon.

At one time, Toycie and Beka asked little more of life than to be on the island, walking up and down the hot sand path to and from Fisherman's Town, to swim in the crawl or nearer the beach, to fish from the slats of the pier with thread and pins, trying to catch one of the cunning long guards that swam in schools in the shallower water near the beach, to curl up on the sand with the family at moonlight listening to a fisherman play his guitar, or to sit on the steps of a house watching older people dance by hurricane lanterns to a mouth organ and improvised instruments. And later, to walk sleepily home, listening to the disjointed histories of families that owned the houses on the caye now, and in the days long gone.

These were the memories they looked forward to reliving all year long. They had been at the caye six days already, but the island in some strange way, seemed to know that it could only show it's treasures to quiet minds, and receptive hearts, and it had turned away, turned away from old friends who needed the splendour of its healing. As Beka hurried towards the beach, the waves beneath the pier rose high to sprinkle water over her feet. The beach front was deserted. There seemed only to be grey clouds, grey island, and empty, grey sea all around.

CHAPTER 9

Three pelicans wheeled low over the sea. Beka jumped off the bottom of the old sailing dory, and walked a few yards to the beach. A wave curled coldly around her ankles and then retreated. She looked south, in the direction of the old cemetery and saw with relief that Toycie was running back, her hair bushing up and around her face. Beka scanned the sea swiftly once again, and then started for the house. Toycie's voice came along the wind,

'Wait 'pon me, Beka!' Beka hesitated for a minute, and then moved towards Toycie, shuffling barefooted amongst the seaweed piled onto the beach. The girls were about two yards apart when Toycie yelled,

'Watch you foot, Beka! Man-o-war!' Beka leaped to sandy

ground, her flesh prickling as she saw the transparent, purple coloured sac, bloated with poison, half-covered by seaweed only a short distance from where her foot had been. Toycie stood beside her breathing hard. She picked up a piece of driftwood and began poking the sac.

'They're all along the beach today,' she said.

Beka felt a sudden distaste for the sea.

'And where's manfish Milio?' she asked.

'He stayed behind to give me time to get into the house, and he doesn't like you calling him that.'

'If Sister Virgil only *hears* you have a boyfriend she'll suspend you, Toycie.'

'Don't say anything to Miss Lilla or your Granny Ivy, *please*, Beka, otherwise they'll keep me inside.'

'Have I ever backed story about you, Toycie Qualo?'

'No, Beka, but I promised to meet Milio for a little while after tea and they might ask, that's all.'

'We'd better go back,' Beka said. 'It's time to help make tea.'

'Let's practise again tomorrow, Beka!' Toycie said in an attempt at cheer. 'Even if Mr Bill doesn't send you back to school, you can still learn to be a politician and give speeches on the rostrum at Battlefield Park.'

'I don't want to be a politician any more, Toycie,' Beka answered, as they began walking single file along the path.

'What do you want to do then?' Toycie asked over her shoulder.

'Pass into second form. Remember that story about the lady and the tiger in elementary reading book. I keep wondering which one will get off that boat when my Dad gets here.'

'Never mind, Beka,' Toycie said, tying the towel more firmly around her hips. 'We'll study again tonight after tea. You must try and get the times tables right though, promise?'

'I promise.'

Toycie grasped her hand, and together they left the path leading to Fisherman's Town and began sprinting towards the fence. The Blanco house, white, with rust-coloured shutters, was set far away from the beach, coconut trees forming a semicircle around the back and sides. The stairs, overlooking the pier, crawl, and sea, descended from an ample verandah to a front yard covered with layers of white shell sand that chinkled underfoot. On moonlit evenings, Beka sometimes sat on the front stairs, conscious of the height of the house hulking behind her, as she listened to the sea and trees trying to hush the island to sleep, or watched the silhouette of an occasional sailboat docking at one of the neighbouring piers that interrupted the flow of the beach to the right of the house.

There were two families in the colony that Beka both envied and admired. One of these was the Blanco family. Beka wished, on the rare occasions when the two families were at the caye simultaneously, that she could somehow observe the Blancos closer at hand. But, as is often the case, wealth, class, colour and mutual shyness, kept the children of the two families apart, although they occupied the top and bottom of the same house.

Beka tried to imagine their life from the little she could see: the Maya Indian servant, long plaits jiggling, running after the four children in the yard waving their anklets and patent leather shoes, an existence where one's father had achieved a status not unlike a Maya deity — raining blessings upon his employees as long as the rituals were ceremoniously enacted, the sacrifices offered, and the commandments obeyed. He was the kind of man that inspired the devotion of people like her Dad who looked on him as a model of what a man could do through hard work, using the opportunities available in a land where, at that time, black models in the commercial sphere were hard to find. His wife, she hardly ever saw, except for the few times Mrs Blanco ventured down the back steps to give her mother a pot of steaming escabeche, the hot tortillas wrapped up in an exquisitely embroidered napkin.

As the girls pushed open the picket gate to the yard, Beka's mother called from the kitchen outside the downstairs apartment,

'It's about time you two came home! Did you see *Mermaid*?'

'No boat yet,' the girls chorused.

'Lay the table then, Beka, and Toycie, please bath the boys.'

Beka fetched the cotton dresses they'd slung over a clothes line, stretched between two dwarf coconut trees to the rear of the yard, while Toycie took her turn bathing in a tall, narrow stall close to the kitchen, pouring tin cans full of silky rainwater over her hair and skin. In the thatched, open fronted kitchen, Lilla continued to fry fish in boiling coconut oil, stepping back quickly whenever oil, mixed with water, spat out of the pan. Beside her, at the firehearth, Granny Ivy turned johnny cakes expertly with her fingers as they browned in the big, black iron pot. When Beka was dressed, Toycie called to Chuku and Zandy racing soldier crabs on the concrete foundations of the pinewood posts of the house,

'Chuku, Zandy, come, let me throw water over your skin.'

'We not dirty, Toycie!' Chuku protested, his hair, cropped to a close cap, grey with sand. 'We bathe all day!'

'One more race, Toycie, one more,' Zandy kept pleading, one arm elbowing his short pants onto his hips, while he held down the cone-shaped shell of his crab with the other.

'Come and wash off that salt water the two of you, or I will fling those crabs to kingdom come!' Toycie called again raising her voice. Irritated, Granny Ivy swung her wide body out of the kitchen, grabbing off its hook the bamboo kiss-kiss used to pluck hot wood and coals from the firehearth. She clicked the long tongs threateningly, and, dropping their crabs, the boys rushed squealing over to where Toycie stood waiting for them with the soap and rag outside the stall.

In the downstairs, built under half the floor space of the house above, Beka spread a red and white cloth on the table, padding back and forth on the bare pinewood floor, setting out heavy cream-coloured saucers and cups from a wire netted safe near the large window at the side of the house. In an adjoining room there were bunk beds built on either side of another large window, with a view of the beach and the sea.

Granny Ivy came in with the hot cakes wrapped in a large piece of cloth. Knotting it tightly several times to keep them warm, she said in a peevish way, the wrinkles in her cheeks deepening,

'I bought fish from Lahoudie at Fisherman's Town this afternoon and we got to talking about the stoning of Mr Hartley's house last year. He insisted only the Hartley house was stoned, but I am sure a few others got it too. Lahoudie is growing old, like misself.' Beka knew that her Granny Ivy didn't enjoy being out at the caye because she was missing several political meetings in Belize, and would have to hear about them second hand from Miss Eila or Miss Flo.

The Hartley family was creole, but they lived lives that had much in common with civil servants from England who headed many of the departments of the colony's Civil Service. The Hartley sons attended boarding schools abroad, returning home only for vacations. From her verandah at home in Belize, Beka sometimes saw them passing by, shirts neatly tucked into trousers with creases as sharp as razor blades. The three light-brown boys stepped smartly along the street in step ladder fashion, hands in their pockets, looking neither to the left nor the right. This ability to look straight ahead was a thing of wonder to Beka who often bumped into irate people on the street as she walked along gazing behind her at some person or object that attracted her attention. Mr and Mrs Hartley attended functions at Government House which meant they had reached the pinnacle of the small creole society. There were a few other families like the Hartleys, who, on trips to England, were invited to parties on the lawns of Buckingham Palace, and they displayed, on their centre tables, framed photographs of themselves with members of the royal family to prove it. Beka observed the Hartleys with envious admiration whenever she had the opportunity, and, curious about anything to do with them, she asked,

'How come, Gran?'

'How come, what, Beka?'

'How come Mr Hartley's house got stoned?'

'Don't you remember anything from one day to the next, Beka?'

'Did it happen yesterday?'

'Are you cheeking me, Beka?'

'No, Gran, no,' Beka said. 'It was only a little joke.'

'All right then, but better save your smartness for school, if there is any schooling left for you to do!'

Beka waited until her Gran had returned to the room with the teapot, cosy and strainer before she said,

'Tell me about the stoning again, Gran.'

'Well, as I was telling Lahoudie, far as I remember, the crowd went to Mr Hartley's house and stoned it because he was supporting West Indies Federation, and they stoned several others too.

Then that night, a crowd marched to Government House and somebody knocked out the guard. That was when the Governor put a ban, for a long time, on our political meetings and the Princess' visit was cancelled which was just as well, for people like us don't like the British anymore.'

This was news to Beka. Things British had nearly always been things best. Beka's notion of British was a glimpse of Sir John and Lady Radison on the Battle of St. George's Caye Day the year before she entered St Cecilia's, when the elementary schools, partly funded by the Government, assembled for their annual march to Government House. The afternoon sun, at its most venomous, sent perspiration trickling down her face and she took frequent swigs from the water bottle slung across her chest. She thoroughly enjoyed marching to the blaring brass bands along the streets packed with crowds of wildly cheering people, their upheld umbrellas undulating and shimmering like an unending rainbow all along the route. She shook her Union Jack vigorously at relatives, friends and acquaintances calling to her from windows and verandahs swathed in red, white and blue cloth.

The Governor and his wife, looking small against the expanse of the house behind them, stood on the top step of the broad verandah inspecting the children streaming past in schools. That day, the whole world seemed decorated in red, white and blue; the bleached whiteness of school uniforms reflected the foam on the sea below the lawns of Government House, her sateen waist ribbon matched the cobalt blue of the sea beyond the reef, and the blood-red hibiscus ringing the lawns was the red of the streamers dangling and fluttering on the hats of the children marching four abreast as far as the eye could see. The Governor's medals glittered against the stiff white uniform, the plumes of his helmet dipped slightly as he saluted the cheering schools. Lady Radison's face was shadowed by her wide brimmed hat, as she waved a gloved hand at the children who shouted, 'Hip, hip, hooray!' A few of the ruder ones amongst them sang under their breaths, 'Dog di walk, and puss di talk and rabbit deh behind, O!' stifling their giggles and swinging their arms with exaggerated vigour as they swept past the Governor and his wife. Beka marched with such enthusiasm that her twice-starched cotton frock scratched her legs like cattle wire . . .

'Did you hear me, Beka?'

'What, Gran?'

'I said, why are you standing there with your mouth open and that cup in your hand?'

'I was listening to you . . .'

'Well, I finished a good minute ago.'

There was a step at the door, and her mother came in with a dinner plate piled high with oval slices of golden brown barracuda and small red snappers fried to a crisp. Setting the plate in the middle of the table she said,

'I was just thinking about what you were saying a while ago in the kitchen, Miss Ivy, and I think one of these days we might well be sorry if we don't federate. Federation would give us all a chance to rise, and it must be better than a Guatemalan takeover. The Indians over the border have a bad time. Think what they'd do to *us*!'

'Just look at my cross now, Jesus!' Miss Ivy said, raising her eyes to the ceiling. 'Who do you hear in their right senses wanting Guatemalan takeover, Lilla Lamb?'

'Well, it's your party talking all the time about how great things are over there, and that's where our destiny is because we are on the mainland, but the way I see it, Miss Ivy . . .'

'That's not it, that's not it at all,' Miss Ivy interrupted. 'The British Government, and the British Lumber Company want federation because they would get more cheap labour. I say, if there is any federating to do, it should be after we are independent and know more about this country. Poor people can't even vote yet!'

'We need more people here, Miss Ivy, and the West Indians would work the land.'

'Which land?'

'There's a lot of land here.'

'Don't fool yourself. A lot of land here is crown land, and the B.L.C. and others like it buy up most of the good land from the time before. They're not using it, but it's to force us to work for starvation wages instead of for ourselves. They keep reminding us that we are hewers of wood, not farmers, and we believe it.'

'I know all that, Miss Ivy, but *eventually*. The British won't want to stay forever and if we band with the other West Indian islands, eventually we would number enough to make a difference!'

'Why is it so dark in here?' Granny Ivy asked. 'Don't we have kerosene now?' Beka went to the door and called,

'Toycie, Chuku, Zandy, tea ready!'

Toycie appeared at the doorway with the hurricane lantern which lit up the room. She hung the lantern on a hook on the ceiling and prepared to sit down. The boys rushed into the house dragging three-legged stools from underneath the table.

'No fish head for me, Ma, just tail,' Chuku said.

'Me too, me too, no head, no head,' Zandy was saying.

'Tail and head go together,' Lilla said, slipping a small snapper onto each plate.

As she sat at the table eating hot johnny cakes, soaked with Australian creamery butter, Beka was wondering who those other British were that Granny Ivy was vexed with. They weren't visible to her around the town except for the soldiers at airport camp. And she knew those weren't the British Granny Ivy was maddest about. As if reading her thoughts, Granny Ivy said, biting into her fish as if it didn't have much flavour,

'I'll never forget that Mistress Tate-Sims, and how she treated me like I had no feelings when I was cooking and cleaning for her. Which is why as much as Bill and I disagree about this new politics we are into, him looking at it from the business side and me from another, I still thank God every night He give me a son to save me from the likes of her.'

'She was something else in truth,' Lilla agreed, 'but you know, Miss Ivy, she was having home problems. Her husband, they say, had a creole girl on the side. And don't you remember Granny Straker telling us that in the old days when the British men didn't bring their wives out here, their creole mistresses treated their servants just as bad as the white people, worse, in fact, sometimes?'

'That was befo' time,' Granny Ivy said.

'And how about that nice bishop who gave all his money to a creole watchman? And Baron Bliss left all his money to the colony for no reason.'

'What does one baron and one bishop have to do with anything, Lilla? Though I suppose with the father you have, you will have to defend them.'

'It's Mrs Leigh that gave me the guitar,' Toycie ventured.

'You were underpaid, Toycie,' Granny Ivy sighed moving the skeleton of her fish carefully to the side of her plate.

The boys were under the table tickling Beka's toes, laughing uproariously whenever she reached under the cloth, trying to grab at them. She strained her ears trying to catch the sound of the *Mermaid* above the noise in the room. Toycie asked, 'Shall we clear now, Miss Lilla?'

'Might as well, if the boat comes, Bill will have a cold tea.'

Somebody was knocking at the fence gate with a stick. Granny Ivy went to the bedroom window and called,

'Who's there?'

'It's me, Lahoudie, Miss Ivy. *Mermaid* coming in now, Mam, she's nearly up to the pier.'

'Thanks, Mr. Lahoudie,' Miss Ivy shouted.

The boys jumped up and down telling each other excitedly.

'*Mermaid* coming, *Mermaid* coming — no bed!'

Beka grabbed the lantern and hurried out of the house ahead of everyone to the pier. Tiny waves sparkled in the early moonlight. Running along, Beka could see the *Mermaid's* light bobbing at the bow of the boat as it drew nearer and nearer to the landing stage. The engine shut off with a tired whoosh, and Cap'n Parks threw a rope to Mr Lahoudie who secured it carefully around one of the thick pinewood posts. Beka called,

'You on board, Daddy?'

'Back here, Beka. Come and take this.'

Beka went to the stern of the boat, and her father passed a single overnight bag, before climbing out.

'Where's your Mama, pet?' Beka smelled whisky on his breath, and he still wore his working clothes.

'They're on their way. We thought you weren't going to make it tonight, Daddy.'

'The engine broke down twice this afternoon, or we'd have been here much earlier.'

He left Beka and began walking down the pier to meet Lilla, Granny Ivy, and the boys. Beka, shouldering the bag, hurried behind him wondering why her Dad hadn't brought them any provisions. As she caught up with them, he put his arms around Lilla's shoulders and said,

'Better pack up, Lilla gial. We'll catch a passage on *Mermaid* at six in the morning. Granny Straker died.'

Her mother didn't answer. She sat down on the edge of the pier, her legs dangling over the side like a little girl. Her father sat down beside her, with Chuku and Zandy on his lap, saying across their chattering heads,

'Don't take it too hard, Lilla. You couldn't have done a single thing. She never recovered her senses, died in her sleep.'

Her mother's shoulders were shaking. Beka patted her mother's hand. Granny Ivy came up and said,

'You made it, Bill! Lilla have you seen Toycie? What *happen*, Lilla?'

'Granny Straker gone, Miss Ivy. My one Granny finally gone.'

Her mother was making a small whimpering sound which tugged at Beka's insides. The boys began to cry. Daddy Bill shoved them over to his mother and put his arms around Lilla's shoulders. Granny Ivy shooed the boys ahead of her in an agitated way, shouting,

'Toycie, Toycie! Where the hell is that gial?'

Beka didn't reply, but she knew. She had seen Toycie walking down the beach towards the old cemetery. Bill Lamb was trying to coax Lilla to her feet and Granny Ivy said to Beka,

'Go find Toycie and tell her to get home, we have to pack up. What she's doing wandering around at this time of night I don't know and just when we need her!'

'Yes, Gran,' Beka replied starting to jog along the pier towards the beach. She didn't want to go. Although it was moonlight, the cemetery end of the island was always deserted at night. In the daytime it was different. It was fun to go then, scrabbling over the broken graves, trying to make out the names and dates, or to gather coco plums from the bushes that grew in thick clumps on that side of the island. When Toycie and herself were younger, they'd sit on the crumbling grave stones eating the fleshy pink and white plums as they played a guessing game, trying to figure out which graves might be buccaneer graves and which were slave people's graves, or wondering whether the early settlers buried treasures in the graves like the Mayas used to do when priests and nobles died. Beka had reached a narrow part of the island where the sea was close on one side and the swamp thick with mangroves was on the other. As she drew nearer to the cemetery she began to shout.

'O Toycie, Toycie O, Granny Ivy says come on home!'

There was no answer for a little while, and yet she knew Toycie must be there with Milio. She left the path and went up to the fence that surrounded the small graveyard.

'Toycie,' she called, 'Are you back there?' The bushes rustled and from behind a clump of coco plum trees, Toycie and Milio came toward where Beka stood peering over the fence. Toycie looked shamefaced, and Milio's shirt tail hung loose over his khaki pants. Beka could tell from their faces that they thought she was interfering again, so she said quickly,

'My Greatgranny dead, Toycie, and we have to go to Belize tomorrow. Come and help pack!'

'Madre de Diós!' Milio said blessing himself. He helped Toycie through the broken fence and she said, not looking at him,

'See you in town, Emilio.'

'All right, mi vida,' Emilio said. 'Condolences to your Mama, Beka!'

The girls ran back along the path, awash now with moonlight. They ran as if all the ghosts of long dead slaves were pursuing them. They ran as they had when they were children except that then it had always been in the daytime with the wind pushing them along at a speed almost as fast, it had seemed, as the gulls flying over the sea. Out of breath Toycie came to a stop.

'Let's walk, Beka,' she said. 'I can't run any more.' Her face looked pinched. They panted along and when Toycie had caught her breath she said,

'Girl, I feel bad about your Granny Straker. But you're still luckier than me. You have Miss Lilla, your Daddy and Miss Ivy.'

'You have Miss Eila, Toycie.'

'Yes, but it's not the same. My own mother scarcely writes to me anymore. I'd feel better if she were dead. She went to America when I was two and has never come back. She's married to a man in Brooklyn who doesn't even know she has me back here.'

'What happened to your Daddy?'

'Miss Eila said that my father was a coolie man. He went to Panama to work before I was born, but he never came back or wrote to my mother. So my Mama lent me to Miss Eila because she had no children and wanted me.'

They were approaching the Blanco house, and the girls started running again. Beka's Dad was at the gate. They could see the glow of his cigarette as he waited for them. He came out to the gate and called,

'That you Beka? Toycie?'

All of a sudden the confused feelings she had about her father began to ease. He must care about her, for he too had gone to Panama for a short time, but had come home. She shouted,

'It's us, Daddy, it's us!' and leaving Toycie behind, she ran, stumbling across the sand, to where her father stood in the shadow of the Blanco house.

CHAPTER 10

Beka sat wedged between Granny Ivy and her Mama Lilla, watching Aunt Tama directing traffic at the front door. The elastic band which fastened a straw hat onto Beka's head was squeezing the undersides of her chin. Her body still felt sun-soaked and water-logged although she had lain across her bed for two hours after their arrival in Belize from St. George's caye shortly before noon.

Aunt Tama's tiny parlour felt like a baking pot. As many mourners as could fit into the room were there. Amongst the women seated on straight backed chairs lining the walls, were Miss Eila and Toycie, fanning themselves with long-handled straw fans. Beka's Dad, his hands behind his back, and her Uncle Curo, in a double-breasted woollen suit, stood on the front porch whispering quietly with other men. The three o'clock sun was not shut out by Aunt Tama's white bobbinet curtains. The sunlight zig-zagged whenever one of the women opposite moved to the right or left, and the light hit Beka in the eyes, making them water. Everytime this happened, Beka sniffed, and each time Granny Ivy passed Beka a handerchief smelling of lemon grass cologne.

Outside, she could hear footfalls as people lined up for the procession to the Holy Redeemer Cathedral, and thence to Lord's Ridge. Through the door to the right of where she sat, she had a good view of the glass-sided hearse, draped in purple. The horse was snorting and shaking its head, depositing large clumps of dung on the pot-holed streets. The Sodality ladies, mostly mestizos, dressed in white and blue, held their mantilla ends over their noses delicately as they passed the horse to join the procession. Beka saw the driver lean sideways in his seat, high up on the hearse, to take a stephanotis wreath from Mrs Villanueva and sling it carefully over a corner knob with black plumes. Mrs Villanueva was a member of Our Lady of Sorrows Sodality, as Greatgran Straker had been.

The sun hit Beka's eyes again, and she used the handkerchief Granny Ivy shoved at her to blow her nose. The coffin was laid in the middle of the room and Beka could smell freshly varnished pine; she had not yet looked in. Beka's Dad cleared his throat at the door, and Aunt Tama, her head bowed and the wide golden hoops in her ears bouncing against her cheeks, moved closer to where he stood. He said quietly, but loud enough for everyone to hear,

'It's time, Tama.'

Granny Ivy immediately gripped Beka's arm, propelling her over towards the coffin. She was shocked to see Greatgran's face looking so slack. Somebody had stuck the curved tortoiseshell comb in the very middle of Greatgran's hair, which was dressed all wrong, and Greatgran's mouth was twisted. The coffin was closed, and carried slowly out of the house and down the stairs by Daddy Bill, Uncle Curo and two other friends. Beka followed behind Lilla and Granny Ivy staring at the men's grip on the silver plated handles of the coffin. She was conscious of the onlookers crowding the neighbouring verandahs, and of the people lining both sides of the street to watch. Crossing the boxboard bridge over the drain to the street, Beka heard a woman say to her companion,

'Old Mother Straker was one of the last. Not too many left now of the old people that remember things from the time before. The young ones aren't interested. All they think about is picture show, motor car, party and clothes.'

Beka looked up into the woman's face, shaped like a cashew seed, and the woman said,

'This one here, she is one of the great grand pickney, no better and no worse.'

Ahead of them, Aunt Tama was tearfully accepting condolences of people lining the street sides, and Granny Ivy was muttering indignantly to Lilla,

'Why is Tama wearing black mantilla with her black skin?'

'That is her prerogative, Miss Ivy,' Lilla replied.

'Prerogative my backside! It's since Tama came back from Honduras Republic that she start acting like pania. Everytime I did something to help her in the house this afternoon she said,

'Gracias Ivy, my corazón!'

The coffin was hearsed, and Beka's Daddy came down the line of people to seat them in a black car Mr Blanco had lent the Lambs for the occasion. Aunt Tama and Beka were put in front and Granny Ivy and Lilla had the back seat to themselves. Beka noticed that Daddy Bill's eyes were bloodshot, the lids swollen and heavy. He had loved Greatgran Straker as much as he did his own mother. He had helped organize the funeral and was paying many of the expenses.

Beka heard the wheels of the hearse crunching on the street as it moved off, the men following on foot, then the women, then the cars. All along the route from Aunt Tama's house on Manioc Road, down Water Lane, where many bars were situated, and over the swing bridge, people lined the street sides. Women and children stood on verandahs. Anyone could spare the time, stopped whatever they were doing to watch the funeral go by. It was a custom. It was important to know who had died, under what circumstances, to whom the person was related, and who the mourners were following the hearse, and why they felt the need to attend this particular funeral. There were few events that commanded the total attention of the community as much as a passing funeral. Its size was commented upon, and the life story of the deceased, whatever was known of it, whispered from person to person. It was more than a funeral they watched. In a way, it was a small lesson in community history, and everyone, for those minutes, was a diligent scholar. Belizeans did not often articulate what they did know of their history, even amongst themselves. By and large, most people preferred to forget the time that had gone before. But on certain occasions, and especially at the funerals of the very aged, through the use of innuendos and euphemisms, a feeling was communicated, and this was understood.

The only song Beka really heard during the service was the one her mother sang, without the accompaniment of the organ, in the choir balcony projecting from the rear wall of the cathedral. Her mother made a false start, but then her voice moved with strength over the assemblage. Aunt Tama was crying, and Granny Ivy kept shoving the damp handkerchief towards her, but she wouldn't take it. Daddy Bill stared fixedly at an enormous statue of St. Joseph, holding a long-stemmed lily, standing on a ledge high above Beka's head. The service was short, and similar to many other Catholic services, and the priest spoke a few words with as genuine feeling as he could manage, a few more songs were sung, and then he led the way out of the church.

The cars kept pace with the pedestrians walking ahead, and on the slow ride to Lord's Ridge, Beka could hardly believe that Greatgran would never talk to her again about buying a small plot of land in the little town of Boom, not far from Belize, where she could tend fruit trees, do a little gardening and teach parrots to talk. Granny Straker had felt close to the earth. Once Greatgran had said to her in the kitchen of Aunt Tama's house where Beka was spending the day,

'There's no need to be so delicate about gutsing that chicken, Beka! You and that chicken made from much the same thing. Push your hand into the hole and pull everything out. You are the earth, and the earth is you, and there is nothing so dirty on or in it that you can't try to clean. Just as long as you wash your hands with strong blue soap after.'

Beka had not replied, but a lot of the time she did not feel like that about the earth she saw and felt around her in town. She didn't enjoy sitting outdoors on grass and hot sand for very long. The earth was often times swampy and smelly. Mosquitoes, fireants, and sandflies always found her. Hurricanes and storms had uprooted many shade trees that would have sheltered the town's streets. The weather was often stickily hot, making a person sweat until she smelt like peccary.

At the cemetery, mosquitoes gathered in their swarms around the hole that Greatgran Straker was finally getting as her own. Family and friends circled the priest as he performed the rites of Christian burial. Beka was glad that Greatgran had died not knowing that she had failed first form. Glancing up at her mother's face, Beka could tell that Mama Lilla was taking comfort in that thought too. Greatgran had been so proud the first time she saw Beka in her convent uniform. 'When you walk up the aisle at Parish Hall for that diploma, Beka, we'll all be walking with you,' she'd said.

Beka watched the grave-diggers lower the coffin into the hole with ropes, shuddering as she heard the coffin hit the watery grave with a splat. She dropped her handful of earth onto the lid and walked towards the gate of the cemetery before the diggers could start shovelling earth on top of Greatgran Straker. She caught up with Miss Eila and Toycie who were walking that way too. Mrs Villanueva was already at the gate, stamping her feet on the ground trying to drive mosquitoes away. Beka and Toycie paused to read a few of the names and dates on the nearby graves, but Miss Eila, her hair neatly combed, and put together under a brown felt hat, a wisp of beige veiling touching her forehead, went up to Mrs Villanueva and said,

'Fly only bad at graveside, comadre!'

'Ay, Diós mio!' Mrs Villanueva replied in agreement. 'And how are you, Senora Qualo?'

Miss Eila paused for a moment looking down at petite Mrs Villanueva who was trying to be kind. Miss Eila observed greying curly hair covered with a lacy mantilla, the fine material of her Sodality dress, the chain around her neck with the golden cross, the stockinged feet, and the white pumps. Miss Eila smelled the cologne and saw the wide wedding band. Wrapping her big knuckles tightly around her handkerchief rolled up into a ball,

Miss Eila replied matter of factly,

'I am not a senora, Mrs Villanueva. I never had the good fortune to get married.' Mrs Villanueva glanced for a second down at Miss Eila's bad foot, then she turned to Beka saying,

'How we will miss your Granny at Sodality, Beka! Her rice and beans stall at our Christmas bazaar always made such a lot of money.' Beka nodded her head and Miss Eila said,

'How is Toycie doing with her guitar lessons, comadre?'

'*So* good, Senora, *so* good. Toycie is already nearly better than I am. Perhaps she could continue on her own now for a little while? I am so busy, Senora, so busy.' Patting Miss Eila on the arm she continued, 'And marriage is not easy Senora, not easy, and Emilio? He is not studing as he should . . . so difficult, so difficult.'

'Oh, I understand, comadre,' Miss Eila said. 'I am lucky with Toycie here. I never have to stand with a stick over her head to make her study. But since you're so busy we'll stop the lessons for a while.'

'Muchas gracias, Senora. I am glad you comprehend. It's a problem for me to do everything.' She turned to Toycie, and putting her arms around her shoulder, looked into her eyes and said,

'I am *so* sorry, reina! Did you see Emilio and his grandfather at the caye?' Toycie nodded her head, and Mrs Villanueva looking worried and half sad said,

'I am so glad. We all love you like our daughter . . .'

'Juana!' Mr Villanueva, his stomach hanging like a pillow over his pants, stood by the cemetery gate beckoning to Mrs Villanueva.

'Adiós, amigas,' she called, and they watched her scrabbling over the uneven and unkempt grounds of the cemetery towards the road where her husband stood by the open car door, waiting impatiently for her to enter. Miss Eila, Toycie and Beka stood there for a long time without speaking, slapping mosquitoes, and watching the grave-diggers make a peaked mound over the place where Greatgran Straker lay buried.

CHAPTER 11

On the ninth morning after Greatgran Straker died, Granny Ivy returned from Bridge Foot market with her everyday straw basket bulging.

'I bring fish for today and some tough beef to stew for tomorrow, Lilla, since we'll sleep late because of the wake tonight. You going to wake, Beka?'

'Mama says no, Gran. I have to study anyhow.'

'Why not, Lilla? Beka over fourteen now and it's holiday time. No harm in it.'

'I don't believe in it, Miss Ivy. How Aunt Tama could plan a thing like this, knowing how I feel and then ask Bill to help pay for it, I don't know. My Grandmother was Christian, and she had a Christian burial. We don't need to protect ourselves from my Granny Straker.'

'Well, whatever else I may say 'bout Tama, I must tell you that she at least don't give up *all* the old ways.'

'That's just a bunch of superstition, Miss Ivy. When a person dies, that's it. No amount of bramming can do a thing more. Granny Straker's spirit isn't roaming around trying to hurt a single soul.'

'It's only a get-together to remember and pay respect to the dead, Lilla. Tama is cooking, and getting the musicians. You should be glad to hear people talking about the days when your Grandmother was young. Moreover, a lot of people over on that side could do with a boil-up from those that have it to give. It's a help to the living.'

'It's not the money to feed people that worry me, Miss Ivy. I know all about the old days when Granny Straker was young. I know it by heart, and I don't need a wake to remind me. I am fed up with it. I don't want to remember. The old ways will poison the new. I don't want Beka getting into the habit of those things. She's having enough trouble right now with school.'

'Lawd, Lill, you actin' like the wake is obeah.'

'It's all connected, Miss Ivy. It's all connected.'

'All connected to what, Mama?'

Ignoring the question, Lilla continued,

'Granny Straker wouldn't have wanted a wake. She was trying to progress. And that's what Bill and I are trying to do with this family. You and Tama as bad that way as the Caribs in Stann Creek that you associate with.'

'Miss Benguche in elementary school says Caribs have a lot of traditions that creoles give up, Mama. She thinks keeping them is a good thing if they don't do any harm.'

'Stay out of this, Beka,' Lilla said. 'Here, start scaling this fish. Start from the tail and go down. You might as well learn kitchen work, because it seems like that's all you'll be good for.'

'You don't know a thing 'bout Carib people, Lilla,' Granny Ivy said, bumping yams, oranges and plantains onto the counter.

'After '31 hurricane, families in Stann Creek sent food to feed lots of people up here, and we were glad to take from their hands then. After service, I don't close my church door. And anyhow, when you get right down to it, Carib and creole are branches of the same African tree, although I am not saying I could marry a Carib man . . .'

'Miss Ivy, let me tell you something,' Lilla interrupted, pointing the butcher knife covered with scales at Miss Ivy. 'Tama practises a lot of things she learnt down there. She even frighten Beka one time when I sent Beka with her for a few days to Stann Creek. All Beka did was take two johnny cakes from the pile she left to cool, but she lied to Tama about it. Tama took Beka to her bedroom with the other children of the house, closed the curtains and set a table. She filled a glass with water. Took a hair from her head, tied it to a wedding ring, and held it in the glass over the water, and then she pretended that the ring bumped against the glass by itself when Beka's name was called. All the time chanting I don't know what all. To this day, Beka believes that ring bumped against the glass by itself!'

'Anyhow,' Granny Ivy continued just as if Lilla hadn't been talking, 'I don't believe Carib people sacrifice children and I don't believe that if they put a doll with pins and a bottle of fowl blood under the stairs . . .'

'Miss Benguche says,' Beka interrupted, wiping the scales off her cheek with her frock tail,

'Shut your mouth, Beka.' Granny Ivy said.

'But, Gran, Miss says . . . Miss says . . .'

'I'll clothespin your mouth as well as your flat nose if you don't shut up, Beka! Miss, Miss, all I hear from you is Miss. Keep quiet for a change.'

Flinging the knife down onto the floor, Beka shouted,

'When I grow up I am going to marry a Carib!' The slap across her face came with such swiftness and strength that Beka staggered back against the stove.

'Don't you ever speak to your Gran like that again!'

In agony, Beka rushed up the attic stairs and flung herself across her bed weeping in confusion, guilt and shame. Why couldn't she be good to her family? Why couldn't she learn to say and do the right thing? 'Why am I so horrible?' Beka whispered. 'What is wrong with me?'

Every year, after Christmas, Caribs wearing masks, painted black and red, and dressed in colourful costumes decorated with jingling shells, danced to drums at street corners, and in yards, for gifts of money. The excitement generated by the drumbeats drew the children of the town in swarms. One year the children in Beka's class returned to school, tumbling all over themselves in their eagerness to tell 'teacher' what they had seen, in whose yard, or at which street corner, the drumming or dancing had been best. To quiet the class, Miss Benguche, a Carib, explained that the Caribs were descendants of African slaves who escaped from West Indian plantations by paddling their way to St Vincent. There, they mingled with the Caribans, originally from South America, adopting much of their language and some of their ways, but keeping many of their African traditions. The British wanted the land the Caribs occupied after a while, and so they were shunted to Roatan, in the Republic of Honduras, and quite a number, over the years, paddled to Stann Creek, and other towns along the Belizean coast, where they established towns and villages.

Lilla climbed the stairs slowly and walked over to Beka's attic space to sit on the edge of the bed. She touched Beka's back with a hand smelled of fish and limes, but Beka kept her face to the window.

'Beka, please look at me.' Beka turned her head around, eyes swollen and rebellious. Her mother's face looked frightened and contrite.

'You can come to the wake with us if you still want to, Beka. Why I am trying to keep you away from the things I experienced as a child, I don't rightly know. But sometimes your Mama have bad worries that she can't explain to herself, let alone begin to tell you. But if you like, I'll try to tell you a little about when I was young.' Beka nodded, turning completely around.

'Remember when you came home from school last year and was so angry to find my father sitting at the table? Well, you shouldn't have been. Granny Ivy used to tell me that after my mother died, and for a long time afterwards, he took good care of me. My mother wanted me to go to the convent, so he used to pay for me to go. I was the blackest and poorest one in my class.'

'But your skin is light, and your hair almost straight.'

'Yes, but in those days most black children used to go to the Protestant schools. The majority of the girls at the convent were white skinned, either mestizos, bakras, or children of foreigners. Nobody's fault, just the way it was. Sometimes my shoes had holes. I couldn't sport gold bangles or golden earrings, my clothes didn't look like theirs did. And although I used to invite a few of them to my house, they wouldn't come, excepting once or twice, because my house was in a poor area and it was almost flat on the ground like Toycie's. I felt out of place many times. Well, one day, I said more or less what I am saying to you to my father and he said,

"Well, Lilla, if those things are more important to you than your education, you'd better leave. My skin looks white, but I am a poor man.' He refused to pay to let me finish school. I never spoke very much to him again until last year when you came home from school and found him sitting at the table. So I had two years of high school. Your Dad never went to high school at all."'

Beka was quiet for a while, watching her mother smooth out the wrinkled sheet and trace the red roses she'd embroidered on the edge of Beka's pillow slip.

'Mama?'

'Mmm?'

'Mama, is it the obeah why creole and Carib don't mix too much?'

Her mother's eyes grew puzzled. Then she said,

'To tell you the truth, Beka, I don't rightly know. I doubt if many creoles could tell you. Nobody really remembers the reasons. We creoles are so different, one from the other, that it's hard for us to mix properly amongst ourselves, let alone among Carib people who have a lot more things in common. Maybe it's because Carib people remind us of what we lost trying to get up in the world. See, in the old days, according to Granny Straker, the more you left behind the old ways, the more acceptable you were to the powerful people in the government and the churches who had the power to change a black person's life. Mind you, many of the old ways were harmful, health-wise and so on. Anyhow, when slavery was over in fact, a lot of people only went to the bush to cut mahogany when they absolutely had to do so. The bush maybe reminded them of the cruelties and forced labour, for little or nothing, which they had endured. Living in town became a habit. Some did want to buy land, but the law didn't encourage it. Things are changing though.'

'Is that why you don't like to go up to Sibun for holidays like Daddy Bill and Granny Ivy would prefer us to do?'

Her mother laughed high, long and joyously like Beka had not heard since the day she failed first form.

'That may be true, Beky Beky. You've maybe put your finger on something. Maybe we'll spend our holiday up Sibun River next year. You'd like that wouldn't you?'

Beka nodded, smiling at her mother's happy face.

'Daddy would come with us then, I think.'

'We'll see, Beka. We'll see. Did you find your present yet?'

'No,' Beka answered, startled. 'Which present?'

'Go look in your drawer.'

Beka crossed over to her work table, and pulled hard at the drawer which always stuck. Today it came out so smoothly she stumbled a little. Lying on top of her jumble of papers was a package wrapped in green kite paper and tied with a bright red ribbon twirled into a fancy bow. She opened the package carefully, and there was the new exercise book from Gordillo's. She picked it up, flicking through the pages.

'What's it for, Mama? I have plenty of empty blanks.'

Something dropped with a clink and Beka picked from the floor a beautiful grey-blue fountain pen which she knew her mother must have purchased from St Ignatius Press on Queen Street. Carrying everything to the bed she asked again,

'Why did you give them to me?'

'Well, the pen *was* to be a present for passing. The exercise book I thought about later.'

'Am I going back to school?'

'Your Dad still has not decided. But that pen and that exercise book are only for at home.'

'To do what?

'Well, everytime you feel like telling a lie, I want you to write it down in there and pretend you are writing a story. That way, you can tell the truth and save the lie for this notebook. And when we tell you stories about before time, you can write them down in there, too, for your children to read.'

'I'm never going to get married,' Beka said.

'Then you'll have it for yourself, then.'

'It's a *nice* pen,' Beka said, uncapping it, gently checking to see if the nib had been damaged by its fall.

'Shall I give you a different hairstyle for the wake tonight?'

'Nope,' Beka said. 'I am going to sit right here and write down what you said.'

Pleased that her gift was a success, Lilla's laugh pealed out again,

'Just don't exaggerate, Beka!'

'I'll try not to, Mama love,' Beka laughed in return, opening her brand new exercise book.

CHAPTER 12

At the wake, later that evening, everything appeared to Beka, as Granny Ivy had cautioned it might, similar to every other creole yard party she had ever attended — except that everyone was dressed soberly in white, lavender, black or brown. Bill Lamb joined a group of men drifting towards the bar; while Chuku quickly found himself a place on the front steps below Aunt Tama's parlour. There, a gathering of children sat listening eagerly to Uncle Curo, a glass in his hand, telling of a day long ago when Brer Anancy, the spider, flattered Brer Alligator into carrying him safely to the opposite bank of the Sibun River. Occasionally, the children laughed in loud bursts of self-recognition, at the knowing twists Uncle Curo gave to the familiar tale.

Beka followed her mother, pushing the pram with Zandy sprawled asleep in it, towards a table beneath the bottom of the house, where Granny Ivy and several women stood filling bowls, plates and dishes with savoury rice reddened by kidney beans, potato salad creamy with mayonnaise and chicken stewed in a thick gravy. Lilla wrapped an apron twice around her waist before taking her place behind the table, and Beka leaned across to whisper in her Gran's ear,

'I managed to get her after all, Gran!'

Miss Ivy pinched Beka's nose, chuckling uncertainly in the back of her throat. She gestured with a long pot spoon at the piles of steaming food,

'The chicken isn't bad . . .'

Beka shook her head looking thirstily at the dozens of pint bottles, surrounding a large block of ice, in an aluminium bath pan on the ground beside her feet.

'Some lemonade and a piece of potato pound?'

'Yes, please!' Beka said, upturning a glass and selecting a red lemonade for herself from the pan. Miss Ivy lifted a heavy brown pudding from a side table, cutting a generous slice for Beka. Munching the soft, spicy pudding and sipping her icy drink, Beka leaned against the table and looked around. The higher ground under Aunt Tama's house bottom had been brushed clean, with chairs and benches grouped at the edges of the square, slightly below which, the grassy area began. Under a tamarind tree in the middle of the brightly lit yard, a group of men, dressed tidily in white shirts and dark pants, played a game of cards on Aunt Tama's washing bowl, which they had turned over like a barrel. Daddy Bill was rocking back and forth, first on his toes, then on his heels, talking politics, Beka was sure, with Mr Phillip and other men at the bar which had been made from several planks laid across two carpenters' horses, near the vat. The yard was filling up by the minute, and Beka spied Miss Eila, Aunt Tama, Miss Flo and a quantity of other ladies greeting each other near the back steps. Swallowing the last of her sweet drink, she hurried across,

'O *good* evening everybody, Aunt Tama, Miss Eila, Miss Flo!'

'Noches, Bekacita, my angelita,' Aunt Tama exclaimed getting up, bangles jingling, giving her a huge hug.

'Ladies . . . This is my grandniece, my only one. Isn't she fine? She is the picture of my Mama Straker, no?' Aunt Tama's body felt like the soft pudding Beka had been eating, and one of the golden earrings was digging hard into Beka's cheek, but Beka hugged her with all her might because Aunt Tama was always so encouraging and thought Beka was gold.

'Beka shure resembles her Greatgranny Straker,' Miss Eila agreed.

'To the life!' a scrawny yellow faced lady called Miss Janie said. 'We can hope she grows with Mother Straker's ways.'

'Shush, Tama, shush,' Miss Eila was calling from her bench. 'Your Ma had a long life, and her spirit will live with Beka here.'

Aunt Tama was weeping on Beka's shoulders, making a wet spot on her dress, but Beka continued to hold her tight and Miss Janie, strands of long, grey hair getting into her eyes, grasped Aunt Tama by the arms and led her over to the bench where she sat dabbing at her eyes with a handkerchief she kept tucked in the cleft between her bosom. The women crowded around Aunt Tama murmuring consoling words and kind remembrances of Greatgranny Straker. Beka plucked at Miss Eila's brown skirt asking,

'Miss Eila, excuse me a minute, Miss Eila, but isn't Toycie coming tonight?'

'Toycie sick, pet, sick! Had big vomiting this morning. I warn Toycie time and again about eating green mango and salt. She must have eat ten at least today.' Limping over to a chair, she eased herself into it.

'But we always eat green mango and salt, Miss Eila,' Beka said, watching Miss Eila suck her lip through the gap in her front teeth.

'Every day bucket go to well, one day the bottom fall out! I never see a body crave after green mango and salt so except when they is . . . well, I can't stay long tonight, pet. I left Toycie in a bad way.'

'I was going to drop by tomorrow to get her to check my arithmetic, but I'll wait till she feels better.'

'Still come on by, Beka. It's only the mango and she'll feel better by morning. I'm shure. What a life this is, from one worry to the next!'

Aunt Tama was recovering herself with an effort, blowing her nose with loud honks. She balled up her handkerchief, scrubbed her nose, which was round like Mama Lilla's, heaved a sigh and said,

'My mother was the best that ever lived, amigos, the best, but she had such leetle happiness, such leetle joy, and I was not the best daughter, not the best.'

'Don't be so hard on yourself, Tama.' Miss Janie said, and the ladies chorused,

'Not so *hard*.'

'I feel so guilty, so-o guilty,' Aunt Tama was crying again. 'I left Mama for fifteen years when I lived in Puerto Cortes with my gentleman, fifteen years, and when he died, and I came home, Mama was old and I couldn't catch up . . . oh my God, my sweet Jesu.'

Miss Flo, a short, fat lady with breasts hanging like hoops over her high waist, looked at Beka standing in the middle of the group and said to Tama,

'Better stop that cow bawling and start think of wedding, Tama. Beka is getting to be a big girl.' Aunt Tama looked up startled and she said,

'Beka only fourteen, Flo, not fifteen till next year.'

'You could have fooled me! But children grow faster than when I was young. No more school, eh, Beka?'

'I don't know yet, Miss Flo.'

'Well, take some advice and watch these young boys and married men around here now. They'll take slave man's revenge if you're not careful!' She laughed her deep, belly laugh and Beka, conscious of her knees sticking way out below her dress and the tightness of her blouse, felt uncomfortable.

'What, Miss Flo?' Beka asked.

'Nowadays we outnumber the men, Beka, not like the days before your Greatgranny's time when we had black slaves and white master competing for . . .'

'How about a little pound, Miss Flo?' Aunt Tama asked.

Miss Flo skinned up her top lip as if she couldn't think of anything worse than a little pound.

'One li slice then, Tama. I am more thirsty than hungry.'

'A little coconut water with a drop of rum and some ice to wash down the pound?'

Miss Flo looked bored and disgusted. 'I am heaty,' she said, fanning herself with her frock tail. 'A *little* rum and coconut water would help me out at that. Just a drop mind you, Tama, I am not what you would call a drinker. And forget the pound.'

'Thank you, but *not* a thing for me, Tama,' Miss Eila said when Aunt Tama turned to her. 'I just drop by to pay my respects. Toycie have stomach trouble and I have to go see to her.'

'Heh, heh,' Miss Flo said, not laughing.

'Night, Tama, Janie, Winny, everybody, and oh, Florence, how are your grannies?'

'I have a new one now, Eila!'

'Tell mi ears now,' Miss Eila said. 'Same daddy?'

'Shame on you, Eila! This one is by my granddaughter's third boyfriend!' And she threw back her head and laughed like a dog choking. Suddenly she stopped and looked around wiping laugh water with her fingertips from the corners of her eyes.

'My, my,' she wheezed, 'things shurely are slow at this wake tonight.'

'Oh, but wakes was lively things when I was young!' Miss Janie said through her buck teeth. 'The body was on a cooling board for everybody to pay their respects. What a good wake we had same night as the death. Not the coffee and johnny cake kind they keep nowadays. Nowadays it's law this, and law that. The body gets buried before a proper wake. Takes the life out of the whole thing.'

'The drumming was hotter too,' Miss Winny piped up, moving her stringy throat up and down, like a peeled necked chicken. 'Sometimes it was only box we had to beat on but everybody sing and dance and punta till we all fall down. We got the spirit. 'Course nowadays everybody so genteel with all this education,' here she glanced at Beka, 'that they shame to do the old things.'

'Eating with fingers is now a disgrace,' Miss Flo said, glancing as if deeply offended, at an empty plate and fork on the seat beside her.

'Food taste sweeter from the fingers,' Miss Janie said. 'Nowadays everything is metalware. Gives food a funny taste.'

'Nowadays, you is all old fowl,' Miss Eila said, 'I want to see *you* punta till you fall down, Winnie!' And Miss Eila laughed at the very thought.

'There'll be dancing later, my corazones,' Aunt Tama said, her arms akimbo, doing a little half-hearted punta in front of the ladies. 'After the children go home.'

'That's what I like about you, Tama gial,' Miss Eila said, picking up her straw bag, 'you don't take offence easy, 'specially from the likes of Florence here,' and she slapped Miss Flo on the shoulder. All the women laughed in agreement calling 'nighty night' to Miss Eila as she limped her way to the gate.

Beka left the group of women, still laughing and joking, and climbed the back stairs of the house to the long bridge leading to Aunt Tama's kitchen. A pile of firewood bumped against Beka's leg. The bridge was dark, but the kitchen was lighted and crowded with women cooking over the huge firehearth. Beka stood for a minute looking over the railing into the yard. She watched Miss Eila pause several times before she reached the gate, to chat or greet this person or that. Then Beka slipped inside the darkened house. Light came from Greatgranny Straker's room, and Beka pushed the door and went into it. Aunt Tama's parlour had once been bigger, but she had partitioned a part of it off so Greatgran could have a little privacy.

A lamp on the bureau, its globe gleaming brightly, diffused light into the small room crowded with mementos Greatgran Straker had collected throughout her long life. On the bureau were many, many photographs, and Beka picked out the one with Greatgran, Chuku, Zandy and herself taken not too long before. Beka had never seen her Greatgran in anything but long-sleeved, printed cotton dresses that covered her ankles, or without thick cotton stockings, and laced up thick-heeled shoes and she was dressed that way in the photograph. Beka put the picture, in its frame, very carefully down on the bureau and went across the room to sit on the edge of her Greatgran's bed, spread with Aunt Tama's best lace-edged sheets, that she had brought all the way from the Republic of Honduras. A huge picture of the Sacred Heart, dripping blood, hung on the partition wall facing the bed. A rosary was draped over the picture of the Sacred Heart. Beka eased off her shoes, and whispered, just as her Greatgran used to whisper whenever anyone entered the room during the bad times when she was too sick to lift her head,

'Are you there? Are you there? I fail, you know, and Miss Florence laugh, and I feel frighten . . . And you remember Miss Flo's granddaughter? The one with her face bumpy like pineapple skin? Well, she has *three* children now . . . with different daddies. And Granny Straker, Toycie *sick*. She's craving green mangoes and salt just like they say pregnant ladies crave dirt, but I'm sure Toycie isn't pregnant. That's just my bad mind remembering those late nights she used to keep with Milio on the beach at the caye by the old cemetery. It's bound to be all that mango, but I just thought I'd mention it. It's failing and maybe having to leave school I'm worrying about. I don't want to turn out like Miss Flo's granddaughter! Whe fu do, Granny Straker, whe fu *do?*'

Beka sat there swinging her legs, listening to the noise below the house. Someone had started singing 'Rock of Ages' and it seemed to her that the entire yard joined in. When the singers reached, 'Let me hide my soul in thee,' the intensity of sound reached such proportions that Beka felt it could lift the floor boards right up, and her with it. She rested her head on the pillow, and the faint scent of Greatgran's hair pomade in the room was comforting. She lay there listening to the hymns for a long time before she fell asleep.

'Bill! Bill! This way, Beka right here fast asleep.'

Beka sat up, her heart jumping around in her chest, but it was only Mr Phillip. Mr Phillip, a civil servant at the Customs House, was half her Dad's age, but he was her Dad's true friend and Beka's. She could tell he was a friend not only from the things he tried to do for the Lamb family, but by the way his very soft, big brown eyes looked at her, and the way his smile curved up to meet his sprawling brown nose.

'You frighten me, Mr Phillip,' Beka said. The ice tinkled in his whisky glass as he laughingly said to her Dad who had come into the room,

'She was right here on her Granny Straker's bed, fast asleep. This girl have bigger heart than we, eh, Bill?' And he laughed again. Daddy Bill's speech slurred a little as he said,

'Weren't you afraid in here, Beka? The mattress not even turned over yet.'

Beka shook her head and stood up between the two men, unable to explain that the scary things she was afraid of were not in Granny Straker's room.

'Put your shoes on then,' Daddy Bill said.

'The wake over yet?' Beka asked.

'For you it is,' Daddy Bill answered.

It seemed to Beka, as she walked sleepily down the stairs ahead of the two men, that the wake was just livening up. The crowd under the house bottom were clapping and shouting,

'Heh, heh, hie, hie,' as a group of women danced and bounced in the circle of people. Miss Flo, sweating profusely, every part of her body jiggling, was in the middle shouting,

'Help me Lawd, Lawd Jesus help me!' The drummer was banging with his fingers and palms hard and fast. A man, sitting next to Uncle Curo, still on the front steps, kept calling,

'She's got the spirit, brother, she has got it.'

Daddy Bill went over to the food table, took Chuku from Mama Lilla's lap and swung him across his shoulder. Her mother started pushing the pram and Daddy Bill called 'Goodnight' to Granny Ivy standing a little outside the circle with Mr Phillip and Aunt Tama. As they left the yard, Beka peeped backwards. The group around the house bottom seemed to have increased in size. People were clapping, stomping and shouting. She couldn't see Miss Flo, but she could hear her voice keening loudest above the crowd.

The wheels of the pram rolled noisily over the tiny stones of Manioc Road. Nobody said a word as they walked down Rum Lane and crossed the swing bridge. The market was shuttered and deserted, and the reflection of the buildings lining both sides of Haulover Creek lay on top of the water. River boats moved quite gently in the reflections and, on the North Side, a fireman sat on a stool outside the fire station fast asleep, his cap slipping to one side of his face.

At Holy Redeemer Cathedral, her mother rolled the pram through the gates and said,

'I'll go in and light a candle,' and Beka kept the pram rolling back and forth as her mother pinned a handkerchief on her head, dipped her hand in holy water at a niche by the door and went inside. Daddy Bill bought a bag of chicharrón from a small Spanish boy sitting by the drainside outside the church gate and gave Beka a handful. Beka and her Dad crunched on the crackly, deep fried pork skin, and at the sound Chuku moved from one side of his Dad's shoulder to the other, but stayed asleep.

'I was talking to Phillip at the wake,' her Dad said.

'Mmmm?' Beka said, her mouth full.

'He agrees with your Mama and your Granny Ivy that you should get another chance at school.' Beka nearly choked but she didn't say anything. The nights were getting cool, and she drew the pram sheet over Zandy's legs.

'Between them, I will have no peace if I don't allow you to go back, maybe I won't even feel at peace with myself if I don't. And your Greatgranny Straker would have been at me too, if she had lived. So, as I told your mother, I'll send you back for one term. But if you don't pass, I'll be compelled to take you out of school.' He passed the bag of chicharrón to her and Beka took another handful.

'You understand me, Beka?' Beka nodded stuffing the chicharrón into her mouth. She chewed on a fatty piece and made a face. The watermelon had dissolved in her chest and she was so excited and happy that she felt like making all kinds of wild promises to come first in class, to make a perfect score in arithmetic, never again be late for school . . . but she knew that any display of that sort would only dispel the closeness between her Dad and herself that night. She struggled to find the right words to say thank you but everything she could think of seemed artificial and wrong. In the end, the best she could manage was,

'I'll try, Daddy.' And her father answered her exactly as if he were talking to an adult,

'That's all people like us can do, Beka, that is all.'

Her mother emerged from the church, took one look at Beka's face and smiled. Daddy Bill hitched Chuku further up onto his shoulder, while Mama Lilla placed her hands on the pram handle beside Beka's, and they began rolling Zandy through the church gates behind Daddy Bill. They continued walking home past shuttered shops and darkened houses, their footsteps and the pram wheels sounding quite loud on the empty street, and Beka could hear the voice of the Spanish boy, following at a distance behind them, calling in a monotone,

'Chicharón . . . chi . . . char . . . rón.'

CHAPTER 13

Three weeks later on the first Monday of the new school year, Beka awoke shortly before the sawmill whistle blew at seven. She waited for the blast and it came almost immediately, blaring hoarsely like a fog horn across Northside blotting out every other sound. Once the harsh noise had subsided, she rolled over to the window, tilted the flaking window blinds and sleepily surveyed the town. A mill hand on his way to work hawked and spat in the drain outside the fence; the wood smoke from somebody's firehearth hung pungently in the air and from a nearby house came a baby's piteous cry. No blue showed in the overcast sky, but ragged sunlight drained through the clouds onto the rusty rooftops signalling a hot, sticky day.

It was to be the kind of day when tempers are short, when eyelids droop after lunch, when the sea stretches flat on its bed for hours; the kind of day that fries the brain making a person dull of eye, heavy of tongue and unable to concentrate. Such a day required keeping cool under the bottom of a house, or under the branches of a leafy tree. It required a good night's sleep or an afternoon nap to last in a sane fashion until perhaps an afternoon breeze, rain or the setting sun brought relief. The excitement of starting school again had kept Beka awake for much of Sunday night, and she regretted the early heat of the morning for she was as tense within herself as the rising tensions of the weather outside.

'Beka! Beka!'

'I am up, Mama!' Beka shouted, slapping down the blinds on a group of men pedalling their bicycles furiously toward the sawmill. Downstairs in the yard, the gate creaked to with a bang. Granny Ivy was home from the market. Beka hoped it wouldn't be conch stewed with okra for lunch today. Quickly she began to dress. The long-sleeved blouse went on first. She drew the jumper over her head carefully so as not to disturb the box pleats in front and at the back. The green bow tie she shoved into her blouse pocket. That she would pin on at school. There was no need to walk through the streets this first morning unnecessarily advertising the fact that she had failed. She couldn't start off late! Why hadn't she dressed the moment she awoke? Hastily she pulled on white socks and her brown shoes. She hated the things and for a guilty minute rejoiced that the factory manufacturing them was breaking down. The shoes creaked, made barges of her feet, and gave her bunions. Still, they were strong, never wore out, and Beka was almost positive she would wear them the night she marched down the aisle at Parish Hall to receive her diploma, if she ever managed to graduate.

'We must support Mr Sampson,' her Dad said as they bought the shoes in the pokey shop littered with scraps of leather, and no amount of whispered pleadings on Beka's part had weakened his determination. At home that afternoon, Daddy and Granny had enjoyed a rare moment of accord on the subject of Beka's shoes.

'Old man Sampson spent a lifetime trying to build up his factory and store,' Daddy Bill said, leaning back in his chair by the radio, watching as Beka tried on the shoes in the hall for Granny Ivy's inspection. 'His store is breaking down, not because he didn't try, but because of devaluation. He can't import some of his necessities from America anymore. Everything has to come from England.'

'The Governor passed the bill right over our heads, Beka, with his reserve power,' Granny Ivy said, standing beneath the archway. 'Sampson can't compete with the big foreign stores any more, everything is more expensive.'

'They'll call me "bargefoot" at school, Daddy,' Beka grumbled.

'Your feet are big, Beka, no amount of fancy shoes can change that. Best accept it, eh?' her Dad had asked.

'Anyhow,' Granny Ivy concluded, 'You have razor blades between your toes. Only families with young ladies that step dainty can afford patent leather shoes from Wincham's on Albert Street. When since you start worrying 'bout whether shoes ugly or not? You thinking about boys or what?'

'No, Gran!'

'Well then.'

As she made neat bows of the cord-like laces, Beka wondered about the shoe factory. It put her in mind of Mr Ulric next door, the only creole grocer this side of Cashew Street. His shop was breaking down too. The groceries on his shelves were scanty while Mr Gordillo not too much further up the street was flourishing. Daddy Bill said *this* was because, much as he hated to admit such a thing about his own people, creole shopkeepers did not seem to consider trade or business dignified, serving customers with an attitude of condescension indicating that shopkeeping was a temporary misfortune, an occupation they would abandon the moment something better suited to their talents turned up. On the other hand, mestizo shopkeepers were not too high to humble themselves to customers, not too proud to live in the rear of their shops, at first, using the profits to replenish their stocks or to add new lines to their business.

Time passes swiftly, Daddy Bill had said, and before anybody could realize what was happening a tiny two-shelved shop became big business like Gordillo's Grocery and Dry Goods, then there was no room on the street for half-hearted shopkeepers like Mr Ulric. It was all very confusing to Beka, and as she scrambled around in her mind trying to fix on a way to prevent her own life from breaking down, her Mama called again from below the stairs,

'You'll be late! Come and set the table, Beka.'

'Coming! Coming!' she shouted. The dreaming around would

have to stop. Today she would start properly. No gazing through the classroom door at the activity of the sea; no smart remarks in Father Nunez's class; no reading of books under the desk during arithmetic. Grabbing her white beanie off the bed, she clumped downstairs. Her mother had finished setting the table.

'Girl, hurry up,' she said, eyes and body anxious, as if she too was starting school again.

'Yes, Mama, yes.' Beka banged the iron frying pan on the stove, poured in too much coconut oil and began cracking an egg, the white sliding over the side of the pan. Her Gran stood skinning liver at the counter.

'Here,' she said impatiently, rinsing the blood off her hands. 'Let me finish this, you'll ruin that uniform and never get out of here this morning.'

While Granny Ivy fried eggs, Beka made tea and sliced bread. Her Dad emerged from the bathroom all ready for work as she was shoving the fat cozy onto the pot, and he didn't have to walk as far as she did!

'You'll be late, Beka,' he said, drawing back his chair. 'What were you doing from the time sawmill whistle blew until now?'

Beka perched on the side of her chair and not waiting for the eggs, began crumbling a piece of dry bread. Before the tea in her cup cooled sufficiently, Toycie called at the gate.

'Bye, Daddy, Mama, Gran!' she yelled dashing onto the verandah. There stood Chuku, his tennis shoes unlaced, on the wrong way, making him look as if he had two left feet.

'Where are *you* going, Chuku?'

'With you.'

'Mama! Gran!' Beka called, her prickly heat becoming fiery in her long sleeved uniform. Her Dad came out, a banana in his hand. He gave the fruit to Beka and carried Chuku inside the house kicking and screaming.

'That Chuku!' Beka said to Toycie as a greeting at the gate.

'He's a nice little boy,' Toycie said. 'Sometimes I wish I had a brother or sister like that at home. It gets lonely when Aunt Eila is at work.'

'See me and live with me is a whole other story, Toycie! You don't know your luck.'

Toycie didn't reply. She was trying to smooth the tiny pleats around the edge of her collar. She didn't wear a tie either. She was going to get senior red this morning at school. It wouldn't seem strange that Beka was not wearing a tie today. All girls promoted to a higher class would buy new ties later in the morning. But tomorrow the whole town would guess who had failed by the girls who did not wear their ties.

As they walked along, the early morning chaos of getting to school began to recede in Beka's mind and she took a peep at Toycie. Toycie did not look at all elated to be beginning her final school year. She seemed to be in some kind of distress, her eyes slightly puffy as if from weeping and her uniform was badly ironed. The two friends had not been together very much during the weeks before this first morning of school; and during the hours they spent under the cashew tree in Toycie's yard, in Beka's attic, or on their walks, there hadn't been much to say. Beka had become obsessed with trying to learn the lessons she had failed, pestering Toycie with questions, and Toycie was always distracted wanting only to talk about Emilio, not listening to Beka, staring into space in a trance as if awaiting some signal that would restore her to normality. They walked quietly along the busy street to school, no longer able to enter the heart and mind of the other with the ease of former times. At the corner of Queen Street and Milpa Lane, where St. Cecilia's was situated, Toycie squeezed Beka's arm saying,

'I am sweating cold, Beka, and I feel so *bad.*'

'Are you menstruating, Toy?' Beka asked.

'No, Beka gial, no, and my stomach feels like it doesn't belong to me.'

'Let's go back home, then Toycie . . .' Beka said, dreading the thought of missing the first morning of school. Toycie hesitated, shoving a limp curl behind her ears.

'Let's go on,' she said finally. 'Maybe the feeling will pass.'

Milpa Lane was jammed with groups of girls in twos and threes chattering and laughing as they made their way towards the open gates of the convent. Toycie and Beka didn't join any group, each girl responding dully when hailed by classmates, or in Beka's case, former classmates. Neither did they shout rude remarks, nor return witty sallies to student cyclists, deliberately pedalling as close as possible to girls on foot, tinkling their bells in unison and calling,

'Make way, make way, behold the bridegroom cometh!'

This last was a reference to the Bible story which Father Nunez was sometimes fond of dramatizing for freshmen at the start of a new school year.

As the girls approached the high grillwork gate of the convent grounds, Toycie shoved her arm through Beka's. She seemed about to faint. Beka lifted her arm into a hook and together they progressed slowly along the uncracked cement walk. A statue of the Virgin Mary, her arms outstretched, dominated the centre of the wide walk, lined on both sides with soaring palm trees. Behind the statue was the convent, two stories high, resembling a Spanish hacienda. The girls skirted the statue, joining the throng of students swerving to the right of the convent's front door. They followed the walk around the building, scurrying across the playing fields towards the modern high school fronting the sea, far away from the nuns' residence.

After the time allotted for purchasing new books, new ties, and the assignment of desks was over, the entire school, according to rank, marched along the playing fields to the convent, where they assembled quietly in the chapel for a short service to mark the beginning of a new school year. The chapel on the top floor was a beautiful, airy place with a high ceiling. The girls knelt on prie-dieus lining both sides of the walls, which were decorated with plaques depicting the stations of the cross. An ocean of polished floor separated the rows of prie-dieus facing the simple altar on which stood a cross glittering in the sunshine streaming through the doors.

Beka, kneeling on a bench with the freshmen in the rear of the chapel, spied Toycie near the altar with the seniors already wearing red bow ties. Beka felt fairly comfortable, as the place where she knelt was cushioned and surrounded by wide open doors. A breath of air touched her forehead now and then, and for the first time in her life that she could remember, she was praying with wholehearted concentration. She had rarely felt a great need to ask God for anything before. Mama Lilla, Daddy Bill and Granny Ivy had always been good enough. Today she bent her head listening to the Glee Club chorusing, 'Re . . . gi . . . ina cae . . . e li, Re . . . gi . . . i . . . iina cae . . . eli, laetare,

laetare, alelu . . . u . . . ia!' and she tried to pray. She prayed not only for herself but for her friend Toycie who she was beginning to suspect was in serious trouble.

Somebody poked her shoulder and she turned around thinking to respond to a new friendship, but the girl inclined her head towards the front of the chapel, and Beka saw Toycie moving swiftly across that ocean of floor in the centre of the chapel. She rushed down the right-hand side, one hand clasped firmly over her mouth. But before she could reach the verandah, bracketing the three sides of the chapel, up came the vomit, squeezing through her fingers and dropping in big dollops onto the gleaming pinewood floor. For a second, Toycie stared in horror and confusion at the slimy mess splattered on the sunlit splendour of the chapel floor before rushing outside, and the entire chapel gasped, girls turning to one another to wonder about Toycie Qualo. Vomiting was never regarded lightly among the women of Belize. It was something to be observed with the utmost suspicion.

Beka whispered 'excuse me, excuse me,' over and over, stumbling over numberless pairs of school shoes in her attempt to reach Toycie. Sister Virgil, the principal, arms crossed, intercepted Beka at the verandah door.

'Go to the kitchen and ask for a bucket of water and a mop, Beka. Kindly return and clean this up. I'll see about Toycie.'

'Excuse me, Sister, but . . .'

'Do as I say, Miss!' Sister Virgil said, her sharp nose twitching as if she smelt rotten meat.

'Yes, Sister,' Beka replied, not daring to say another word or to look directly at the short, beady-eyed, pidgeon-chested nun the school had nicknamed, 'Mighty Mouse.'

By the time Beka returned to the chapel verandah with the mop and pail, the watermelon had returned to her chest. She stood for a minute staring over the concrete verandah railing watching dozens of girls in dazzling white uniforms and round white caps, walking silently in crocodiles toward their classrooms, many yards away, near the sea. Toycie emerged from an outside latrine near the playing fields where Sister Virgil stood waiting for her. As Beka watched, she saw Toycie turn to follow Sister Virgil up the steps to her office.

CHAPTER 14

Deep in thought, Beka flopped the wet mop on the slimy vomit already hardening on the floor. Rattling rosary beads startled her and she looked up to see a tall, old nun observing her from the chapel door nearest the altar. Transparent hands with thick knuckles and curling blue veins, fingered wooden rosary beads looped around the broad leather belt encircling her waist. Each rosary bead was the size of the coco plums that ripened on lush green bushes growing in and amongst the ancient graves at St. George's caye.

Water tumbled through Beka's head making her slightly dizzy, and she was on the island waiting for Toycie and the pelicans were flapping their wings as they sailed slowly over the sea. Beka's face was one big ache, but she tried to smile at Sister Bernadette who taught straw handicrafts when Beka was a small pupil at the elementary school near Holy Redeemer Cathedral. Everyone said Sister Bernadette was going crazy.

'Not a very nice job is that, my dear?' the nun asked enunciating her words slowly and carefully as from long practice. Sister Bernadette picked up the aluminium bucket and brought it with a clank nearer to where Beka rubbed at the splatters.

'I don't mind,' Beka replied, mopping carefully so that the water would not mar the varnish of the prie-dieus. 'My friend threw up.'

'She wouldn't mop it up, you know . . . too much the Brahmin that one.'

'Excuse me, Sister Bernadette?'

'Stopped me teaching . . . said I was talking politics, frightening the children. You aren't afraid of me, are you, my dear?' The nun resumed her stance at the chapel door, but her voice had gone soft, slurry and sad. Yellowed teeth showed through wrinkled lips briefly.

'No, Sister Mary Bernadette,' Beka replied with conviction.

It was true. She wasn't afraid of Sister Bernadette who used to be patient with her clumsy attempts to plait straw into mats. But she was certainly afraid of Sister Virgil.

'Twenty-five years I've been in the colony . . . she's only just come. It's because I'm Irish you know?'

'Excuse me, Sister?'

'Not teaching, I may go mad in truth . . . may the Sweet Jesus help me,' and she bowed her head.

'I'm a little bit, too, Sister,' Beka said. 'Is everybody?'

But Sister Bernadette did not hear. Clasping the rosary against her breast she resumed whispering her beads, genuflecting to the altar cross, before walking across the chapel to kneel at a far prie-dieu.

Beka returned the rinsed out bucket and mop to the black cook in the convent kitchen, unpinned her beanie and hurried to class. She was barely in her seat when Father Nunez entered the classroom to give his weekly catechism lesson. The girls rose as one and said in a loud, overly respectful chorus,

'Good morning, Father.'

Father Nunez was a Belize mestizo, well known as a pious man, who whenever he made the sign of the cross lingered over and savoured every syllable of the accompanying prayer.

'Good morning, girls. Please be seated,' he said in his hoarse voice, waiting, hands behind his back, until the last girl had neatly folded her pleated skirt before sitting down, and until the last chair scraped to silence. Father Nunez surveyed the forty heads, smacking his lips and smoothing back a lock of black hair separating itself from the rest that remained obedient on his head that reminded Beka of a mongoose's. Somebody cleared her throat, and the priest looked around at each face, almost every one a different shade of brown, black or white.

There were only a few locally born priests in the country, and Father Nunez was one of them. A man of humble origins, he had made the journey from beans and tortillas almost every day, to ordination as a Jesuit priest in Rome. This was not an ordinary accomplishment. However, in Belize, where almost everything locally reared or made is suspect, where everyone's childhood misdemeanours are known, where family circumstances and prejudices are well documented, Father Nunez was in a difficult position. His life and the lives of his generations before him were set alongside the lives of foreign priests who arrived in the country full grown, with no known past, freeing them publicly to assume new identities, and to write fresh scenarios for themselves, limited only by their personalities, intelligence and of course, the laws of their order and of the Church. In certain areas even these laws were occasionally circumvented or ignored, sometimes wisely.

Father Nunez tried to make up for his constraints by being more pious than his counterparts.

'Though how could this be,' people asked themselves, 'when he was born in Xaicotz?' a village notorious for settling disputes in ways vaguely reminiscent of the Wild West.

More dedicated.

'Isn't it a shame,' people asked one another, 'how hard he is working to please this foreign bishop, leaving his poor papa to slash and burn the milpa plot as best he can?'

More concerned about the moral fibre of the community.

'And you know, his aunt lived with that black man right in Belize City all her life with no wedding?'

These comments, overheard, perhaps misunderstood, no doubt misconstrued, formed the basis of the young people's attitudes toward Father Nunez. The majority of students in St. Cecilia's could not be expected, at their age, to perceive the underlying conflicts in Father Nuñez's personality. They had a romantic notion of how Belizeans ought to behave, and to them Father Nunez was hypocritical adopting the mannerisms, language, and style of living of his foreign counterparts — faults they, of course, would seldom be guilty of as adults. The young people within and without the gates of St Cecilia's were looking for local models of whom to be proud. If Father Nunez had been a little more open, a little more understanding, a little more self-confident, a little more Belizean, it is possible that he could have performed a miracle greater than his lonely journey from Xaicotz to Rome.

But he was human and not only that, he was a pioneer and pioneers in non-traditional fields of endeavour generally inhabit an uncertain place. They are faced with complex choices. Should they forsake the old for the new? This seems simpler, at first, but the emotional cost of attempting to reject one's nurture is dear. Should they hold tightly to the old and shut out the new? How can this be done when they are no longer entirely 'the old'? It is only time, experience, and emotional maturity that teaches some pioneers to try and graft the best of the old onto the best of the new. What is the best of the old, and the best of the ever-changing new? That selection takes generations to evolve, and the task is never done.

As far as Father Nunez' religious vocation was concerned, he stuck to the old path. It was a rough one, and he was not entirely sure of its twists and turns, but since it was well trodden, he believed it would take him, eventually, to his ultimate destination which was not of this world. So that first morning of the new school year, he did not attempt to deal, except obliquely, with the temporal problems seething behind the bland young faces turned toward him. He began to speak again in a way that for him was becoming a pattern.

'My dear hearts in Jesus Christ, we shall all be happy working together in this beautiful classroom, built in part through the aid of our friends overseas. I see my old friend Miss Lamb . . . and one or two others . . . here with us again this year. We shall be happy, all be happy getting to know the Lord Jesus Christ. Of course, we must have faith, faith in God the Father, God the Son, and God the Holy Ghost. We must have faith also in the infinite wisdom of Mother Church who has observed mankind down through the ages, and knows all, *all* the evil we are capable of . . .'

He took a quick look at Beka, but Beka was apparently staring straight back at him with a steady, clear-eyed, attentive gaze.

Last year in that very classroom, Father Nunez had said,

'Of course, dear hearts, we all want to go to heaven when we die. This is why we must mortify the flesh, do penance always so that we will not burn in purgatory, or worse, be damned to everlasting hellfire. Remember the story of Eve. As young ladies you must walk always with an invisible veil about you so as not to unleash chaos upon the world. God, in His infinite goodness, gave us the Blessed Virgin to erase the memory of Eve, and to serve as an example to the women of the world. He has also given us free will which places us above the animal kingdom. Who would not want to sit in heaven on the right hand of Our Father?' Father Nunez did not really want an answer, but Beka couldn't help herself, and in the pause raised her hand,

'Yes, my child?'

'Excuse me Father, but it's nature that produces the chaos, Father, and women and men are part of nature, and my Gran says that no matter how hard we try, sometimes, like bad luck, things break down. She says to do the best I can and not worry too much about living in heaven or hell for the guilt might frighten me crazy.'

'Don't you believe in heaven and hell, my child?'

'I wasn't saying that, Father. My Gran says . . .'

'How about you, child, what do you say?' Father Nunez had come right down the aisle of rows to her desk, and she could see fine particles of chalk dust whitening his black cassock. Beka hung her head and didn't reply.

'Come now, Miss Lamb, do you believe or don't you believe?'

'I don't know what to tell you, Father.'

'You don't know,' the priest said. 'It seems you need time for meditation to consider what you do believe. I will request Sister Mary Virgil to allow you that freedom.' He turned to the class.

'All the girls in this classroom who believe there is a heaven and a hell please raise your hands.' Every girl in the room raised her hand and Beka sat down. That was the moment Beka first heard the roar of seawater in her head. She felt like smashing her fist straight through the desk. She began to fear there was something within herself that was spoiled, something that caused her to continuously do and say things against her own best interests. What was the memory teasing the edges of her consciousness, obliterating her ability to think clearly? If she could only lay it on her desk and look at it, perhaps the salty water blurring her vision would recede and she could understand.

Later that morning, Beka had been sent home to give her time to consider her beliefs. Sister Virgil wanted to suspend her indefinitely, but Father Rau, a friendly American priest at the presbytery to whom Daddy Bill appealed for help, interceded with Sister Virgil and Father Nunez.

At the meeting in the school office, Sister Virgil told Father Rau that Beka was 'a heretic at worst, and a rough diamond at best.' Her home life was such, Sister Virgil said, that it was doubtful whether Beka should be educated at a Catholic school. Daddy Bill had sat there sullen and insulted at this reference to his Protestant upbringing, for a long time traditional among the black population.

But Father Rau, a tall, skinny man, with joking ways, a humble manner and an aptitude for persuasion had somehow afterwards managed to gain permission for Beka to return to school a few days later.

Beka blinked with alarm when Father Nunez said,

'For next week's homework, I want you to read pages three to five in your catechism.' Beka made a note of it. She would check with somebody to see if she had missed anything important. She heard the recess bell with relief.

'So far, so good,' she thought to herself, climbing the stairs to the senior classroom to find Toycie. 'I didn't concentrate, but at least I didn't say anything.'

Sister Gabriela, Beka's English teacher, and Toycie's homeroom teacher, sat at the desk in front of the empty classroom correcting papers. The noise from the playing fields below echoed loudly in the classroom.

'Oh, hello, Beka,' Sister Gabriela smiled. 'Toycie went home after chapel this morning. She's unwell today.'

'She went by herself, Sister?' Beka asked.

'Sister Virgil sent her home in a taxi. Now don't look so worried. She'll be all right I'm sure.'

'I'll telephone my Dad then, Sister, for Toycie's auntie is at work. He'll send a message to Miss Eila.'

'All right, Beka, but please, would you return here afterwards? I'd like to speak to you.'

After the telephone call to her father, Beka returned to sit on the edge of a chair opposite Sister Gabriela. It was the first time she'd been this far inside the senior classroom. It looked very grand as it overlooked the sea to the horizon and posters of exotic places were spaced at intervals along the four walls of the room. Beka swivelled her head trying to see them all. What a pity Toycie wasn't here to enjoy her first day as a senior. She should have been outside parading the school grounds with her friends showing off the red bow tie at her throat. Instead, she was probably lying down on the hard straw mattress at Miss Eila's house. Sister Gabriela was saying,

'You did well in my class last year, Beka. I was extremely upset to learn you had failed the school year.'

Beka stared at a poster above the blackboard. The dancing girl on it had flowers twined in her hair, and bells on a chain around her ankles. The features of the dancing girl reminded Beka of National Vellor. Beka observed the poster closely and began counting the pleats in the dancer's gracefully draped scarlet costume.

'Beka?'

'I am listening, Sister.'

Sister Gabriela had come out to Belize from Rhode Island only the year before, and Beka was grateful she did not know her history at school as well as many of the other nuns did. She tried hard to concentrate on Sister Gabriela's words.

'The Sisters of Charity will be celebrating their seventy-fifth year of service in the colony in November. The Mother Provincial will be coming from America to celebrate this anniversary with us. As part of the celebrations, I am having an essay competition for the high school. The topic is 'The Sisters of Charity in Belize'. I'd like you to enter when the notice is posted on the bulletin board later today.'

'Me, Sister Gabriela?' Beka asked, looking at the nun to see if she was serious. Everything about Sister Gabriela was tremendous: her large frame, her eyes, her gigantic nose, but especially her smile which made Beka think, 'With her all things seem possible.'

'Why not?' Sister Gabriela asked. She had an unusual amount of space between each of her front teeth.

Beka poked her tongue into one side of her cheek. A punctuation exercise on the blackboard written in Sister Gabriela's large, bold writing, read, 'time flies you can't they fly too fast,' and Beka was trying in vain to figure it out. She said,

'I won't win, Sister Gabriela, if the seniors and juniors enter as well.'

Sister Gabriela sighed. She rose from her chair and came to lean against the front of her desk. She ran a big, blunt finger under the starched white part of her habit that stood like a tiny mountain on her forehead. Beka glimpsed a deep red welt before she removed the forefinger. Wrapping the ends of her gauzy veil about her Sister Gabriela said,

'Perhaps you are missing my point, Beka.'

'Oh, yes, Sister?'

'Mmm. It is *possible* for you to win, but so what if you don't?'

'So everything,' Beka wanted to shout but she kept quiet. Sister Gabriela was new.

'I hope lots of girls will enter this contest and I will try to encourage many of them even as I am encouraging you. I feel strongly that you should understand a little more about your country and about yourselves. Our present curriculum, because of the London examinations, does not leave much scope for that. As a person you can't lose.'

Beka thought of the notebook her mother was helping her to fill, and something within her moved with interest.

'I'll try, Sister Gabriela,' Beka said.

'That's the spirit!' Sister Gabriela exclaimed, moving about with girl-like enthusiasm. 'I hope to learn something from all this myself. Wait!' She selected a holy picture from a pile in her desk drawer and presented it to Beka. It was a picture of a man with a baby on his shoulders struggling in a turbulent river.

'St. Christopher will help to carry you across.'

'Thank you, Sister,' Beka said. She slipped the glossy picture between the pages of her arithmetic book and raced down the stairs, the bell signalling the end of recess clanging in her ears.

CHAPTER 15

Sunday lunch was almost over. Beka fidgeted impatiently waiting for the right opportunity in the conversation to request permission to visit Toycie. The science of studying correctly was something Beka was only beginning to learn, and the daily struggle to retain her place at St Cecilia's strained her resources continually, narrowing her focus to a point, where, while she was not oblivious to the erosion of Toycie's spirits and confidence, she was inclined to murmur consoling platitudes rather than to enquire too deeply into the cause of her friend's distress. At home, Beka studied as much as she could between chores, squabbles and interruptions. The near-silence between Toycie and herself was becoming uncomfortable, however, and she grew determined during Sunday lunch to make amends that very day.

'If you're still hungry, Beka, use the spoon, don't take rice out of the bowl with your fingers. It's a nervous habit. And stop shaking your knees.'

'Yes, Mama.'

'And, Bill,' Granny Ivy was saying, 'I managed to iron two guayaberas yesterday so they're ready for the coming week. I've never seen shirts with so many tiny pleats.'

'I may not wear those shirts for a while, Ma, thank you all the same, though I must say the style is useful.'

'That's sudden. You said you preferred them for meetings instead of coats and neckties!'

'I don't want the town to assume I favour Guatemala. Rumour has it that P.I.P. received aid from the Guats to help start the party. Anybody wearing guayaberas, nowadays, is suspected of Latin leanings.'

Granny Ivy forced her ugly laugh, always painful to hear. She asked,

'What have you got against the party, Bill? They are fighting hard in the City Council, the only place they can, to improve conditions in this country. Our leader was right to say we wouldn't hang any picture of King George in the Chamber until the British Government keeps its promises and listens to our complaints.'

'I am not *against* any group, Ma. I am just afraid Guatemala may use P.I.P. for her own ends. Apart from that, I work for Blanco's. Local businessmen have to be careful not to lose what ground we've gained. Civil servants are in a similar position.'

'They think they are British,' Granny Ivy said, curling her lips. 'They talk British, act British, and go on "home" leave.'

'Well, the British *did* help creoles gain a monopoly in the civil service. Many of them fear losing their positions to other races in the country if local politicians begin to run things.'

'A little competition wouldn't hurt,' Granny Ivy said. 'I

waited two hours at registry one morning to get Beka's birth certificate when she started convent school the first time.'

'I wouldn't have minded being a civil servant myself,' Daddy Bill said, the dimples in his cheeks showing in a rare smile. 'Regular hours, a pension, and dignity. You know, Ma, I studied nights, worked hard all my life in what Lilla calls a high-minded way. One day, I encouraged myself, one day, Billy boy, you'll make the property qualifications, be able to vote, and be one of the few black men exerting a little influence on the way things are done in this country. If this new constitution takes effect, age and a literacy test will be the only qualifications for voting.'

'Your work isn't in vain, Bill.'

'I am not saying that, Ma. I don't really mind that everyone may soon be able to vote. It's one of life's little turns — and I'm turning with it. Hatred of British colonialism unites us now. There are so many races here I wonder what will keep us together once they leave.'

'A man brought a petition to the door while you were at customs shed this morning,' Lilla said. 'The petition is asking the Governor to dissolve City Council because certain members showed disloyalty to the royal family.'

'That's from the loyal and patriotics,' Granny Ivy said. 'P.I.P. has a petition out, too, and we are getting hundreds of signatures from the poorer classes begging the Governor *not* to dissolve the council. I signed already.'

'Those petitions are a farce,' Bill Lamb said, examining a chicken bone. 'If Governor Radison feels threatened by the City Council, he'll dissolve it, and the Legislative Council will support him, backed by British interests represented there. The few local men on the Legislative Council will support the Governor too, because they haven't decided yet whether they are British or Belizeans.'

'This whole picture incident, seems to me, was a trap to give the Governor reason for dissolving the council,' Granny Ivy said, scraping the bones from her plate into an empty bowl. 'And P.I.P. members had little choice but to walk into it.'

'The '31 hurricane shoved us into a deeper pit,' Lilla added, stacking the plates with sharp clicks. 'We agreed to give governors from then on reserve powers in exchange for aid.'

'Don't say "we" Lilla,' Granny Ivy snapped. 'How many people in this country can vote?'

'Anyhow, Miss Ivy, we were grateful enough for the aid then.' Rising to carry the dishes to the kitchen she said, 'I can't understand why so many of us huddle like loggerhead turtles below sea level decade after decade. Do you see any Maya pyramids in this swamp? Trying to build a decent life on this hurricane ridden coast reminds me of the second little pig with his house of sticks. And don't talk to me about love of the sea because anybody who can goes to America!'

'We're here, Lilla,' Granny Ivy said, 'and not likely to leave.' She chuckled. 'It would do my old bones good to see you in rubber boots carrying buckets of well water for rose bush in Sibun jungle.'

The family roared with laughter and Chuku and Zandy playing under the table stamped on the legs. Lilla, looking a little shamefaced, said,

'There's lots of nice land in this country, Miss Ivy. Mountain Pine Ridge, for example, and the Stann Creek hills . . .'

'That's true, Lilla.' Daddy Bill agreed. 'One day everything might change that way for the better.'

A good family feeling was in the silence that followed so Beka said,

'I am going to Toycie's now, Mama, Daddy, Gran, to see if she's feeling well enough to come with me when I take the boys for their walk.'

'Is Toycie still sick?' Lilla asked surprised.

'A little, Mama.'

'Still vomiting?' Granny Ivy asked, her spectacles catching the sunlight from the window beneath the attic stairs.

'I'm not sure, Gran.'

'Tell Eila there's another meeting at Battlefield Park tomorrow night, Beka, only I don't suppose she'll go if Toycie's sick.'

'Yes, Gran.'

'Take us, take us Beka!' the boys clamoured, pulling on Beka's arms.

'You boys will bathe and sleep,' Granny Ivy answered, rapping knuckles on the tabletop. 'Go on, Beka.'

97

'The dishes will be waiting right here for you,' Lilla called. 'So don't stay long.'

Cashew Street, between the Sunday hours of noon and four, was a dismally quiet place. Not even a john crow showed its face. Chico's Saloon and Bar was closed and the Cashew Street Unemployed Boys' Ballet Corps disappeared behind some invisible shade, as did many other characters like Hicky Chick, a very old, poor half-crazy lady who wandered from shop to shop begging for pennies. Mandolyn Jawbone Greasy was not at her usual lamp-post trying to persuade strangers to buy bottles of coconut oil which, experienced housewives on the street knew, were likely to be rancid. There was no tinkle of Mr Martin's fresco bell to entice Beka into buying one cent's worth of shaved ice dripping with brown cane syrup, and Gordillo's Grocery and Dry Goods Store was tightly shuttered although Beka guessed Mr Gordillo was in there restocking his shelves, and would sell anything needed, from a side door, to the special customers who provided the bulk of his business. The muted slap of cards behind Abrero's Wood Shop assured Beka that the gamblers were not idling Sunday away.

Beka found Toycie under the umbrella-like cashew tree, sitting on a stack of planks Miss Eila was slowly collecting to build a kitchen. As she crossed the well broomed yard, Beka looked around carefully. For the first time, it seemed to her, she saw, with unmisted clarity, the rusty water drums, the rotting planks of Miss Eila's house. She allowed herself the truth and understood that the Qualos were very poor, and there was no romance in it. Toycie had provided the enchanted quality in her environment. She was the one who touched each humble item in that yard, embellishing everything with bright sparkles of what she believed could be. Toycie's blazing spirit turned petty financial contrivances into minor adventures, and Beka had chosen to see the Qualo house and yard through Toycie's eyes, and had often envied the fairytale like atmosphere conjured up there, out of almost nothing, before her delighted eyes. These last days, however, the glory of it all had diminished, the spirit of the magician seemed quenched.

'Hello, Beka gial,' Toycie said, moving over so Beka could also sit in the shelter of the tree.

'Feeling any better?' Beka asked.

'I'm still feeling queasy, but at least I didn't throw up my lunch. Aunt Eila is watching me.'

'No walk today, then?'

'Well,' Toycie replied, looking up at the sunlight shifting on the undersides of the cashew tree leaves, 'I'm going to Mass at St Joseph's this evening. Can you come with me, Beka? I haven't been to that church before, and I might feel shy by myself.'

'I went to Mass at Holy Redeemer this morning, Toycie. Why are you going all the way back there?'

'Beka, girl, I haven't seen much of Emilio since we came home from the caye. All I get is a quick hail and a wave when he flashes by here on his bicycle. He goes to church at St. Joseph's and I must speak to him.'

'Why do you want to see him so badly?'

'He's got to marry me, Beka, because I am pregnant.'

'Pregnant? Pregnant?' Beka sprang off the planks as if she'd been bitten by a scorpion.

'Shut up and stop squawking like macaw parrot. Aunt Eila will hear you!'

'How do you know such a thing?' Beka pleaded, looking into Toycie's eyes, black as the seed of a mamey apple; noticing how thick eyebrows touched over her nose, watching pink lips trembling against the rich brownness of her skin. Mama Lilla always said Toycie's fingers were made for music they were so tapered and strong. Beka usually felt overgrown and overfed beside Toycie's slenderness.

'How do you know such a thing?' Beka asked again.

Toycie licked her lips.

'Well, I feel sick in the mornings, sometimes *all* day, and I haven't had my periods for the second month. I was reading about it in a doctor book at Bliss library.'

'Why don't you tell Miss Eila?' Beka whispered fiercely into her friend's face. 'Maybe you read wrong!'

'I can't tell. I can't, Beka. Aunt Eila thinks I'm a queen.'

'What do you think Emilio will do — marry you — Toycie gial?'

'He'll marry me . . . he always said if anything happened he would marry me.'

'But he's in school.'

'So am I!'

'What about graduation?'

Toycie put her head down on her knees and her shoulders were shaking,

'What to do, Beka? What to do?'

'Maybe it's not true, maybe it's not true. Maybe it's some other kind of sickness. I hear about plenty of ladies who think they're pregnant, and it turns out to be only a tumour. Let's talk to Granny Ivy then?'

Toycie grabbed Beka's wrist and held on tight. Her fingers were cold.

'Don't you tell Miss Ivy or anybody, Beka, you hear me!'

'Do I ever back story, Toycie?'

'Are you coming to church with me or not?'

'Yes, Toycie, yes. But we'll have to take the boys, and wait outside until Mass is finished. Mama wouldn't send me out today without Chuku and Zandy.'

'All right then,' Toycie said.

'Is Miss Eila asleep?'

'No, she's reading about the City Council fight in *The Bulletin*.'

Beka went to the front of the house and called,

'Miss Eila? Oh, Miss Eila!'

The door opened halfway and Miss Eila peered out. Her hair was loosened from its tight corn rows, her feet were bare, and she held the two-page newspaper between the fingers of one hand.

'Afternoon, Miss Eila. Granny Ivy says to remind you about the meeting tomorrow night . . .'

'I know about it, Beka. Tell Miss Ivy I'll meet her at your gate about seven depending on Toycie's feelings.'

'And, Miss Eila?'

'Yes, pet?'

'Can Toycie go out for a walk with me and the boys this evening?'

'Toycie sickish all last week, Beka. I am planning to take her to doctor tomorrow if she doesn't feel better. You don't look so good yourself this afternoon, Beka.'

'Please, Mam?'

'Toycieeee,' Miss Eila called.

'Coming, Aunt Eila.'

'You feeling good enough to go with Beka?'

'Maybe the walk would do me good, Auntie.'
'All right then, but don't you girls stay out too late.'
'See you later, Toycie,' Beka said. 'Bye, Miss Eila.'
'Bye, Beka,' Toycie said, 'don't forget now.'
'I won't but I think you *must* be wrong,' Beka replied. She felt Toycie's eyes on her back as she walked across the planks to the gate. On the way home, Beka tried to compose her face, but the effort was unnecessary for she heard her father's snores from the bottom of the stairs. The boys were stretched out in bed beside Lilla and there was no sound from the attic. Beka took a long time cleaning the kitchen, and when she was finished she looked at the stove in surprise — she didn't remember washing the pots, but she had.

Later that evening, Beka, Toycie, Chuku and Zandy, left Beka's house to go for their walk. The girls wore Sunday dresses but they had not taken the trouble to titivate. Toycie hadn't washed her hair, and a smoky, firehearth smell was about her. A plastic barrette clasped Beka's hair at the back of her head in a stubby tail and she hadn't borrowed Lilla's clip-on earrings. It did not occur to the girls, as it once would have done, to transform the pot-holed streets into tree-lined boulevards or to pretend that the dilapidated houses in cluttered yards were painted mansions surrounded by smooth green lawns. They shoved the cumbersome pram, its wheels squeaking loudly, straight ahead, responding to friendly greetings and innocent enquiries from verandahs and yards, with uncharacteristic suspicion. Beka was feeling guilty again, for as usual, Lilla had cautioned her to walk with the boys 'out front', and Cinderella Town, a few streets to the rear of Barracks Green, was not what her mother meant. It was a kind of lie, and Beka felt she was breaking her resolution after a short time. But what could she do?

It was a fairly long walk to Cinderella Town, where the small, wooden houses on stilts were freshly painted, but many streets were waiting to be paved. The area was swampy. Crickets screamed in the grass growing waist-high on empty lots. Beka and Toycie took turns pushing the boys as they strolled back and forth along St Joseph's Street trying to appear unconscious of the questioning stares of householders and children taking the evening air on their verandahs. Chuku and Zandy whined continuously about mosquitoes and sandflies eating them and the girls flicked handkerchiefs above their heads in an effort to keep the boys from being too badly bitten.

A bell tolled when Mass was ended and the little group stood near the church door watching to see if Emilio was amongst the people filing out of the pews. This new activity kept the boys momentarily quiet, and Beka rubbed her fingers over the dusty fronds of a coconut tree growing near the path to the church door. Father Mullins, the pastor of St Joseph's, stepped briskly across the threshold of the church, stopping to chat to parishioners as he made his way to the street. Beka glimpsed a newspaper vendor, Miss Arguelles, a pile of *Bulletins* under her arm, talking to a customer and gesticulating with plump arms towards the church. Toycie gazed fixedly at a clump of grass near her feet. Beka poked her arm,

'Emilio and his mother are coming out now, Toycie. Don't act so poorthingfied. People will wonder and begin to watch.'

'Let them wonder,' Toycie replied. 'I am fed up worrying about what people think!'

Emilio, hair water-slicked and greased into a stiff roll above his forehead, and his white hand-embroidered shirt hanging over his Sunday pants, guided Senora Villanueva, fingertips under her elbow, through the church door as if she was crafted from some fragile substance and would shatter if she stumbled on the two steps from the church door to the yard. Toycie, skirt swishing, left Beka's side and approached them saying,

'Good evening, Senora. Hello, Emilio. May I see you for a minute?'

Emilio glanced about him as if seeking refuge, then he smiled, the reluctant prince, long lashes brushing smooth olive cheeks as he looked down at his petite Mama dressed exquisitely in a sheath fashioned of sharkskin material. Her tan patent leather shoes matched her dress, and the glass beads of her rosary sparkled like crystal. Senora Villanueva's face lost the exalted look of a recent communicant and a frown of annoyance pleated her forehead. She forgot to call Toycie 'reina', looking her up and down with open hostility. Beside Senora Villanueva, Toycie appeared a trifle scruffy in her lavender, waterwave taffeta dress with its overskirt of billowing lavender bobbinet. Unravelled to one side, her frock tail drooped around her calves. Shoe whitening smeared Toycie's brown ankles, and her worn flat-heeled shoes keeled over, on the outer sides, like sailing dorys on a rough sea. Emilio adjusted the beige lace mantilla carefully around his mother's shoulders, touched greying curls and said,

'Talk with Father Mullins for a while, Mamacita. Un minuto por favor.'

Senora Villanueva inclined her head to Toycie and Beka as if they were rebellious campesinos on some rancho, as she stepped daintily away, her high heels sinking twice into the dust of the path before she reached the church gate. Then Emilio and Toycie, walking as far apart from each other as possible, disappeared around the corner of the church.

Beka and her brothers joined the last trickle of people leaving the churchyard. The boys began whining again, demanding that Beka take them to the park for they wanted to swing. On the street, groups of churchgoers and passersby had formed and Miss Arguelles stood in the middle of the street glowering at Father Mullins as he listened respectfully to Senora Villanueva and other pious lady parishioners. Miss Arguelles' voice boomed above the after-church chatter. The crowd fell silent and Miss Arguelles was pointing at Father Mullins and saying,

'You Keatolics are the ones encouraging our boys to have talks with Guatemala! You are trying to make one big Keatolic nation!'

Beka heard Senora Villanueva suck in her breath and murmur to a friend with a body like a mammoth tortilla,

'Madre de Dios, Dolores, mi amiga, no respect for the Padre!'

Her pasty faced companion wrinkled her face and shrugged.

'Only the creole, no culture.'

Father Mullins shrugged his shoulders with embarrassment as he said,

'Come, come, Miss Arguelles. We've always been friends.'

'Don't miaow at me with your puss face, Father. Today is Sunday so I won't tell this crowd out here what I know about your deeds!'

Father Mullins made no further attempt to mollify Miss Arguelles. He began moving on long legs through the crowd, pressing about them, towards the church gate. Miss Arguelles, feeling dismissed before she was good and ready to go, pushed her way in front of him, turned around, bent over and hoisted her skirt exposing a fat, black bottom encased in a long pair of white drawers.

'Aie, ya yie!' and 'Yohooo!' yelled the crowd pressing closer, and a few rude boys in the centre of the ring whistled shrilly. Father Mullins, stopped, lifted his long arm with deliberation and described, in the air, an exaggerated sign of the cross at the broad expanse of white against black. He nodded a curt good evening to the crowd and running his fingers through red-brown curls, slipped swiftly into churchyard. Miss Arguelles screeched after him,

'You are American but I know you have Spanish blood!'

Once upon a time, Beka would have found the whole scene jaw-breakingly funny. She would have memorized every detail, and then some, to enact for Granny Ivy the moment she reached home. Today, she glared viciously at Miss Arguelles, and shushed the boys who didn't know what they were laughing about, from aie, ya yieing with the rest. It was a burning shame, Beka felt, that Miss Arguelles was letting creoles down. Senora Villanueva was pressing a handkerchief delicately to her temples. Following her gaze, Beka saw Toycie hurrying across the churchyard, ahead of Emilio, who lagged behind at a sedate saunter, hands in the pockets of his trousers, head straight up, like a grandee. Beka rolled the pram in front of Senora Villanueva and, in conscious imitation of Lilla's hauteur, bowed good evening before going to meet her friend Toycie, at the gate.

'What did he say?' Beka demanded, regretting not treating Emilio with more deference when she'd had the chance. Toycie looked pinchfaced and old.

'He took the note,' Toycie panted, 'but he couldn't talk to me long because today is his mother's birthday and friends are having an escabeche supper. But we arranged to meet at Battlefield Park tomorrow night.'

'Tomorrow is a school night!'

'I am not asking you to come, Beka Lamb.'

'But how will you get away from Miss Eila and Granny Ivy to talk to Emilio if I don't come?'

'I'll find a way.'

Beka hesitated for a minute, then she said,
'I'll come.'
'Nobody is forcing you.'
'I want to.'
'All right then.'
'How do you feel now?'
'Like I could burst wide open.'
'Let's walk out front for a while.'
'Not over this side by Crazy House.'
'No, we'll go up your side by the lighthouse.'

'All right then,' Toycie said. 'Let's go,' and squeezing the boys into the pram, the girls began the long walk to Baron Bliss' grave.

CHAPTER 16

The time appointed for the meeting at Battlefield Park had come and gone . . . yet, men, women and children continued to pour onto the small, sandy piece of circular ground in the centre of town where meetings, rallies and celebrations had been held for a longer time than anyone could remember. The majority of people, hundreds deep around the elevated rostrum in the middle of the park, did not have very much in the way of material goods, and they were excitedly looking to the politically aware, racially diverse leaders, busy on the platform, to provide them with the possibility of having more.

Granny Ivy and Miss Eila sat on three-legged stools, in the company of Miss Janie and Miss Flo, under Battlefield's only tree, an ackee, the roots of which burrowed beneath a wall, six feet high, separating the Canadian Bank Compound from the rest of the park. Toycie and Beka, faces sombre, leaned against the trunk of the ackee tree scanning the crowd with anxious eyes. Toycie glanced left at the domed clock atop the roof of the two-storied court house building. Cupping her hand over her mouth, she whispered to Beka,

'Do you think it's eight o'clock already? Emilio said he'd be here the latest seven thirty.'

Beka plucked at a man's blue and white striped shirt.

'Excuse me, Mr Cassian, excuse me, but what time is it?' Mr Cassian, a warder with Beka's Uncle Curo, at His Majesty's Prison was one of the few civil servants supporting P.I.P. openly.

'What time is it, pet?' His bald head shone from the naked bulbs strung all around the park, and his voice, usually soft and conciliatory, shook with patriotic fervour. 'What time is it?' he asked again, shaking a pale brown fist into the night air. 'It's time for freedom, for independence! Let's hear it for our boys, my countrymen! Hip, Hip!' and a group of his friends responded with a resounding 'Hooray!'

'Bally!' Beka muttered to Toycie. 'Touch anybody nowadays and what do you get? Speech!'

The girls ducked through the crowd of excited people until they reached the edge of the pavement. Across Regent Street, more people crammed the court house steps overlooking the park.

'Let's wait right here, Beka,' Toycie said. 'He's got to come over Big Bridge and we can see.'

'Do you think he'll go looking for us on Albert Street?' Beka asked, referring to the main shopping thoroughfare flanking the park on the right.

'I don't know, I don't know,' Toycie replied.

The girls stood for about half an hour peering down the street towards Market Square. Each bicycle lamp, moving like a dim spotlight down the middle aisle of Big Bridge, made them step into the street to see more clearly. A barefooted Carib, a basket of cassava starch topping a circle of cloth on her head, sauntered by calling,

'Starch, starch, want to buy starch?' Lilla always needed starch but Beka didn't have a five cents in her pocket. The woman's headscarf of muted reds, blues and greens, her plaits peeking out, curving up over the ears, reminded Beka of the Stann Creek holidays when she swam in Dangriga River. She said,

'Not tonight, sister, not tonight.'

The vendor moved slowly along the fringes of the crowd, her full length skirt, brushing the street, showing a total disregard for style. Swinging her head fully around to look at Beka, she asked,

'Next time?'

'Maybe next time,' Beka said, wondering how she managed to prevent her starch basket from falling off her head. Toycie touched Beka with icy fingertips,

'He's coming, Beka,' and she was off, crossing the street swiftly before an oncoming car could delay her. Beka watched as Emilio swung long legs over the bicycle seat, switched off the lamp, wheeling the cycle alongside Toycie as they started down the short lane separating Scots Kirk from the court house. Beka stayed where she was, until the two figures rounded the corner leading to Southern Foreshore, then she manoeuvered her way, through the rapt crowd, towards the ackee tree. She touched Granny Ivy lightly on the shoulder, tempted to confide in her, but Granny Ivy said,

'Shu, Beka! I want to hear.' Beka returned to the streetside afraid Miss Eila would question Toycie's absence.

A brown man, big as a bear, wearing a short-sleeved shirt, stood at the microphone, arms upraised to silence the cheers and handclaps of the receptive crowd,

'My people, for centuries we have probably been the most subservient subjects in the entire British Empire. Unemployment, sub-human wages, malnutrition, slums, and all the other social evils of which you know, forced us to send that memorial to King George. Why did we send it? My countrymen, our backs are to the wall. Over the centuries colonial exploitation took and is taking abroad the little wealth we possess, leaving us impoverished and destitute. Imperial preferential tariffs, and the control of finances and other vital issues by the Imperial Government through the Governor's reserve powers, cannot but degrade us further.

'What did we ask for in that memorial, my countrymen? We asked for the restoration of our dollar to its traditional parity with the American dollar, the discontinuation of all endeavours to federate with the West Indies at this juncture in our history, the removal of the Governor's reserve power from the constitution, an elected majority in the Legislative Council and increased aid for development.

'The Governor, my friends, and some of our own misguided people, are saying that we are communists, that we are selling the country down the river to Guatemala. In the past few days, the Governor has accused us of disloyalty to the royal family because we refused to hang the portrait of the King in the only place we can demonstrate how we feel. In a blatant misuse of his power, the Governor has dissolved our council, nominating nine people of his choosing to concentrate on street and drain issues until he sees fit to refer the matter back to the electorate. What have we got left? National unity, my people, that is what we have left. Let us present a united front to the world. We must show, as was said in the memorial, that a poor, suffering, homeless, undernourished people can stand together until our not unjust demands are met. National unity, shoulder to shoulder . . .'

On and on the speeches went. The court house clock struck ten — that meant it was nine thirty and Toycie had not returned. Sodie's Department Store, directly opposite the park, was already closed, only its huge glass showcases remained brightly illuminated. Beka noticed clerks in pink skirts and white blouses dawdling near the curb looking and listening. They wouldn't dare linger long or they'd probably all be fired. Beka crossed the street and began running down the lane to the sea. There was no moon and the lap, lap of the waves against the sea-wall kept pace with her heartbeat. She kept running until she drew opposite Baron Bliss Institute . . . was that Toycie leaning against the door?

'Toycie?' she called softly. 'That you, gial?'

The figure turned around. It was Toycie, and by herself!

'Toycie, what happen, what happen? Where's Milio?'

'He's gone, Beka, Beka, he's gone.'

Beka pushed the Institute door, what a blessing, it was open, always a sanctuary. Leaning heavily on Beka, Toycie allowed herself to be led into the auditorium. They fumbled around quietly, as they found seats to the rear. A light, burning in the librarian's office, showed up a section of the stage curtain which hung loose. Beka itched to go up front and adjust it, so that it would hand as it should. Toycie, quiet for a few minutes, was convulsing again.

'What did Milio say to you, Toycie?'

'He said he can't marry me because he has to finish school and go to university in Mexico.'

'That's all?'

'No.'

'What else?'

'He said he doesn't believe the baby can be his, if I am pregnant, because his body didn't go into me and anyhow he could never marry anybody who played around with him like I did, because if I can do it before marriage, after marriage I would do it with somebody else and his mamacita would collapse if he married somebody that wasn't a virgin because she's so religious and she raised him to be a modest Catholic boy . . .'

'But you and Milio know each other for two years, Toycie. You never had another real boyfriend. And Toycie? Didn't Miss Eila tell you when you were having your period first time that sometimes if the sperm from a man touches your vagina, sometimes it can go into you and become a baby?'

'No, Beka, no. I didn't know and maybe Aunt Eila doesn't know either. And Milio said nothing would happen and now he says he loves me but can't marry me. But he couldn't even like me, Beka, to treat me so badly.'

Beka pulled Toycie's head onto her shoulder and caressed the crinkly hair whispering,

'I love you though, Toycie gial. And I think Milio likes you very much, too, but he's frightened, that's all. Maybe when the baby is born, if you're pregnant, which I don't believe, and Milio sees how much the baby looks like him, he might change his mind.'

'I don't want it, Beka. I don't want it. I don't care if I never see Emilio Sanchez Villanueva ever again in my life! *You* didn't see his eyes! All I want now is to graduate. Aunt Eila works too hard.'

'I'll help you if it's a baby, Toycie. We'll live together when I leave school and raise it as best we can, and if it's a girl, we'll explain everything carefully about everything so that her life doesn't break down that way. And if it's a boy, we'll do the same.'

Toycie was convulsing in Beka's arms again and Beka heard in her mind a childhood game song Toycie and herself had played as children: 'There's a brown girl in a ring, tra la la la la,' as she was shoved into a wide circle of girls holding hands in the play-yard at Holy Redeemer school. She stood there in the middle listening to them shouting at her in unison, 'Now wheel and take your partner, tra la la la la!'

Beka pushed Toycie up into a sitting position.

'Now listen, Toycie, why don't we *please* tell Granny Ivy? She can keep a secret, I swear, and she'll know how to help you maybe. Granny Ivy knows lots of things.'

'Please not yet, Beka. I feel ashamed and dirty. Maybe it's a mistake, what you say? Maybe it's a mistake, eh? Can you tell I was crying?' she asked, her face close to Beka's.

'You'll have to try and hide your face. Wipe it with your frock tail. Let's go quickly, I can hear "Land of the Gods" blasting over the loudspeaker already. Come on now, let's go.'

'My period may come this month,' Toycie was whispering hopefully as the girls scuttled out of the auditorium into the street.

At the park the crowd had lessened. They found Granny Ivy and Miss Eila standing to attention singing, 'God bless America' instead of 'God Save the King' which was another thing Governor Radison had against Granny Ivy's party.

As they left Battlefield Park, Toycie and Beka trudged silently behind Granny Ivy and Miss Eila, who discussed the speeches all the way home. Toycie kept glancing about her, as if she expected to see Emilio waiting to smile goodnight to her, from a darkened store front, at Market Square, on Big Bridge, near the post office, at Holy Redeemer Cathedral, everywhere, but there was no sign of him at any of the usual places, and Toycie's disappointment was pitiful.

Beka felt heavy with Toycie's trouble as well as her own. She had promised herself to stay home and study, but how could she let Toycie down? They accompanied Toycie and Miss Eila to their house, waited until the lantern was lit, and then continued home. Bill Lamb was working at his desk, Granny Ivy immediately climbed the attic stairs to bed, complaining, 'my veins are killing me.'

'Maybe you should stay home more then, Ma,' her son replied.

Beka went into the kitchen and using her Dad's thermos made herself a drink of coffee. The clock on her Dad's desk, which was always right, said eleven. She removed her books off the archway shelf and sat down at the dining table. Her Dad peered at her over his glasses and said,

'Coffee and homework at this time of night? If I was at home, you wouldn't have put a foot out of this house. But as usual, you sneaked off with your Grandmother's encouragement. For the life of me, I can't see an end to all of this.'

Beka looked pleadingly into her Dad's face, so much like her own. She looked at the clock and the work piled up on *his* desk.

'You'll be late for school again tomorrow, mark my words.'

'I don't have much more to do, Daddy,' Beka said humbly. Bending her head she continued to memorize Theorem One.

CHAPTER 17

Sister Mary Virgil paced the lower verandah one Monday morning two weeks later, inspecting students as they streamed across the grass, burnt a rusty red by the scorching August sun. Any girl without a written excuse for not wearing full uniform, would be sent home to get such a note. Beka and Toycie reached the top step to find Sister Virgil's pacing had brought her to meet them. Toycie's uniform belt broke, the botton rolling off the verandah into the grass below. Clutching at her waist to prevent the belt from falling to the floor, the textbooks slipped out of her arms, and papers, covered with Toycie's neat, upright script, scattered in every direction. Toycie stood there, under Sister Virgil's steady scrutiny, as if every sensible thought had left her. Beka set her own books down, rushing about to gather Toycie's, aided by two freshmen who detached themselves from a group goggling outside the classroom door. Beka placed the books and papers in the crook of Toycie's trembling arm. A freshman passed Toycie her belt, and Beka watched Toycie's hand jerking violently as she placed the coil on top of everything.

'If you're quite finished, Miss Qualo,' Sister Virgil said, 'I'd like to have a word with you.'

Toycie swallowed and nodded, following the Principal who

was stepping briskly towards her office. The verandah became noisy again as soon as Sister Virgil and Toycie were out of earshot, and Beka walked into her classroom buzzing with all manner of girlish conversation. In those days, St. Cecilia's was almost another world from the rest of Belize. The majority of students, among whom were the poor, the rich, the brilliant and the mediocre, acquired the art of suppressing segments of their personalities, shedding the lives they led at home the minute they reached the convent gates. They managed, somehow, to leap through the hoops of quality purposely held high by the nuns, rarely, however, without awkwardness, determination and intense effort. There were others, many times of the highest intellectual capacity, who could not, did not, would not, for a variety of reasons, learn to switch roles with the required rapidity. Their upbringing, set against such relative conformity, was exaggerated into what was perceived to be vulgarity, defiance, ingratitude, lack of discipline or moral degradation. These were the ones who stumbled and fell, often in utter confusion, and sometimes were expelled from school.

As Beka strove to bring order to the jumble inside her desk, a shadow at the door, blocking the sunlight, made her spring to her feet nervously. She expected to look into Sister Virgil's accusing face, but Sister Gabriela stood at the door, a sheet of paper in one hand.

'Good morning, Sister Gabriela,' the class chorused, forming queues alongside the six rows of desks.

'Good morning, girls. Before the bell rings, let me remind you that the closing date for submitting entry forms for the essay contest was last Friday. We had three entries from this room, Elizabeth Tate-Sim, Guadalupe Rosado and Beka Lamb. I want to wish the contestants good luck and to remind them that the essays must be handed in to me at three o'clock on the last Friday of October.'

'Thank you, Sister. Good morning, Sister.'

During prayers, led by Sister Frances, homeroom teacher to the freshman class, a note was passed to Beka. It said, 'Hope you win. Thomasita Ek.' Thomasita had failed first form as well. Beka glanced surreptitiously along the first row. At its beginning, the Maya Indian girl's head was bent low, her thick plait swaying from side to side as she thudded her breast with the rest of the class intoning the closing lines of The Confiteor,

'Through my fault, through my fault, through my most grievous fault.'

The note comforted Beka, who had not yet found a place amongst the new freshmen, but by the time prayers were concluded, she had made a resolution to inform Sister Gabriela that she would not be able to enter the contest after all. The first two class periods of the morning fled by in a blur and at recess, Beka was the first out of the room rushing upstairs, downstairs, all over the school yard in her search for Toycie. A group of seniors studied in the shade of several coconut trees near the sea, lapping quietly against the rocks piled into a wall. Beka went up to a classmate of Toycie's asking,

'Stella, do you see Toycie about?'

Last year when Beka had been on the freshman basketball team, she used to guard Stella Beaufort, who had arms of a remarkable length, and stopping her from sinking too many balls into the basket had stretched Beka's guarding capacities to their utmost. Stella got up, blonde hair swinging about her face,

'Girl, Beka, I think something terrible must be going on! Sister Virgil sent Toycie home!' She led the way to the rock wall away from the other girls.

'Did she have her books, Stella?'

'Every last one. What did Toycie do, Beka?'

Beka wished to confide in someone but it couldn't be Stella. She was the sweetest person, but all Toycie's business would be over the school yard in no time at all. Stella told secrets only to her friends but almost everyone in the school was her friend. So, looking into the kindly grey eyes, fringed with black lashes, Beka said as normally as possible,

'I'm not sure,' but inside her, voices were screaming, 'Toycie got expelled, *expelled!*' She moved away from Stella, then moved back to her side again.

'Tell me when you find out, eh, Beka? Toycie helped me with my English and Maths otherwise I would never have made it into fourth form.'

'Sure,' Beka said, 'Sure.'

Around and about the yard, the chattering, laughing, joking girls all seemed to belong to exclusive groups. The turmoil within Beka convinced her, quite irrationally, that everyone was withdrawn, hostile, out of reach.

'Well, I can at least tell Sister Gabriela I am not entering her contest,' Beka said to herself. 'Nobody can expel me for that!'

Sister Gabriela was writing test questions on the blackboard that covered the entire front wall of the classroom.

'May I help you, Beka?' she asked, one hand continuing to write while the other kept her gauzy veil from brushing against the writing on the board.

'I came to tell you I can't enter, Sister.'

The chalk dropped with a click on the ledge, and the nun crossed the room, quickly, to where Beka stood pushing four fingers through the gap between the classroom door and the wall.

'Why ever not, Beka?' Sister Gabriela asked reaching out to straighten Beka's faded green bow tie.

'If I don't pass first term, I'll have to leave school, Sister, and the work is too much. I am getting behind already.'

'That's understandable, Beka,' Sister Gabriela said, spanking chalk dust off her hands.

'Do you know what's to happen to Toycie, Sister Gabriela?'

'I don't know very much about it, Beka,' Sister Gabriela said, busily adjusting her glasses. 'And what I do know, I can't talk about. Is Toycie a relative of yours, Beka? I know you are very close.'

'Not a real relative, Sister, but I've sometimes pretended she was my sister or my cousin. She lives close by my house.'

'Have you managed to do any work on the essay at all?'

'I was planning to go see Mr Rabatu. He is a very old man now, but he still massages people when they have backache and so on. Granny Ivy told me he was one of the acolytes that went to Fort George to welcome the first Charity nuns.'

'That's interesting, Beka. I had no idea there was anybody like that still about.'

Beka's heart was full so she stooped down and began to tighten her shoe laces.

'Have you done anything else, Beka?'

'Not much, but my mother talked to the librarian at Bliss and he said he would look up some papers.'

'Interesting, interesting! What a plan you've got, Beka. It sounds so exciting!' Her tone changed as she watched Beka tying the laces of her other shoe.

'But I know how worried you are about your work . . . and about your friend Toycie.'

'Yes, Sister,' Beka said standing up.

'I tried to make friends with Toycie during the few weeks she was with us but she seemed a little withdrawn.'

'That's not her usual way, Sister, but she is in trouble.'

Sister Gabriela sighed and said,

'Look, Beka. I won't scratch your name off the list just yet. Later on, if you feel differently, let me know. There's no harm in keeping your name on it indefinitely.'

'All right, Sister Gabriela, but I didn't want you to depend on me.'

'Beka, I know what it's like to be poor, like Toycie is right now, materially and spiritually, and I know the panic failure sometimes brings. On the farm in Wisconsin where I grew up, when the crops failed, we had to start again, without knowing whether the drought would continue into the following year.'

'Sometimes I feel bruk down just like my own country, Sister. I start all right but then I can't seem to continue. Something gets in the way and then I drift for the longest while.'

'Sister Mary Frances and I were teaching out-district last weekend, Beka. On the way to a village, I saw machinery standing useless alongside the road. They lacked parts and the driver told me that's why they aren't being used. What my father would have given for a tractor when I was a girl — after the Great Depression, my family broke down too. But when a good piece of machinery lacks a part, Beka, you don't give up on it or leave it alongside the road in the swamp, and the rain and the mud. You shelter it and try to find some way to make it work, even if you have to learn to make that part!'

'People out district are poor, Sister, and they don't have education like Americans.'

'I know, Beka. I know. I am not trying to criticize. Let me put it another way. You are lucky, Beka. You are being given advantages most young people in this country far smarter than you are not going to get. Therefore, you have an obligation to serve, a responsibility to produce under the most adverse circumstances. You must go as far as the limitations of your life will allow. Find a way to do what you can, even though things seem to be crashing all around you. Sometimes they are not breaking down at all, sometimes things are taking a different shape. Try to recognise the pattern even if it is one you don't like, then maybe you can do something about it.'

'My Dad feels a little like you. He feels the whole world depends on the whole world. That's why he doesn't go around shouting "Independence now" because he feels that even after we're independent, we'll still be dependent.'

'Independence is just another relative thing, Beka. It's better to be more than less though.'

'Well, if you're encouraging me about the contest, I'll try, but the prizes will go to one of the bakras or pania girls anyhow.'

'My goodness, don't do *me* any favours! How do you know, anyway?'

'My Granny says that's how it's been from before time. They have all the advantages.'

'You are *here*, aren't you? You now have some of those same advantages. Only your attitude hasn't changed to match!'

The recess bell clanged and with a small exclamation, Sister Gabriela hurriedly said goodbye. Beka flew down the stairs feeling slightly giddy. Attitude? Attitude? What did Sister Gabriela mean? Halfway down the stairs she braked, the prolonged ringing of the bell vibrating in her ears.

Daddy Bill, Miss Eila and Toycie were coming single file down the walk. Beka's insides churned sourly in a way becoming sickeningly familiar. Toycie's problem remained. That hadn't gone away. If there's a pattern to all of this, Sister Gabriela, Beka said to herself, then we've lost it.

CHAPTER 18

Daddy Bill stomped up the steps, a sound like steam escaping through his clenched teeth. Miss Eila limped behing him, her eyes half wild with stress, her face powder blotchy from tears and sweat. Beka continued down the stairs and her father, the brim of his felt hat skinned up in front, said immediately,

'Shouldn't you be in class, Beka?'

'Yes, Sir,' Beka said, looking at Toycie, still wearing the unbelted school uniform. Toycie, who was always so gaily optimistic, so brave, so encouraging to others, whose eyes were usually lively with the anticipation of tomorrow's promise, looked at Beka with a dull resignation that Beka could not believe. She slumped against the verandah railing, too nauseated, too disoriented to recognize or appreciate anyone's concern or sympathy. She turned her head away from Beka to stare at the sea, indicating that she had lost her main hope, and for that, there could be no consolation. Beka wanted to go over to her friend and say,

'Never mind, Toycie. Maybe you can open a store or a shop and still get to build your house at Fort George by the sea. We'll plan it tomorrow. Maybe Mr Blanco will give us a loan!' But her father led the way into the waiting room and Toycie never glanced her way again.

Beka could not go to her classroom. She leaned against the side wall of the office, listening to after-recess prayers resounding throughout the school. After a while, she peered through the space between the door and the wall. A two-foot statue of the Virgin, her arms outstretched, her stone eyes expressionless, stood on a table beside Daddy Bill's straight chair. He removed his hat, straightened the brim, twirling it once, twice, around his fingers. Sister Virgil emerged from her office, the wooden cross of her rosary in her hands. Daddy Bill and Miss Eila sprang to their feet. Toycie didn't move, just sat there, feet slightly apart, hands in her lap, hair in disarray, her head tilted slightly to one side,

'Good morning, Sister Virgil,' Daddy Bill said, 'Miss Eila tells me we have some trouble about Toycie, and she asked me to come along and discuss what can be done.'

'Good morning, Mr Lamb, Mrs Qualo. Please be seated.' Flicking the tail of her veil out of the way, she placed herself opposite them.

'I am glad you are here with Mrs Qualo, Mr Lamb, although we always seem to meet in unfortunate circumstances. I know how busy you are and it is good of you to help out at this time.'

'It's no trouble, Sister Virgil. Miss Eila and Toycie are like a part of my own family. Toycie helped my wife with Beka and the boys for many years. It's only right they should turn to us now.'

'Of course, yes, of course. It's a delicate matter we are to talk about today, Mr Lamb. I don't know whether you are aware of all the circumstances?'

'Not delicate at all, Sister. Yes, I am aware,' Bill Lamb said, placing his hat upside down on the Virgin's table, carefully, as though afraid his hat might damage the statue. 'Miss Eila and myself took Toycie to Doctor Clark for confirmation as you suggested in your note to Miss Eila. Dr Clark said she's about three months pregnant, although you couldn't tell to look at her.'

Miss Eila's head was bowed to her chest, her bad foot sticking out on the floor in an awkward position. Sister Virgil turned to her,

'Mrs Qualo, let me come straight to the point. I will have to ask Toycie to leave school.'

'For how long, Sister?' Miss Eila was pleating the skirt of the work dress she hadn't had time to change.

'For good, Mrs Qualo, and I am sorry about it. Toycie is one of our best students.'

Miss Eila's gnarled fingers wiped the tears impatiently from eyes narrowed to puffy slits. 'Sister,' she was saying, 'I beg you, Mam, I get down on my knees to you,' she said, slipping to one knee on the floor, dragging herself along to clutch at the heavy gown flowing about Sister Virgil's boots, 'Give my Toycie a chance, Sister. She will go up to my brother's at Sibun River till her time comes. My family will take good care of Toycie's baby so Toycie can come back and finish next year. Please, Mam, please!'

'I can't do that, Mrs Qualo, you know I can't do that. I have the parents of the other students to consider. They would be shocked if I allowed Toycie to return to school after bearing a child.'

'Shocked, Sister, shocked?' Bill Lamb was asking in his most reasonable voice. 'Why should anybody be shocked? Toycie is an excellent student. She alone is not to be blamed for this accident, and Mr Villanueva's son will not be expelled from school. This is the last year before she graduates. She could leave school now and come back after the baby is born. I personally would see to it that all this does not become a scandal.'

'This country remains Victorian in a number of ways, Mr Lamb, and there is little you can really hide, as you well know.'

'You'd be surprised at some of the things hidden here, Sister. Toycie needs shelter, not another stick to beat her down. Look at her! She needs hope.' Sister Virgil did not look but she said,

'And then, of course, there is my conscience.'

'Your conscience, Sister?' Bill Lamb was trying to be polite, but Beka could see his eyes getting feverish and his lips beginning to curl.

'Please, dear God,' Beka begged, 'don't let him fight with Sister Virgil. Please, dear God.'

'Yes, my conscience, Mr Lamb. In cases like this, we believe it is entirely up to the modesty of the girl to prevent these happenings. Our girls are warned of this likelihood, and the possible consequences. Not all girls who get into trouble here are of Toycie's calibre. Believe me I hesitated, waited, praying we might be mistaken. One day, these things might change, but right now these are the rules, and I am *truly* sorry.'

The silence in the room had a frightening quality and Bill Lamb, taking his hat off the table said,

'Well, Sister, Miss Eila and I will leave you now with Toycie, as I can see, as you say, there is nothing you can do. Maybe in your position I would do the same. Who knows? My daughter is in this academy and I pray to God she makes it through school. But because of Miss Eila here, and because of Toycie, I feel I must tell you this: you have been principal of this academy for two years so maybe you don't yet realize the financial strain people are under in this country. Families without resources have no strings to pull when their children get in trouble.' Bill Lamb's voice was rising, 'Miss Eila here, has worked from morning to late night for Toycie's education, making bread and buns for sale, after cooking all day in other people's houses. She is a simple woman, like many of our women, in certain matters, and she had one ambition, to see Toycie graduate from your wonderful academy. You say things will change, Sister. It'll be too late for Toycie here, and others like her, but the woman brave enough to make that change should be crowned Queen of the Bay at Battlefield Park!'

Sister Virgil's blue eyes reflected the glint of the window panes sparkling in the room. Swinging her cross like a pendulum, she said,

'We women must learn to control our emotions, Mr Lamb. There are times we must stand up and say "enough" whatever our feelings. The rate of illegitimacy is quite high and has been high for a long time. The women will have to decide for a change in their lives, otherwise they will remain vulnerable. Under prevailing conditions, I cannot see much hope for the long term development of this country. This, Mr Lamb, is in large part, what we try to teach in this academy.'

Toycie fell forward onto the floor, and Daddy Bill and Miss Eila began shouting instructions to one another. In the confusion, Beka slipped into the room to cradle Toycie's head as they carried her out of the room. Sister Virgil was saying,

'Put her head between her knees, Mr Lamb, put her head between her knees,' but neither Daddy Bill nor Miss Eila paid any attention. Bill Lamb gave Beka his handkerchief, and she raced to the vat to wet it, stumbling over the stones. The handkerchief seemed too little to be of much use so Beka pulled off her half-slip and soaked that too. When Toycie revived, her sorrowing eyes looked at the heads bent above her, as though they were revolting apparitions in some incredible nightmare. Daddy Bill picked Toycie off the floor and began walking with her across the school without a backward glance. Miss Eila dragged herself behind him and her uncontrollable sobbing rose and fell in the windless, brilliantly sunny morning long after they had reached the cement walk beneath the chapel and long after they had left the convent grounds. Sister Virgil went into her office, turning the key in the lock, leaving Beka standing on the verandah.

She crunched across the stones to the vat, washing her face, over and over, in the full force of the water rushing from the faucet, but the tears continued to spill in rivulets down her cheeks. Her head spun, she couldn't think clearly, her knees refused to work with their usual co-ordination as she made her way to the rear of the school building. Spreading her half-slip in the sun to dry, she found a shady spot in the shadow of the school and looked at the sea, almost level with her eyes. A clump of grass, with the tiniest purple-white flowers, grew nearby. Each dainty, olive-green branch supported a dozen, tiny oval leaves. She touched one branch watching the shy leaves close like the wings of a butterfly. She touched another, and another, counting as she touched. When the bell clanged for lunch, and chairs scraped, as one, all over the building, she had counted over three hundred branches. She sat there waiting for everyone to leave. In the midst of listening to footfalls marching down the stairs, she sprang upright, pulling on the warm half-slip in haste,

'Yes, yes,' she muttered to herself. 'Yes, *I* know how to punctuate Sister Gabriela's riddle! It's: 'Time flies? You can't. They fly too fast!'

The school yard was deserted by the time Beka made her way to the front of the school. She stood on the path Toycie had walked for the last time, unwilling to accept the fact that Toycie *was* expelled. She wouldn't flick a ball into the baskets, over there on the field, with her usual graceful, off-handed precision. They wouldn't link arms and stroll about at recess time, exchanging gossip about girls and nuns, sprawling in the shade of the tall pine trees, where the grass stayed green and cool, to laugh in wicked glee over somebody's minor misfortune. Toycie was going to have a *child,* and Beka suddenly realized that Toycie herself was childlike, in ways Beka could not remember ever being. But just supposing she was? The fields were silent, the nuns must all be sitting down to lunch, and gloom suffused the gloriously sunlit day.

Rounding the corner of the nuns' residence, she spied Thomasita Ek, her short, stumpy body propped against the tall, wrought iron gate in the shade of a palm tree. She was turning the pages of a book open in her arms. A lump rose in Beka's throat as she observed Thomasita sucking on the tail of her blue-black plait, her circular face solemn. Thomasita's best friend, a girl from her own village in the south, promoted to second form, did not seek Thomasita out very much anymore. At Beka's approach along the walk, Thomasita's birdlike eyes, with eyelashes straight as a stick, looked at her sharply as she stated flatly,

'Gecmetry test this afternoon, bally.'

'Sister Virgil didn't warn us!'

'Mighty Mouse strikes again, taraaa!' Thomasita said.

'Did she ask for me in class, Thomasita?'

Thomasita shook her head, then said,

'Do you know the theorems, Beka?'

'Some. You?'

'Some,' Thomasita replied, giggling as she suggested,

'If you say what you know, I'll say what I know and maybe we can do a quick review.'

'Good idea, you start,' Beka replied, as they stepped into Milpa Lane. All the way home, oblivious to the noon-time traffic of impatient cyclists, pushing pedestrians, beeping cars and trucks, braying mules pulling loaded carts, and gangs of heat-maddened men shouting furiously as they spread boiling, stinking tar on the streets, the girls repeated the theorems to each other, pausing every now and then to consult the book when their statements conflicted, and Beka discovered it was soothing to fix her mind on lines and angles. By the time the girls parted to go their separate ways for lunch, Beka had reached a calmer plateau, and could wave to her mother anxiously looking out for her from the verandah of the house on Cashew Street.

CHAPTER 19

It was report card day, and Beka was unwell. She had menstrual cramps, a headache, and part of her wished to flee the school never to return. A quiet, almost the same as if it were closed and empty, descended on the classroom after morning prayers, and youthful faces, distorted by excitement and tension, turned attentively to the front of the room. Outdoors, sailboats bounced cheerfully on a playful sea. Sunlight, muted and friendly, sent feelers along the whitewashed classroom walls, splattering handfuls of sunballs on the blackboard, the ceiling and the floor. The brush of mellow trade winds on Beka's legs created in her a sensation of floating on the blue, beyond the barrier reef, towards the horizon.

The aquamarine sea, the pale blue sky, netted by a gauze-thin spread of clouds, the wide open classroom, almost a part of the environment, close to the edge of the sea, the reddish glow of glossy desks, the shelves of books near her seat, all the things that made St Cecilia's a special place, assumed an exaggerated beauty and value that morning, and Beka felt uncertain of her ability to keep watch over a treasure generations of crippling work had placed within her reach.

Smoothing the thin moustache above her top lip, Sister Mary Frances rose behind her desk, where yellow allamanda nodded in a bowl of clear water. She snapped the rubber bands off the cards, a bilious pink, striding as if on a long hike, to the centre of the room. The discs in Beka's neck ached, as though they supported an enormous calabash, so she rested her head on the desk, straining to hear the almost inaudible voice of the British nun, six feet tall.

'First in our class of forty-four, with an average of ninety-five, Alicia Lacrois. Second, Guadalupe Gonsalves, ninety-three. Third, Thomasita Ek, ninety-one point five.' The roll of names continued in Sister Frances' emotionless murmuring. Then there it was, 'Twenty-first, Beka Lamb, with an average of seventy-five, point five.'

The nun's abundant lashes shielded sapphire eyes as she handed over the card, and at her desk Beka scanned the row of figures anxiously. The lowness of her maths scores had pulled her average down, but she had passed every subject. She released her breath with a whistling sigh, but her relief at passing was tempered with regret that she had not done better. Still, she would stay in school and that fact she tried to keep before her as she waited for Sister Frances to finish handing out the remainder of the cards. She couldn't wait, now, to get home.

After tea, later that evening, Lilla and Granny Ivy sat with Beka on the back steps scrutinizing the report card as if it were the most complex legal document, reading the fine print, savouring the idea that this time Beka had 'praises be', passed the term. As Lilla called out each subject and it's accompanying score, Granny Ivy grunted in varying degrees of satisfaction, giving Beka pegs of sugar cane from the growing pile in an enamel dish, on the steps between them. Clouds, golden red like oranges, hung suspended in the sky. The splitting sound of Granny Ivy's butcher knife stripping joints of cane, the stickily sweet juice dribbling down her chin, and the chiming sing-song of her mother's voice, lulled Beka into a relaxation she had forgotten existed. The sun which had turned the crimson ixora, growing near the middle of the yard, into a burning bush departed reluctantly, leaving coral trails all over the west, to flash on the other side of the world. The pile of sucked out cane trash in the basket at Beka's feet had grown higher than the mound of cane in the dish, when Miss Eila rounded the corner of the house, dropping with a groaning weariness on the bottom step.

Lilla quickly hid the card in her apron pocket and Granny Ivy heaved herself down the steps to sit at Miss Eila's side. Since Toycie had been expelled from school, Beka rarely saw her anymore. She wouldn't leave the house during the daytime and avoided any contact with Beka. Miss Eila told Granny Ivy that the only times Toycie went on the street was after sunset, when Miss Eila's bad foot was aching and stiff, to empty the slop bucket.

'Have a piece of cane, Eila,' Granny Ivy was saying. 'What's up then, gial?'

'Toycie's not eating much, Miss Ivy,' she said, her voice unnaturally high. 'Course, she never was what anyone could call a big eater, but I bought hot corn and pork tamales for tea this evening, and most of it is still sitting on her plate.'

'She's got to begin thinking of the child,' Granny Ivy replied.

'Hardly says a word all day long. Works a bit in the house, or sits in my chair rocking back and forth. I try to tell her it's not judgement day and she isn't the first and she isn't the last. If she would talk, we could plan!'

'Is Nurse Palacio still seeing her?' Lilla asked.

'Oh, my, yes, Miss Lilla. Nurse comes by twice a week with tonic, pills, and books, but Toycie just listens and it's hard for me to get her to take the medicine regularly. Nurse tells me she's anaemic and what they call depressed, and I must get her to the doctor, but Toycie's turned stubborn on me.'

'Let me come over there tonight, Eila,' Granny Ivy said. 'I will try and talk to her. Tomorrow I will get Bill to compel her see Doctor Clark.'

'All right, Miss Ivy,' she answered moving off the steps. 'But I am getting tired, and not a word from her mother. Right now I am going to see an old woman living on Southside they tell me knows about conditions like Toycie's.'

'Why not wait until *after* she's seen Doctor Clark?' Lilla asked placing a restraining hand on Miss Eila's arm.

'I have to try everything, Miss Lilla,' Miss Eila said, dark eyes anguished.

'Miss Eila! Miss Eila!' Beka called, running down the steps, 'Please give Toycie this note for me. I dropped by again after school today but she wouldn't open the door!'

'All right, pet. But those other notes and things you give me, I give her, but she just leaves them on the table till I have to clear them away they are so much.'

'Why is Toycie vexed with me, Miss Eila?'

'Toycie's not vexed with a soul, pet. I think she's gone someplace so far inside herself she forget us back here, that is all.'

'Did you hear any more from the Villanuevas?' Lilla asked.

'Mrs Villanueva comes by for a minute or two, off and on. And one evening Emilio came by himself. He offered to marry Toycie after he graduates, but I don't think Toycie can understand anything much anymore, and if she did understand what that Villanueva boy was saying, I don't think she believes he really intends to marry her, nor do I if the truth be known.'

'Bill and I will go see the Villanuevas tonight when he comes from the club, Miss Eila. Maybe we can at least get a promise of maintenance for the baby. What do you say?'

'Thank you very much, Miss Lilla, thank you, Miss Ivy, night, night.'

'Nighty, night,' the Lamb women called.

After the dishes were washed and put away later that evening, Granny Ivy stood before the small rectangular mirror above the chest of drawers in the attic, sticking the final hairpins into grey plaits tucked under, over her ears. She stepped into a freshly ironed brown print, bordered with narrow white imitation lace around the sleeves and collar. Deep in thought, her movements were slow, and she uttered, now and then, little agreements with herself. Down the street, from Chico's Saloon and Bar, the night's first pop tune ripped through the quiet of the evening and Granny Ivy said briskly,

'It's seven, Beka, come and zip me up, please.'

Beka uncurled from where she sat at the window overlooking the street. Granny Ivy squeezed her waist an inch smaller and Beka pulled up the zip watching the pleated skirt fall neatly into place around her Gran's bulk. Granny Ivy tucked a handkerchief, folded into a dainty triangle, in the belt hidden by her bosom. She had her bag, and was preparing to leave, when there was a frantic banging on the back door. Daddy Bill, Mama Lilla, Chuku and Zandy were on the way to the Villanueva house, so Beka tore down to the kitchen hoping it was Toycie come to visit at last. She pushed her whole weight against the door which always jammed. It flew open unexpectedly and Beka shrieked. National Vellor stood in a pool of moonlight, sopping wet, clad in a blouse and skirt instead of the velvet gowns she wore at night.

'Come quickly,' she said, grabbing Beka's wrist. 'Miss Eila not at home!'

She wouldn't let go but pulled Beka down the stairs, through the yard, across Cashew Street, into the lumber yard and down towards the creek. Their feet squelched in the muddy sawdust, and Granny Ivy shouted from the verandah,

'Bekaaaaa! Beka!'

'Help me, help me with Toycie,' National panted.

In the moonlight, Beka saw her friend spread-eagled in the mud, beneath the rickety bridge leading to the latrine over the creek.

'Toycie! Toycie O!' Beka screamed. 'What happened to you? What happened, Toycie?' Stooping beside her friend, she put her arm under her neck and shoulders watching the ugly cut ooze blood onto her nose, mouth and throat. How Toycie's stomach had grown! The moans she uttered were too much for Beka's self-control. Whimpering with fright, she looked at National who ordered,

'Lift her!'

Toycie was so heavy, and Beka, remembering her grace and slenderness, wanted to kneel in the mud and bay mournful remonstrances at the moon. In National's shack, they laid Toycie gently on the blue chenille spread. National turned up the kerosene lantern and Beka watched in panic as the blood trickled onto the pillow from Toycie's forehead. National pushed Beka, sobbing with fright, through the door and she ran full tilt to find help. At the edge of the lumber yard, she saw Granny Ivy hurrying across. As she reached Beka, an army truck screeched to a stop inches from where they stood.

'Bloody British!' Granny gasped to the soldier who hopped down from the cab of the huge truck.

'Toycie drownded, Granny Ivy, Toycie drownded!'

'My sweet Jesus Christ!' Miss Ivy exclaimed, breaking into a swift walk, pushing Beka along the path in front of her. The soldier, his blonde hair slicked flat on his head, picked his way behind them asking repeatedly,

'What's oop then? What's *oop*?'

Inside the shack, National was holding a cloth tightly over Toycie's forehead, fanning her ashy face with desperation. The soldier, without saying a word to anyone, grabbed the cloth, tying it tightly around Toycie's forehead. He lifted her off the bed and began stumbling with her in his arms toward his truck. Granny Ivy rushed after him shouting,

'I am going with Toycie to hospital. Find Eila first, then get Lilla and Bill. Tell them to hurry!'

'Yes, Gran, yes,' Beka said, hovering uncertainly at the doorway. She was stunned. National removed her wet, muddy clothes.

Blood had made a bib on her blouse. The room stank of creek water. Her hair hung in tendrils onto her shoulders. Above the bed of rough sawmill planks, hung an old, fly-stained calendar showing a giant tree, its roots above the ground. Behind the tree, flowed unending fields of what looked to Beka, like emerald grass. Women, resembling National, wearing veils on their heads, walked through the fields, pottery vessels on their heads or in the crook of their elbows.

Beka glanced around swiftly noticing the velvet dress lying in readiness across a chair beneath a window overlooking the creek. National poured water into an enamel basin and then turned her palms upward, following Beka's gaze around the room.

'You see,' she said. 'No mother, no father, no school. What can I do?'

'Toycie,' Beka said, swallowing her spit. 'Toycie had school.'

National flung her wet clothes over the window ledge and stood looking across the lighted creek to the other side of the town, then she came over and pushed Beka gently through the door.

'Please,' she said, 'you go now and run!'

Beka stepped out the door into the merciless moonlight and said 'thank you' to Vellor standing in her underclothes, framed by the doorway. In front of her, as she raced across the lumber yard, loomed Vellor's luminous, glowing black eyes, her bedraggled hair, the green fields of grass. Vellor's face melted into Toycie's, Toycie's face merged into Vellor's and then Vellor became Toycie, as she had been, her mouth open in song, and there on the narrow path between sheds piled high with lumber, the flapping noise began again in Beka's head and she said aloud,

'No, dear God, no!' Clamping her hand over her mouth, she stifled the desire to lie on the path, abandoning herself to the hysteria that threatened to engulf her. She reached the streetside, busy now with lights, people, the horrible, raucous music, and she stood there not knowing which way she should go. Looking towards Toycie's house she saw Miss Eila unlatching the gate, and Beka pounded the street towards her, heart beating rapidly, not knowing how to break the news to poor Miss Eila.

CHAPTER 20

What seemed like hours later, Beka, her parents, and Miss Eila arrived at the hospital. Toycie had been taken to a ward upstairs and was receiving attention from the nurses, but she had not yet been seen by a doctor. Nurse Palacio, a trained midwife, was doing her best, Granny Ivy said, but Toycie was miscarrying. Daddy Bill rushed away quickly to try and locate the doctor who was supposed to be on night duty, and it was quite another age before the doctor arrived, and Toycie was taken to the operating theatre.

'I couldn't get Dr Clark,' Daddy Bill was saying over and over to the little group standing in suspense in the emergency room. 'I couldn't get Dr Clark, he's working out district, he would have been the best, so I had to bring this young one from home. He should have been in the hospital! Some doctor should be here at all times!'

Granny Ivy said,

'That gentleman soldier brought Toycie in here and I said to the nurse looking at us as if she didn't know what to do, I said to her, she fall down off a bridge into the creek and she's pregnant, and where can we put her down, and she said to me, put her on that table in the corner so I can clean the cut, the doctor went home to eat, and I said, please, nurse, can you change the filthy pillow case because the cut is bad, and she said, that's all right, it doesn't matter if she dirties it!'

'All she meant, Miss Ivy, was that there are no clean ones to put on the pillow or that the person with the keys to that cupboard isn't around.'

'I *know* what she meant, Lilla Lamb, but if things are so bad in the emergency room, what are they like up there in that so called theatre we can't see.'

Miss Eila's hand, with an ugly whitlow on the thumbnail, gripped Beka's arm so hard she could barely stand the pressure. Miss Eila's voice was shaking as she said,

'Toycie gone to that bridge over and over. How you think she managed to fall down? I can't think of a way she could fall unless she was dizzy . . . she complain sometimes that her head swings. You think my Toy will live, eh, Miss Ivy? Miss Lilla? Mr Bill? Tell me you think Toycie will make it through.'

Everyone muttered consoling words to Miss Eila excepting Granny Ivy who glared through the door at the nurse sterilizing instruments in another room. She jerked her chin in the nurse's direction and said,

'If she hadn't been so afraid to call that doctor from his dinner, I could say.'

A hunched-over black woman, with a bucketful of dirty water and a mop with bits of rotten string dropping all over the place, began sloshing dirty water on the floor, and the water mixed with droplets of Toycie's blood, which mingled in, drying in a matter of minutes upon the floor. All the while she mopped, she grumbled about the long hours of work, poor pay, starvation, and going on strike. As she sloshed the mop about Beka's shoes, a husband and wife, looking distraught, burst through the door, the wife hugging a screaming child, while the husband held the little hand firmly, a napkin wrapped like a miniature turban around the child's fingers. The plump little nurse bustled over and the man said,

'A door slammed on his fingers, get the doctor.'

'Let me see the finger,' the nurse said. 'Put him on the table over there.'

The woman, a fastidious creole housewife, took one look at the messy table and shook her head. The nurse stooped before her trying to unwrap the napkin, but the husband, shorter than his wife, and twice as broad, bellowed,

'The top is holding on by a skin thread. We won't take that cloth off till the doctor comes. Where is the doctor?'

'He's in the emergency room. We can't do anything until he comes, if you don't want me to at least clean and disinfect. You should go to a private clinic if you're so fussy.'

'None is open,' the wife spat nastily, 'or believe me, we wouldn't be sitting here. My husband is a civil servant and we can afford it!'

The little boy continued to scream at the pressure on his hand, the room stank of dust, dirt and medicine, and Beka was sure the odour of death flowed through the airless room from the Dead House to the rear of the emergency room. Every minute, she expected to see an orderly wheeling Toycie to the Dead House, at which point Lilla got up, the sobbing child reminding her of Chuku and Zandy.

'I'd better relieve Miss Boysie, Bill. She's been with the boys since eight and it's after eleven now. Are you coming, Beka? There's nothing you can do.'

'I'll stay with Miss Eila and Gran,' Beka said.

'I'll take Lilla home, then,' Daddy Bill said. 'I'll come back soon.'

The night grew stale, and sick and injured people continued to trickle in. The nurse, looking exhausted and ill herself, helped those she could, the others sat or stood around waiting for attention. Daddy Bill returned with a thermos of sweetened tea which nobody could swallow. Around midnight, Nurse Palacio came to the emergency room on another errand, and saw them still sitting there. Her eyes widened behind hornrimmed glasses and she rubbed the black mole on her brown chin as she took a seat beside them conscious of the pleading eyes of sick people sitting and standing around the walls. She said in the sweet, quiet, consoling way that made her the town's favourite nurse,

'We had some trouble with Toycie, Miss Eila. She lost the baby, but she will be all right, the doctor thinks.'

'How long did the operation last, Nurse?' Miss Eila said, holding onto Nurse Palacio's hands.

'About two hours or so,' Nurse Palacio replied. 'The cut had to be sewn up, too.'

'We sat here waiting and waiting thinking she was still in the theatre, Nursie,' Granny Ivy said.

'Oh, I am so sorry, Miss Ivy,' Nurse Palacio said. 'A trainee was sent to tell you, but maybe she was detained. We are so understaffed, and so many sick people tonight, and only the one doctor to do everything.'

'Can we see her now?' Miss Eila asked, recovering a little of her customary vigour.

Nurse Palacio looked at her sadly for a minute then she said,

'It's so late now and the other patients might be disturbed. But you come first thing tomorrow and you can peep at her then. Go home and get some rest now, eh, Miss Eila? I'll visit you when I can.'

'Thank you very much, Nurse,' Miss Eila said, pressing her

cheek against Nurse Palacio's. 'Thank you'. And with her head bowed she left the room followed by Granny Ivy, Daddy Bill and Beka.

One evening, a few days later, Beka accompanied Miss Eila on one of her constant visits to the hospital. They were early so they stood outside on the verandah of Toycie's ward peering at her through the window. Toycie wore a hospital gown of white cotton with strings at the back. Her long hair looked matted and unkempt. A nurse was holding her down on the bed while another tried to give her an injection. Toycie's screams were ear-shattering and she rolled, fought and struggled to a sitting position. She sank her teeth into the nurse's arm and the tray of needles and medicines crashed to the floor. It took four nurses and an orderly to restrain Toycie while another nurse gave her the injection.

After Toycie lost consciousness, Miss Eila and Beka were allowed to sit beside her bed until visiting time was up. The doctor who operated on Toycie came over to talk to Miss Eila. He looked harassed and kept twisting his stethoscope around in his hands. His pale, brown, hairy arms were sweaty, his eyes bloodshot from lack of sleep. He leaned against the bed where Toycie lay and gazed down at his shoes.

'Miss Eila,' he began.

'Yes, Doctor Meighan?' Miss Eila said, looking apprehensively at his serious face.

'Miss Eila, your niece needs help we can't give her at this hospital.'

'What do you mean, Doctor?'

'Physically she's doing well. But I hate to tell you this, Miss Eila, but she hasn't yet recovered her sense of reality.'

'Are you telling me Toycie's gone crazy?' Miss Eila said, her voice rising in anger.

'I am not saying anything,' the doctor said. 'She's becoming generally uncontrollable. She imagines she's at school and keeps asking when the recess bell is going to ring. You saw yourself her behaviour earlier this evening. I am going to recommend that she be put in the Belize Mental Asylum where she can be better treated and controlled.'

'When, Doctor?' Miss Eila asked, her voice nearly a whisper.

'Just as soon as I consider her physically fit.'

Miss Eila's racking sobs echoed in the ward and the other patients and visitors were quiet, looking at her. A nurse led her away to be given a sedative, and Beka went to the streetside to find a taxi.

CHAPTER 21

It was a sober Sunday the evening Granny Ivy, Miss Eila and Beka set out to visit Toycie at 'Sea Breeze Hotel' the town's euphemism for the Belize Mental Asylum. Along Victoria Avenue, acquaintances on verandahs nodded to them respectfully in deference to Toycie's condition, waiting until they were well along the street before passing the news to other neighbours, curious perhaps, about their destination. At the barracks, the wind blew roughly off a choppy sea, lifting high the skirts of mothers and girls walking children along the town front.

Beka licked the salty spray from her lips as they entered the courtyard of the asylum, built to resemble a brick mansion, their feet rattling on the loose cobblestones. Everything appeared clean, and there was a strong medicinal smell in the air which, Granny Ivy muttered was 'the smell of drugs — of a somewhat dangerous kind'. Beka trailed her elders, heart beating fast, marvelling that the men and women gripping the bars at the windows no longer seemed all that fearful to her. She gazed at an attractive young man with brown, curly hair in striped pyjamas. His lean face alternated between extreme seriousness and riotous laughter making him double over it was so painful.

There was little to complain about with regard to Toycie's cell. The room overlooked Barracks Green, a pleasant area, where soldiers drilled long ago, and where, so Beka was told, a small concentration camp had been set up for a few German residents of the town during that last war of the world. From the barred window of Toycie's room, Beka could see a latrine protruding over the sea. To Beka's eyes, hoping as she was for the best, Toycie seemed more or less like her old self, excepting that her hair was cropped so short not a curl was visible. The scar on her forehead pointed in a jagged line to her eyes moving weakly back and forth. Toycie's face was plump, and her hands were cupped in front of her face in a most peculiar fashion, and when Beka sat on the bed beside her and said,

'Hello, Toycie gial.'

Toycie said angrily, 'Shush!' and Beka realized that she was pretending to study.

The three people watched her, the tears rolling down Miss Eila's face which, during the last harrowing weeks, had shrunk to skin and bone. Visiting time over, they left Toycie in the same position as they had found her and walked to the gate where Matron Sedasey waited to talk with visitors. Matron's silken plaits were pinned around her ears in flat round buns, and her jowly cheeks seemed a part of her neck. Her tan face was creased and the eyes looking out of rubbery folds of skin expressed automatic sympathy, not unkind, but unsurprised and a trifle detached. She greeted them saying,

'Don't take things so *hard*, Miss Eila. I've seen cases worse than your niece and sometimes they recover, given time.'

Miss Eila perched her scrawny body on a boulder near the gate, gazing across the green to the chiffon-grey sea. Her greying hair was puffed out in an invisible hairnet, and her black water-wave taffeta Sunday dress was shiny from many washings and ironings. The flat nose looked too broad for her face now it was so thin, and her dark eyes were sunken in their sockets. Selecting a hairpin anchoring the net, she examined it, then tucked it in again at the top of her head.

'I failed Toycie, Matron,' Miss Eila said. 'I was trying and working to give her the life I never had, but I failed her. But, you know, Matron, she never was a child to give any trouble. She appreciated everything I did and that gave me the strength to do more. Nurse Palacio tells me she was starved for loving words, but I gave deeds, and didn't realize.'

'Now about the loving words, I don't know, Miss Eila, there I just couldn't say. Men and boys about here, married or not, pursue certain young ladies, especially the pretty ones, ambitious and proud like your Toycie. After they catch them the men, not all, mind you but some, start treating the girls like dirt, confusing them. The girls get desperate because they've lost their virginity and they try to prove constancy to one man by forgiving the bad treatment. Many girls wind up pregnant. This makes the men *somebody* in the eyes of their friends, it gives them status, as they don't see how else to get it around here. It's a kind of revenge, don't ask me for what, Mislady, especially if the girl skinned up her nose at them at first.'

'I wish some of them knew what I know,' Granny Ivy said. 'It's sad if you lost your virginity unmarried and to the wrong man, but if you lose it, you lose it. There's no need to degrade yourself.'

'No man ever approach me for any such reasons, Matron,' Miss Eila said. 'Of course, with my crooked body none would, so I couldn't tell Toycie much on that score. If her mother had been here, she, maybe, could have said.'

'Don't you believe it, Miss Eila. It happens in all kinds of families and mothers always hope things will be different for their daughters. You see that boy laughing his head off over there? Nice family, good education, but what happened? He was to marry a girl, the girl got pregnant by his worst enemy, and he stabbed the girl nearly to death.'

'You've been here now, what is it, Matron, going on for twenty years?'

'Yes, Mam, and I won't be sorry to retire. I am getting too old to help people with their heartbreak.'

'How long do you estimate Toycie should stay here?'

'Now that depends, Miss Ivy. She hasn't been violent lately and some days she seems almost better. If that continues, and there was a quiet place she could go with people to watch her, administer the drugs and so on, maybe, after a while, I can get permission from higher authority to let her out.'

'Tell me ears now!' Miss Eila said. 'She could go to my brother's place up the Sibun River, and I could go with her!'

'Yes, Matron!' Beka exclaimed. 'Toycie enjoys it there. I used to spend holidays with her there and it's nice.'

'Send your son to see about it then, Miss Ivy,' Matron said. I'm not promising much, mind you, but send Bill, and we'll see.'

135

Straightaway Granny Ivy suggested they hurry further up the barracks to fetch Beka's Dad from the town club. Few women frequented the club, unless it was a special occasion like a Saturday night dance or a wedding, so Granny Ivy shouted for him from the street below the verandah of the unpainted, dilapidated house. Daddy Bill leaned over the railing, and seeing them, descended the stairs soberly, expecting bad news.

'We can't talk here, Bill,' Granny Ivy said, referring to the crowd of men seated at the verandah tables enjoying their Sunday evening spree.

'Let's go to the sea-wall then,' Daddy Bill agreed, and the four people walked past the asylum to sit on the broad cement wall that kept the sea at bay in normal weather. They chose the end nearest the latrine where they could see lights being switched on in the asylum as evening approached. The older people sat facing the 'kept up' residences in tidy yards with grass and flowers, while Beka swung her legs over the wall, letting her feet dangle above the sea, welcoming the spray sprinkling her face and clothes.

Beka thought of the days Toycie and herself spent in the little house at Sibun, south of Belize, set in a clearing surrounded by mango and cashew trees. Miss Eila's brother and his wife, a childless couple, were early risers, and as soon as dawn turned the sky from black to grey, they were up firing coals in the outside hearth, sweeping the clearing around the house, feeding chickens and turkeys meant for the Belize market. By six o'clock, Toycie and herself had breakfasted on hot johnny cakes and scalding, sweet tea, after which they dashed outdoors to shuffle ankle deep amongst gold, yellow and rust mango leaves allowed to accumulate beneath the soaring trees so that in the evenings smoky bonfires could be lit, the fragrant leaves raked into burning hills, to drive mosquitoes away.

Mangoes lay all around them on the ground, some with tear-shaped sap, a clear golden colour, still undried on the perfumy skins of the rich fruit. The sweetest of all the mangoes in the cool grove grew on a giant tree, whose most productive branches overspread a deep sloping hole in which house garbage was thrown and burned. In ragged cotton frocks, the girls would slide down the sides to capture these prizes called poopsies. The skins of these mangoes were not lemon coloured or golden red, they were green when ripe. Back up the sides the girls would scramble, their frock tails bulging with poopsies, sweet as syrup. Next, they went after those mangoes shaped like dimpled chins, sweet also, but with long hairy fibres that stuck between the teeth. It was only after these were collected that they searched out the commoner mangoes, extravagantly selecting one here, another there, biting into each to see if it was to their, by now, jaded taste. Soon they were full and could eat no more. Only then would they begin their daily chore of searching out unbruised mangoes hidden amongst the leaves, setting each carefully, one on top of the other, in straw lined boxes which were dispatched in river dories for sale in Belize.

After the noon lunch, the girls were usually free to do as they wished. If the grown-ups were too tired to walk with them down the long muddy route to the river for a swim, they clambered into the branches of cashew trees which didn't grow nearly so high as the mango trees, plucking the yellow or red cashews, depending on the tree, chewing upon the pulpy flesh, the tart juice dribbling down their chins onto their dresses leaving a stain that never washed out. The girls had their own industry. They collected the grey, kidney-shaped seeds, drying them for days in hot sunshine on a zinc sheet they set upon stones. Some evenings they built a fire, under Miss Eila's supervision, poking the seeds beneath the ashes to roast, pulling them out with sticks, laying them aside to cool, before cracking the charred shells open with heavy stones to remove the nuts. Miss Eila claimed the girls ate more nuts than they bottled in jars which also went upriver for sale, the profit from which was entirely their own.

One evening as they stooped around the fire turning nuts to roast evenly on every side, Miss Eila sat on the steps telling them stories. These were mostly stories about some of the small settlements along the Sibun River, established by runaway slaves; about how much better things had been at Sibun before her parents died when the mango grove really prospered. The present house had once been a sprawling two storied home, but as with many other things, the 1931 hurricane flattened the house, killing her parents. Miss Eila, her older sister, Toycie's mother, and her brother had been raised by friends farther down the road until they were old enough to make their own living. After their brother married, Miss Eila and her sister went to live in Belize, although Miss Eila still owned a part of the property that now made a small income during the mango and cashew season. Toycie's mother sold her share in the land to her brother before going to America. Much of the land cleared by Miss Eila's parents had gone back to bush. This particular evening, more to amuse them than anything else, Miss Eila added a tale they had never heard before.

'When I was a girl,' Miss Eila began, laughing delightedly at the memory, 'roasting cashew nuts just like you are doing now, my mother and father told me a story about Tataduhende.'

Tears, caused by the smoky fire, streamed down the girls' faces and the heat made their cheeks fever hot. They knew Miss Eila would continue talking when she was ready, so they kept busy, Beka turning the nuts, and Toycie breaking them open. Toycie's job was the more dangerous because the nuts contained a substance that burned the finger like acid if the nuts weren't properly roasted.

'This property was cleared a good mile all around,' Miss Eila said, 'excepting for the fruit trees and our ground food plantation of course. We had chickens, turkeys, ducks, pigs, all manner of dooryard creatures, and my father used to do hunting, bringing home gibnut or big birds sometimes. Fishing he did too, he was the best around. Joyce, Leroy and me were never allowed to go by ourselves beyond sight of the house. You know why?'

'Why?' the girls asked together.

'Because my Mama said that there's a little man roaming about this Sibun bush barely one foot high. You'll know him if you ever see him. He wears a wide sombrero, is very red-faced, and doesn't have any thumbs. You know why he is roaming round, maybe this very minute?'

'Why?'

'Because he is looking for unprotected little girls and boys, to break off their thumbs because he is so jealous, and then he forces them to follow him forever looking for other thumbs to break.'

Sitting there on the sea-wall, the darkness over all the sea and not a star in sight, Beka remembered one particular baking afternoon when Miss Eila, her brother and his wife lay asleep after lunch. The girls grew bored chasing the chickens clucking through the leaves under the cashew trees; they were tired of waiting for their promised swim, and so Toycie and herself had wandered away from the clearing — a thing forbidden — not intending to go very far, only as far as the well forming the border between the Qualo's and the property of a bakra family nearby. This was a family of deaf-mutes, and the girls scurried quickly by their tumble down house where the blue-eyed children squatted in the dust making peculiar noises, gesturing at them as they went by. The girls reminded each other of Miss Eila's stories about lactating mothers, living in runaway slave towns long ago, who awoke to find snakes suckling their breasts.

It was a big adventure, for a while, seeing mango and cashew walks they had never seen before, stopping to chat with pipe-smoking old women, their heads tied with smoky old rags, or to exchange greetings with bent old men, along the path, returning from ground food plantations with sackfuls of yams and cocoas or plaintains and bananas. They plucked handfuls of limes for juice thinking how pleased Miss Eila would be. Quite suddenly, they found themselves in the dreaded pine ridge, where a person could get lost, far from their own clearing, and they were hopping up and down on the blindingly white sand, panic rising in their hearts, wondering which was the right path home, all trees and all paths looking alike to them. The girls had become fearful and Beka asked,

'Toycie love, do you believe in Tataduhende?'

'Don't be so fool-fool, Beka! Aunt Eila just trying to frighten us so she can sleep afternoons in peace!'

'I believe, though, Toycie, right this minute I *believe*. Suppose he's waiting for us round that bend?'

'Then, Beka Lamb, since *you* are so fraida, why don't we do what Aunt Eila said we should just in case we meet Tataduhende. Mind you, I don't believe for a minute any one-foot man without thumbs is roaming about this bush. The only things I worry about are snakes.'

'Maybe you're right, Toycie,' Beka said, but as they rushed headlong along the path they hoped was the right one which seemed to stretch for miles ahead of them with no clearing or recognizable plantation in sight, the girls pitched the limes into the towering bush, hiding their thumbs inside fists clenched with all their might.

There on the sea-wall in Belize, Beka wriggled her thumbs, resurrecting the ecstacy Toycie and herself had felt on arriving home safely that particular afternoon to find the three adults still snoring. Beka's thumbs, since that time, had always seemed the most vulnerable part of her body. Turning away from the sea, she began listening to the discussion, fast turning into an argument.

'I am still against moving Toycie, Miss Eila,' Daddy Bill was saying. 'Things aren't the best in there, I admit, but at least she's here in Belize where we can personally see to her.'

'But those people in there are lunatics, Mr Bill, and Toycie not in the least bit crazy.'

'Eila,' Granny Ivy said, 'sometimes we get head doctors passing through Belize, and even if I have to stand before where-ever he be from sun up to sun down, we'll get whoever it is to see Toycie.'

'I can't sleep nights thinking of Toycie in that place. She'll get worse mingling with the far gone, and I myself need to go away from Belize for some time. I am afraid I may do that Villanueva boy an injury. Some days I feel like throwing a bucket of lye into his face.'

Beka, putting her arm around Miss Eila's frail shoulders, said,

'Don't take Toycie to bush, Miss Eila, please don't take her. I beg you, Miss Eila, don't take Toycie to bush.'

Miss Eila sucked her teeth shaking Beka's arm from her shoulders impatiently.

'You are just a young girl,' she said, 'what do you understand about all this?'

It was quite late when the group walked to the Lamb house, and after listening for a while, Lilla joined in persuading Miss Eila to let Toycie remain where she was, at least for a reasonable length of time, but Miss Eila was adamant, refusing to believe that anything 'could be so wrong with Toycie that good hard work, a strong talking to, and going home to the place she belonged,' wouldn't cure. In the end, Miss Eila had her way. Daddy Bill recruited Mr Philip's help. As a civil servant, he better understood the procedures necessary to have Toycie released.

One afternoon after school, shortly before Toycie was due to leave the asylum, Beka entered Holy Redeemer Cathedral, near the canal that flowed into the creek. She set her books on a pew right at the back of the church and knelt to pray. At first she had been unable to decide which person in the Trinity to ask for help. In the end she chose the Holy Ghost. His reputation was very much like that of an obeahman's and Beka was in desperate need of a little supernatural intervention for her friend, Toycie, that very afternoon. Needed as it was, the miracle did not occur. Toycie did not come to her senses by the time the little putt-putt cast off its ropes below the swing bridge and set out for Sibun River. Beka stayed at the railing, on the left side of the bridge, staring at the boat's wake until it disappeared from view.

During the days following the Qualos' departure, something inside Beka altered although there was no way she could tell whether the change was for the better or the worse. At first it was impossible to shut off the events of the previous weeks in that special cavern of her being where she stored great hurts, like Great Granny Straker's death, because at school, the girls were curious to know exactly what had happened 'to send poor Toycie Qualo to Sea Breeze Hotel'. But after a while, they grew discouraged as Beka evaded questions and kept to herself, concentrating on school work, which wasn't difficult to do, as the subjects she read had little to do with the world of Cashew Street.

Beka was catapulted back into reality one afternoon, when she arrived home to find that Granny Ivy had decorated the entire front of the house with blue and white flags, given out or sold by the People's Independence Party, in preparation for September Tenth, the National Day. That evening Bill Lamb came home from work and tore down every flag, streamer and bunting. Waving a bunch of flags in his mother's face, Bill Lamb said,

'Look here, Ma! If you want to associate yourself with people selling this country down the river for a bunch of quetzal, it is your privilege to do so, but outside this yard. So long as I am the provider of bread in this household, we will continue to fly the Union Jack until *I* decide it is time to do differently.'

Sucking her teeth, Miss Ivy clumped off into the kitchen and began singing, as she rattled dishes and pots, in a sad, high wail, turning the song into a hymn, all about the 'Baymen's Glory' and how it made 'this land my own'.

Beka had been sent to the attic, to haul from a cupboard under the zinc roof, an old straw clothes basket stuffed with Union Jacks, red, white and blue streamers and buntings that had decorated the verandah ever since she could remember. What with her Dad's hammer beating into the posts on the verandah as he hung up the decorations, and her Gran in the kitchen banging pots around, Beka couldn't find a quiet spot and so she retreated to the bathroom, locking the door. Until the incident of the flags, preparations for the year's biggest festival had bypassed Beka's notice completely.

Saturday evening of that same week, the Union Jacks flapping loudly on the windy verandah, Beka overheard Granny Ivy complaining about Daddy Bill to Uncle Curo on the front steps below her parent's room. Uncle Curo was a joker, and didn't seem to take the business of living as seriously as his brother. He was quite proud, though, of his status as a warder at His Majesty's Prison on Milpa Lane, near St Cecilia's, and he kept the wide leather belt around his pumpkin waist well polished and the brass buttons and buckles of his uniform always highly burnished. Putting fresh sheets on the beds in her parents' room, Beka heard him laughing, and she peeped through the blinds to see him slap his ham hands on Granny Ivy's knee saying in his easy-going appeasing way,

'Cool down there, Mother Ivy. I understand how you feel, old girl. Guatemala hangs like a sword of Damocles over our heads. Bill worked hard for everything and no pension to come. Suppose he was to lose it all to the Guatamantecans? Where would you be, Mother Ivy, or me?'

Beka giggled behind her hand. Uncle Curo was a real Anancy when it came to using words he didn't altogether understand. But in spite of Uncle Curo's skilful efforts at mediation, Granny Ivy and Beka's father spoke to each other only through the mouths of other family members for a long time afterwards.

CHAPTER 22

The house was in costume as befits the National Day. On the verandah the flags snapped and the morning wind blew them against the stephanotis vine, causing the new tendrils to quiver tremulously as if fearing the next slap of the fading flags. Lilla's best cream satin curtains puffed sedately at the windows, and on the dining table was a ziricote bowl of roses with the biggest curving thorns Beka had seen anywhere on a rose bush; her mother never feared the thorns of these deep red roses with black-tipped petals, which grew in the shelter of the vat on the shady side of the house. Beka worked all morning at the table, jumping up once or twice from going through her algebra when the rattle of maracas or the commanding blare of brass bands drew her to the window. But she never stayed away from the table for very long. She had this fear that if ever again she stopped working at her lessons when there was work to be done, something terrible would happen, although no matter how hard she tried, the algebra refused to allow her to progress as swiftly as she would like.

At lunch time her family returned and Beka sat down to her rice and beans, chicken and salad. The boys were so excited by the carnival atmosphere of the town, they couldn't eat, their hands scattering rice grains and soft beans over the sides of their plates. Chuku said,

'You should have come, Beka! The Queen of the Bay was on a big truck all dressed up with a crown and she was waving a stick with a star . . .'

'And, Beka,' Zandy said, stuttering a little, 'there was a man dressed like a crab dancing in front of a big, big band.'

He spread his arms wide to show how big and Chuku corrected,

'Not that big! And you know, Beka, Daddy held me up so I could see Granny Ivy marching and when I shouted at her, she waved her blue and white flag at me.'

The adults at the table picked at their food without much appetite and Beka's Dad seemed concerned that she eat a little more chicken so he passed a leg, his favourite, onto Beka's plate. She ate the chicken leg to please him, feeling a little guilty at her parent's concern, for strive as she might, she could not help but remember all the years Toycie and herself had enjoyed the Tenth together. It was less disloyal, she felt, to stay at home than to parade without Toycie. After the dishes were cleared and washed, Lilla said to Beka,

'If you scrape the comb through your hair and hurry and haul on a dress, we can still get out town in time for the school children's parade. We can watch it from Rectory Lane near Government House.'

'I wouldn't enjoy it, Mams.'

'Tell you the truth, Beka, your Dad and myself are not enjoying it much either. He says this is the worst Tenth he's ever spent. But Chuku and Zandy wouldn't understand about staying home.'

'I know,' Beka said, watching her brothers prancing about the living room, straw hats already on their heads.

After the family left the house Beka sat down at the table again, and since she couldn't concentrate on the algebra, she tried writing, in the notebook Lilla had given her, everything she could remember of the conversation with Mr Rabatu, the Cashew Street masseur, about the arrival of the Sisters of Charity in Belize. Lilla had taken her to Mr Rabatu's house shortly before Toycie's fall off the bridge. Mr Rabatu lived in a two-room downstairs apartment, the bedroom of which was also his massage parlour. The room was crowded with all kinds of dusty jars, ointments, half-empty bottles of coconut oil and salves that Mr Rabatu called 'my unguents'. Mr Rabatu's bed, with a board covering the length and breadth, was his table and sufferers from all over town had lain there, 'from the highest to the lowest', Mr. Rabatu told them. Mr. Rabatu was not an idle man, he said, and so they should not mind if he continued his work, the most important part of which was 'the laying on of hands'. While he talked in this way, he massaged a man's back with a pungent balsam. Mr Rabatu's hair was grey-white and his face absolutely black, creased by a thousand wrinkles. He had looked toward her, eyes dimmed by cataracts, and said,

'When they stepped off the launch, my girl, all those nuns' faces were covered with veils!'

'Veils, Mr Rabatu?' Beka asked, the sound of Father Nuñez's voice echoing in her brain.

'Veils, my girl, veils. Certain women, even here in our town, when I was young, understood their nature and didn't walk brazenly about with bare shoulders in satin and taffeta like they do nowadays! Remember the Bible! Eve gave the fruit to Adam and he did eat!'

Lilla's face closed tightly and Beka could see by the way she looked away from Mr Rabatu that she was getting annoyed, but she tried to joke off the tension saying,

'Now look here, Mr Rabatu, don't you go filling my one daughter's head with that kind of talk! Tell us what happened after they came.' But Mr Rabatu could not seem to remember much more.

Beka stopped writing, studying the few sentences as she sucked on the cap of her pen. The sun was sloping westward, and she put her hands to her head, muttering,

'Now, let's see, on this street Miss Flo had a daughter named Miss Glory, and Miss Glory had Miss Ruby, that's the one with the face bumpy like pineapple skin, and now *she* has three daughters. Then there's old Miss Boysie in the alley and she has a daughter named Miss Prudence, and Miss Prudence has two daughters and one son; then there is Miss Blossom and Miss Queenie living with their mother down the street, and they have no children, and Granny Ivy always says about them 'that it's not want of tongue why cows don't talk', and then there's Miss Lucretia, that's Miss Dotty's maid, and she has three sons and one daughter, Miss Hortence, and she is pregnant; and then there's Miss Eila's sister who had Toycie and went to America and never came back and then . . .'

'You talking to yourself *again*, Beka?'

'Gran, you come home, you come home!'

'Where else would I go?' her Gran asked, sitting down on the cane two-seater near the doorway where the breeze could catch and cool her sweaty forehead.

'Where did you eat lunch?' Beka asked. 'You hungry?'

'I ate a big lunch with Women's Group,' Miss Ivy replied. 'I couldn't eat another thing today to save my life.'

'You thirsty, then?'

'No, Beka, I am not thirsty and please stop jumping up and down like the floor was hot coal. You stayed home all day?'

'Yes, Gran. Did Women's Group have a good crowd to march in the parade?' Her Gran was unpinning the broad blue ribbon from her white dress.

'The best ever, but Eila was missing.' She eased her shoes off with a groan and said,

'My veins are killing me. Why don't you close that curtain in the passageway, Beka? That sun striking me right in my eye.'

Beka ran to do her Gran's bidding and when she returned her Gran was rifling through the papers strewn all over the table.

'If I'd known you were going to stay home all day, I'd have compelled you to go to Women's Group!'

'Daddy would have been vexed if I marched with P.I.P.'

'Since when I worry whether your Pa vex or unvex?'

She moved slowly back to the settee and began ruminatively,

'Governor Radison didn't go to Battlefield today. First time a Governor do that on Tenth, far back as I remember. Must have been afraid. But a few of the "Loyal and Patriotics" went to Government House to read their address of loyalty. Remember last year, Beka, when he said that the party leaders were encouraging us to be disloyal and to insult the Union Jack which flies for British justice and fair play? Well, he's not playing fair now. Imagine calling the leaders Communists?'

'What's that, Gran?'

'I don't rightly understand but the Governor says it's an upside down philosophy or some such thing. He said that, I bet you, because the party talks about buying up foreign-owned land.'

'Oh . . . Gran? Her Gran was staring through the door at the Union Jacks still snapping gaily against the vine so Beka said again,

'Gran?'

'Yes, pet?'

Beka sat cross-legged on the floor.

'Gran, when I graduate, I am going away.'

'Going away to which part?'

'I don't rightly know.'

Miss Ivy leaned her head against the wall, closing her eyes.

'Why not go to Mexico? You can learn more Spanish, since you like to speak it, and come back and be the first black girl to work in the bank. The party will see to it. Course you'll have to do better with your sums.'

'That's too close,' Beka said.

'Too close to what, Beka Lamb?' Granny Ivy said, sitting up.

There were no words ready for Beka to explain to her Gran that, if, as she was beginning to suspect, her nurture was such that her life would probably break down, maybe in Toycie's way, she wanted it to happen in a far away corner where she could maybe pick up the pieces, glue them together and start all over again. So she said,

'All I meant was that it is too similiar to Belize for my liking.'

'But it's not similar at all, Beka! Didn't you listen to Lilla telling you about Merida and Chichen and all those temples and that university and what not all?'

'I heard her, Gran, and we have the same kind of temples here. Daddy took me to Xuantunich one time remember? And the man digging up the ruin told me that word means "Virgin Rock" in Maya. Anyhow, I decided, just before you came in, as soon as I save up, I am going.'

'You are becoming an ungrateful girl, Beka Lamb. You look as if you are going to turn out like Dr Lyban who, just because he couldn't get Government to give him a fancy office to practise in like expatriates get, went off in a huff to England. Look at all the work and money this family is putting into your education — which we still don't know you'll get. Seems like all we are doing is aiding outside countries instead of our own. Bill is right. All these schools around here teach children to do is to look outside instead of in! One day you'll realize that everyone's own home is paradise!'

Beka rubbed the side of her nose and sniffed.

'The climate doesn't agree with me anyway, Gran. Every time sun shines, I get prickly heat and dizziness.'

'There are certain things in people that seldom change, Beka, no matter which place you go and no matter how fancy they talk and no matter what they wear. But you have to find that out for yourself. When you do, maybe you and I will be able to converse. Right now, you are too smart for me.' And she swung her head away from Beka, not understanding what Beka had been trying to say.

A burst of revelling started down the street. As it drew nearer, merely for something to ease the tension between them, Beka and her grandmother went to stand at the verandah railing. A group of drunken men, twirling straw hats trailing exaggerated fringes, were shuffling back to the centre of town, dancing to the rattle of maracas, the beat of nails against empty bottles, and the scraping of glass chips against graters. As soon as Beka and her Granny Ivy leaned over the railing, the lead dancer, a young, light-skinned teenager in a cape of scarlet satin, began whirling his beautiful body in the middle of the street, and the group serenaded Granny Ivy and Beka with a popular West Indian calypso,

> Brown skin gial, stay home and mind your baby,
> Brown skin gial, stay home and mind your baby,
> I'm going away in a sailing boat and if I
> don't come back, throw away the damn baby!

Beka leaned over the verandah railing, laughing and laughing till she thought her jawbone would break. The revellers, offended stopped singing, making a mock display of anger as they waved their fists toward the two people on the verandah before shuffling off down the street. Granny Ivy was beginning to say to Beka,

'I fail to see what's so funny 'bout that song, Beka...' when Chuku and Zandy stampeded up the steps, Lilla and Bill following more slowly. The boys talked for a long time to the group of adults around them about the so big parade and which school had marched the best, whose mother had to pass a bottle of water to whom, and how a truck loaded with school children, waving their flags, had to pull out of the parade because its tyre burst.

After tea was over that evening, Beka went out on the verandah to catch a little air. Her Gran sat in the swing, moving it slowly back and forth. The boys were crouched on the floor near the stephanotis vine hoping to see more revellers, commenting on the passersby in their various costumes streaming past on their way home. The flags drooped on their thin poles. When it was completely dark and the street quiet, her Gran said,

'Why don't you sit down by me here on the swing, Beka?'

'No, Gran, I am going upstairs to work some more.'

'Don't count on winning, if it's that competition you are fretting about. I tell you time and time before...'

'I know, I *know*' Beka said, 'but I am going to try anyhow.' And as she entered the house she heard Chuku say,

'Tell *us* 'bout before time, Granny Ivy.'

CHAPTER 23

Lilla tried her very best not to give herself, Granny Ivy or Beka very much time to brood over Toycie and Miss Eila living in the Sibun Bush out of the holiday season. As soon as marketing was concluded for the day, Lilla encouraged Granny Ivy to hover around Battlefield Park, or near the tiny office of *The Bulletin* to bring home, for family discussion, everything she gathered about the political situation in town. As for herself, Lilla decided overnight to master the cooking techniques of every ethnic group in the country from Maya to Carib, and the amount of slicing, dicing, chopping, grinding, pulverizing, frying, stewing, boiling and roasting she kept up in the kitchen was staggering. Every afternoon the family sat before yams, pounded to stickiness, smothered with red snappers stewed in coconut milk, or a mound of homemade corn tortillas with side dishes of black beans, greens and chillies, or a bowl of escabeche soup chocked to overflowing with onions. One afternoon Bill Lamb called from the table,

'Any left-over rice and red kidney beans in the kitchen, Lilla?'

'No, Bill Lamb,' Lilla replied coming to the table with the pot and spoon in her hand. 'Is something the matter with the relleno?

I made it with pork, onions, recardo, burnt peppers, chimole spice and tomatoes. It's all healthy.'

'I believe it,' Daddy Bill said, looking at his bowl, 'but some of these dishes burn my stomach. I am not used to so much of it everyday, that's all.'

'We'll have to *get* used to it, Bill. Don't you hear what the politicians are saying out at Battlefield Park? We must unite to build a nation, learn about our country, study the names of trees, flowers, birds and animals; flora and fauna, I already know, but you and Beka don't!'

'I must remember to give my stomach the word,' Daddy Bill replied, grimacing as he dunked a rolled tortilla into the savoury black soup speckled with egg yolks.

After a day of news gathering around the town, Granny Ivy's veins were usually just about killing her. Returning from school most late afternoons, there were any number of pots and pans remaining, from Lilla's day of continuous cooking, for Beka to tackle before she could settle down to her lessons or work on the essay. Her sore feet soaking in a pan of warm water, Granny Ivy talked to the family non-stop about the people she met on the streets who worried about annexation by Guatemala or wondered whether federating with the West Indies was wise. One day Granny Ivy reported that she was nearly knocked out by an empty pint bottle, that flew inches from her head, when she stopped to listen to two men quarrelling, at the foot of the Big Bridge, about the right to vote, starvation wages, and unemployment.

According to Granny Ivy, if everyone couldn't vote, all people believed it was their right to talk, from housewives shopping at market stalls to street cleaners shoving their brooms, between conversations with passersby, along the narrow, shallow drains. It was all new, all different, all exhilarating, and the young politicians, tottered, like men on stilts, above the people they had brought to political awareness, uncertain at times how best to use their new power.

A few weeks before the essay was due to be handed in, Granny Ivy came upstairs where Beka sat at the attic table juggling the notes the librarian had sent to her, Mr Rabatu's disjointed story and all she had learned from the older nuns at school.

'I was at court house nearly all day today,' her Gran said as soon as she reached the top of the stairs. Beka looked up but didn't reply. Her Gran was puffing and blowing in a greatly agitated way. Looking expectantly at Beka, she continued,

'They sentenced three out of the four to prison for eighteen months, Beka, because of Mr Prichard's speech reported in *The Bulletin*. With them in prison, I don't know how the new City Council election will fare . . . the crowd at court house is in a hot mood. I wouldn't be surprised if there was a riot tonight!'

'What a boil-up,' Beka said, beginning to lower her head again. She had always been interested in most things her Gran related to her about the struggles of the politicians to gain control over the country's affairs, but nowadays any kind of political talk, and the turbulent atmosphere churning about the town and especially at Battlefield Park and around the court house, reminded her of things she would prefer to forget. Offended at Beka's seeming indifference, Granny Ivy said,

'You are wasting precious time trying to win that fool-fool contest. What I am telling you is important, but you are becoming Miss Biggety, and Miss High Mind, and I am weary telling you over and over again a pania, bakra or expatriate will win! Who ever heard about any black girl winning so much as a pencil at that convent school? Do you see any black nuns at that convent?'

Stunned by her Gran's vehemence and passionate anger, Beka raised her eyes to her grandmother's great heaving bosom, to the sagging cheeks with perspiration rolling down the creases, and finally to her dark eyes, which reminded Beka of rainwater caught in a deep drum, and there was hurt in them. Granny Ivy was at loggerheads with her son, Miss Eila was gone, and she feared losing Beka too. Beka rested her chin on her elbows puzzled as she watched her Gran examining the stained lining of her straw hat. Inside herself, she was beginning to feel detached from the family concerns and activities, finding consolation, for the death of Great Grandmother Straker, and for Toycie's absence, by working at something beyond her natural capacity. Instead of finding the work irksome, as she once would have done, she found she enjoyed it; there was satisfaction in the challenge and she was growing less dependent on the family's praise to make her feel whole. In school, whether she agreed or disagreed, she tried to listen respectfully to the teachers instead of thinking up mischievous comments for the entertainment of the girls sitting around her. In spite of everything, her school work showed improvement, and she was positive that her average would be a little higher next report card day. Best of all, her classmates treated her with new respect making Beka forget, almost, that she was a repeater. Still, Beka reflected, Granny Ivy *is* important to me, too. So she said,

'What was the speech in *The Bulletin* about, Gran?'

'Don't you recall a single thing from one week to the next, Beka? That speech was the one about revolution being the right thing if there was suffering and little else to do! Sometimes, Beka, I am convinced you're turning simple.'

'Oh, yes, yes, that's right, Gran, and in it Mr Prichad said that if the British could make war on China people to force them to use opium, the colonies could fight Britain to force them to surrender more rights.'

'That's right, it did say that bit, didn't it? Although I never did quite understand about the opium and what that had to do with anything here.'

'Mr Prichad's speech was reported long ago, Granny. Why is the Governor digging all that up *now*, when he didn't have anybody arrested then?'

'Because P.I.P. is getting stronger every day, which he could clearly see on National Day gone by. He's looking for an excuse to put our boys in prison so his supporters will win the City Council election . . . which he may announce the day for any time. What Governor Radison is afraid of I fail to see. At most, there are ninety thousand of us in this entire country. Who does he think we could make war on?'

'Maybe he's afraid that if all colonies like us go, Britain may break down, eh, Gran?'

'Sometimes, you know, Beka, I feel I'll not live to see Belize get on its feet. I could die happy knowing you and the boys are growing up in your own country and that it had a chance to become something. I could die . . .'

'You're not going to die,' Beka interrupted, laughing. 'You've come to turn rockstone!'

'Rockstone, eh?' Granny Ivy grunted, moving towards her

attic space. She stood at the window looking up at a sky suffused with the strangest mixture of red and orange.

'It's October, isn't it?' Granny Ivy asked.

'Mmm,' Beka said.

'Anyhow,' Granny Ivy continued, 'even nature is forgetful at times. People like us helped to build up that empire though we didn't choose to; now, we have to help break it down, though there was no need for all this wrangling. We know our situation. People out in those countries forget the time gone before, they forget the wars, they forget all kinds of things to do with us. After all, what do you do after you suck the juice out of sugar cane?' Granny Ivy glared at Beka as if she, too, was guilty of spitting out the trash, and forgetting the juice she had swallowed.

From the bottom of the stairs Bill Lamb called to his mother, speaking to her directly at last,

'Ma! Ma! A hurricane flag is flying from Government House mast!'

'I am coming down, Bill,' she said, pulling on her slippers. 'I'm coming, son, I'm coming.' When she reached the window over the attic stairs, she shook her fist at the sky and said,

'That's right, come on, that's all we need now. Come on bloody hurricane! Come on, choose this time, big October, when you have no right in these waters and Eila, Toycie and the rest out there in the big bush!'

Granny Ivy stumbled, half-sobbing down the stairs, and the sound drained Beka's energy. Her father was shouting at the top of his lungs,

'I am going to buy lumber to brace the windows and doors. See what you and Lilla can do about food, and we must brace Miss Eila's house, too, although that house will collapse with any gale force wind at all.'

The boys tore up the stairs shouting,

'Hurricane, hurricane,' the marbles in Chuku's pocket clicking as he jumped up and down as if something wonderful were about to happen.

Beka heard the yard gate slam behind her father. Downstairs Mama Lilla and Granny Ivy were calling to each other from room to room about how many people to shelter, which clothes to pack and how much food to cook. It was only five o'clock, but the reddish tint in the sky was swiftly fading. It would probably be hours before the hurricane came, if it didn't veer in another direction, but nobody could say for sure when it would forsake the sea which gave it its life, to sweep destructively overland taking hundreds of lives as companions in its own violent death.

The sky was black when Beka scraped back her chair in surrender. The uproar inside and outside the house increased by the minute, and her mother had yelled at her twice already to mind the boys. Beka collected Chuku and Zandy from the yard, and they perched on the back steps watching Daddy Bill and Uncle Curo clambering up and down the coconut trees, chopping off the nuts, in their emerald green outer husks, so the ferocious winds couldn't fling the nuts through anybody's window panes. Beyond the Lamb yard, all around the neighbourhood, people were scurrying back and forth swinging hurricane lanterns, or flashing torches as they tried to secure everything that might be torn loose or blown away.

After a while, the Lamb yard began to look, feel and sound like market square on a good fish day. A few people, with bundles on their backs, and children in their arms, on their way to Government buildings for shelter, stopped to ask if they could stay. Some Daddy Bill urged quickly up the stairs, others, he told no room. In the kitchen, Lilla and Granny Ivy cut sandwiches and prepared other portable food in case they were forced to abandon the house. Granny Ivy brought a bucket clanking to the doorway indicating that Beka should start filling the bathpans with water. Handing sandwiches to the boys, Granny Ivy explained to them carefully, how she had a rope soaking in a bucket of water, and if they so much as moved a big toe off the steps, she would beat them with it until they couldn't stand on their feet.

Beka put the bucket under the faucet and turned it on fully. From all around came the cries of shouting people, the clucking of hens, the anxious peeping of chickens, the barking of dogs, and above everything, worse than the tolling of bells at a funeral, was the doleful banging of hammer on nail, hammer on nail, spreading in increasingly louder waves across the town.

The living and dining rooms were jammed with relatives, friends, acquaintances and their belongings. Uncle Curo's wife commandeered the corner nearest the radio, propping pillows against the wall and spreading her blanket like a small pink sea around her. A man Beka recognized as a worker at Bond Shed near the Customs House, turned her Dad's desk to face the cupboard under the attic stairs and his small daughter lay asleep underneath, guarded by the wife, while the man stood over them both smoking a cigarette. As the work of settling down for the long wait progressed, people talked about the 1931 hurricane. Beka heard snatches as she carried her bucket to and fro.

'A zinc came sailing through the air before my very eyes chopping a man's head right off his body.'

'The Crazy House blew out to sea with all the patients in it.'

'All those school children marching on that Tenth of September up at the Barracks were washed out to sea. Some of the parents went crazy.'

'Water rose twenty feet high in some places. Many of the town's best families were washed away in that hurricane.'

The frantic activity in the house and yard abated after a while. Daddy Bill turned the radio up higher as the announcer interrupted the mournful music to say the storm was still heading for the coast of Belize, but that it was not expected to hit until early morning. People relaxed a little, unpacking stores of food and making their temporary camp more comfortable. Chuku and Zandy fell asleep on the porch and Beka carried them to the bedroom, tucking each under the mosquito netting, their clothes and tennis shoes on, as Mama Lilla had instructed her to do. Then she went to the attic, mercifully empty, to sit down with the pencil and essay again. It wasn't long before her mother came to order Beka's immediate return downstairs.

'The attic is the worst place to be during a hurricane, Beka. The roof is certain to go.' She crossed to the table,

'How much have you done?'

'Nearly all, but I can't get the history before the nuns came, and the history after they came, to fit into this bit about how it all looked to Mr Rabatu, as an acolyte, standing in his robes waiting for them at the wharf.'

'Let me see it,' Lilla said, taking the few pages. After reading them several times she said,

'Why don't you put all that business the librarian gave you, about the history of education, in a separate section at the beginning, put Mr Rabatu's story in the middle, although half of those things he told us, I don't for a minute believe, then put the history of the convent and the growth of the school after they came, at the end?'

'That's it, Mama love,' Beka cried. 'That's it!'

'But come on downstairs right now. You can finish writing on the floor in the boys' room. That way we'll all be together in case we suddenly have to leave the house,' and she looked around as if the attic was dissolving before her eyes.

Beka gathered all her books and papers off the attic table, wrapping them in the heavy oilskin tablecloth Granny Ivy had given her for that purpose, and she secured the bundle tightly with thick twine. Then she picked up the pencil and the essay, hoisted the bundle over her shoulders and started down the stairs to her brothers' room.

CHAPTER 24

The rain, which quickly developed into a violent, whirling storm, started to fall at first with hardly any display at all. Then the howling wind whooshed inland, the lights went out, the radio went dead, and soon tons of rain deluged the town. Beka had not expected such a ferocious sound. The house shook and Beka was sure the wind would tear it right off its concrete foundation. Granny Ivy, Beka and her parents sat in the space between the boys' bed and the bathroom wall. A single kerosene lamp burned on the floor and Beka kept her eyes fixed on that. There were about twenty-five people in the house, but everyone was absolutely quiet. Beka laid her head in her mother's lap, listening to the lashing wind and rain. She meant only to drowse for a while, but the next thing she knew, Lilla was shaking her shoulder,

'It's all over, Beka. Come and help me give these people tea before they go out into that mud and water.'

Beka staggered into the dining room confused by the number of people milling about, their voices loud with relief, as they gathered their possessions and prepared to leave. The house looked grey and unfamiliar and Beka's head ached from the stench of kerosene lanterns and the lack of air. Someone had wrenched the planks from across the front door, and Beka pushed it open, stepping barefooted, onto the wet verandah. The stephanotis vine was gone and the verandah looked naked. The two planks, which had been used to bar the door, stood where the trellis had leaned. Clouds still towered menacingly about the sky and people paddled dories through the streets filled with water over four feet deep, checking to see that relatives and friends were all right and offering transportation to those who needed it.

As she passed cups of hot, sweet tea around the room people babbled at her about the mercy of God, grateful that this storm had not been a repetition, at least for Belize City, of the gruesome hurricane of 1931. Beka gave her Dad a mug, asking,

'Did we get the worst of it, Daddy Bill?'

'No, thank God, it shifted its course at the last hour, but other parts of the country must have taken a battering. As soon as the water subsides a little, I am going out town to find out. But, let me tell you something, Beka. This is the last time we stay in Belize during a hurricane. Next time, as soon as we get a warning, we'll go to El Cayo in the west. No more waiting about to see whether it will come and praying it will not. Let the looters do their worst!'

It took days for the water, debris and fallen trees to be cleared from the streets and yards, and for the swollen rivers to return to their normal level. A muddy stench lingered in the air, and no matter how the Lambs cleaned and scrubbed and polished, it would not go away. All the drinking water had to be boiled, and to get enough clean water to wash clothing was a problem. And through it all was the worry about Miss Eila and Toycie, for by now the storm was known to have devastated the Sibun area, and there was a sense of waiting in the house. The schools were still closed, and in the middle of one work morning when Daddy Bill was supposed to be supervising the salvaging of imported foodstuffs from the mud in the warehouse, he walked through the door, blowing breeze through his teeth, and holding a letter in his hand. Bill Lamb only hissed through his teeth when he brought bad news. Beka, on her knees in the dining room polishing the floor, felt her heart thudding in her chest. The dishes in the sink stopped rattling and Lilla said,

'What brings you home so early, Bill?' Daddy Bill removed his hat and said quickly,

'Toycie gone, pet.'

And the tidal wave crashed in Beka's brain and she was screaming and screaming, the wax splattering all over the floor and her Daddy was holding her tight. Granny Ivy tore out of the bedroom, the broom clattering against the wall and she was shaking Beka and asking,

'What happen, what happen, for Christ sake somebody tell me what happen?' And Beka was wailing,

'Toycie gone and dead, Granny Ivy, Toycie gone and dead on us!' And Miss Ivy picked the letter out of the wax and was reading it to Lilla,

'Dear Mr Bill, just these few lines to let you know that Toycie died the night of the heavy storm. She was buried this day instant. My Toy wandered away in the confusion of preparation and a mango tree fall to break her skull. We are all in good health. Hope this finds you same. Ever your Miss Eila.'

There was no staunching Beka's grief. She was in a state of hysteria and Granny Ivy slapped her, shook her, cajoled her, threw water into her face, but Beka could not regain control. All of a sudden, Miss Boysie appeared at the back door, arms akimbo and she was pointing a floury finger in Beka's face,

'That bougainvillea stump put out shoot, Beka Lamb!'

Stunned, Beka gaped at the wizened old woman standing before her, eyes flashing, black face sweaty from the heat of her firehearth. A dirty, tattered headscarf was tied low over her forehead and she smelt smoky.

'Now see here, Boysie,' Granny Ivy said, 'we are in the middle of grief over Toycie, and as there's a God above, I don't want to fight with you today 'bout no bougainvillea stump.'

'The news about Toycie Qualo reach me before it reach you,' Miss Boysie was saying in her most quarrelsome manner, 'and if it hadn't reached me, the cow bawling stretching from here clear to my kitchen would have let me know. I don't come here to quarrel, Ivy. I watch Toycie and Beka grow, and I am saying to Beka here that her boungainvillea sprout and I want to know from her what she intends doing about it!'

'My Dad will dig out the root when he gets time, Miss Boysie.'

'There's no need for that, Beka,' Miss Boysie said, wiping her eyes. 'I miss the boungainvillea same as you. It was a pretty thing. I figure what with all that board in this yard left over from the hurricane, maybe we could saw it up for a trellis. We could rebuild the one in front, too. My daughter's boyfriend was apprenticed to a carpenter and he's not doing anything now. He's waiting at the fence side to hear whether you agree to build it or not. He'll do it all free, he says, as a remembrance for Toycie.'

'Answer Miss Boysie, Beka,' Lilla said.

'Where is this girl's manners?' Granny Ivy asked.

'Beka?' her Dad said, passing her his handkerchief so she could blow her nose.

'I have no objection to it, Miss Boysie,' Beka replied.

'Then come on downstairs and tell us how big you want that trellis to be,' Miss Boysie said, grabbing her wrist, 'and hurry up, I am baking creole bread for tea.'

Miss Boysie's daughter's boyfriend, Agapito, was as cantankerous as Miss Boysie. He had a bullet-shaped head and eyes that bulged out of his head like a boiled fish. He kept Beka at that fence side all afternoon wanting to know how big the trellis should be and he didn't want any vague estimation of distance, it all had to be measured with a two-foot ruler. Then he wanted to know how high, how thick the slats were to be. Beka had to show him the precise pieces of wood in the yard and he told Beka he wasn't going to wash that muddy wood alone. And he still wasn't satisfied by the time Granny Ivy called Beka indoors to drink her tea. First thing next morning, Miss Boysie called Beka to the fence again. Beka fetched and carried wood and nails, held down boards to be sawed, admired, criticized and scrubbed boards till her fingers were raw. Finally at the end of a week the trellis was up, then the whole thing started again, for the stephanotis vine on the front verandah of the Lamb house.

Once the two trellisses were up and waiting for the vines to begin curling around the slats, the Lambs didn't realize when it was that they took to bolting the front and back doors to discourage unexpected callers. They didn't open the shutters during the daytime very much either, and in the gloom, dust and dirt weren't noticeable. Granny Ivy stopped going to policital meetings, Daddy Bill came straight home from work and didn't go to club after tea, and Beka decided there was no sense walking all the way to Miss Doodie to straighten her hair. The women kept quite busy but apart from food of an everyday nature, there wasn't much to show for all the turning around that went on in the house. The boys grew cranky and tired of playing only in the back of the yard. They wanted to go the park, but Beka said she didn't have the heart to get dressed up and walk all the way to Baron Bliss' grave.

One Friday afternoon Beka sat between Lilla's knees on the bottom step of the attic stairs. Lilla was wrenching the tangles out of Beka's hair and commenting how the hot combing had coarsened the texture. Granny Ivy sat nearby, ready to apply coconut oil to Beka's scalp and to superintend the corn-rowing to take place afterwards. Lilla complained her fingers were out of practice as Beka had been straightening her hair for so long. A gentle rapping of fingernails sounded at the front door galvanizing the three women into action. Beka dashed into the bedroom where the boys were sprawled fast asleep, Granny Ivy immediately closed the kitchen door on herself to hide the greasy stove and the mound of dirty dishes and pots. Lilla shoved her bare feet into house slippers, knotted her hair at the nape of her neck and went to the front door.

'Oh, good afternoon, Sister Gabriela, come right in,' Beka heard her mother say in a faint echo of what used to be her best tone. 'Won't you please sit down? You must excuse the state of the house.'

'Oh, please don't worry about the house, Mrs Lamb,' Sister Gabriela said, 'we are in the same situation at the convent since that terrible storm. We can't walk in the corridors properly what with books and papers half in and half out of boxes. Is Beka at home?'

'Yes, she is, Sister Gabriela. Wait here. I'll get her.' Lilla entered the room and gave Beka a headscarf to tie around the tangled hair bushing about her face. Beka wiped her face on a mouldy towel and went outside. From the kitchen she could hear the stealthy sound of Granny Ivy washing dishes.

'Hello, Beka,' Sister Gabriela said. 'My, but you've lost a lot of weight. I wouldn't have recognized you! What a nice home you have. Is the archway made of mahogany?'

Beka nodded her head, ashamed, wondering why it was that when the house was clean and tidy, with no cobwebs hanging from the archway, nobody like Sister Gabriela ever came to visit. She looked at the dead red bells on the dining table giving evidence of neglect. She ran a trail across the dust on the dining room table.

'Thank you, Sister,' she said.

'Today is the final day for handing in the essay and I wondered if I might collect it, if you have finished it?'

'I finished it the night of the storm, Sister,' Beka said, 'so the last page is scratchy.'

'That doesn't matter. Let me have it.'

Beka went to her attic table and pulled the pages out of the drawer and returning to the living room, handed them to Sister Gabriela. The pages still stank of kerosene oil. The nun put the pages into her briefcase and sat waiting for a bit, but since neither Lilla nor Beka could find anything to say, she stood up, brushing the folds out of her habit.

'When are you returning to school, Beka?' Sister Gabriela asked suddenly. Beka, looking at her directly, caught a glint of disrespect in Sister Gabriela's eyes and she thought to herself, 'If you think all Belize people break down so easily you are mistaken!'

'Well, Sister,' Beka replied in her best creole drawl, 'I was thinking of going back Monday morning.'

Her mother didn't give any evidence of surprise except to look quickly at Beka with a glad smile that squeezed her heart. Granny Ivy bustled out of the kitchen with glasses of limeade, and Sister Gabriela sat down delighted, thirsty, she said, after her long walk.

'I am so happy you are coming back to school on Monday, Beka,' she said, drinking half the limeade in a gulp. 'I need someone to help me with a medley of folksongs in honour of the Mother Provincial's visit.'

'Isn't the Glee Club doing anything!' Beka asked.

'They've already prepared a programme of classical tunes and feel they couldn't do the songs justice with such short notice,' Sister Gabriela said, smiling into her empty glass.

'I don't sing or play music, Sister. My friend Toycie was the one . . .'

'I meant the whole freshman class could sing a medley of the songs and you could help me by finding out which songs are most popular and generally organizing everything. As you know, I'm quite busy with the essay contest and other things to do with the Mother Provincial's visit.'

'Everyone knows the words and tunes, Sister. It would only take a few practices.'

'That's what *I* thought, Beka! Here's my plan.'

All that afternoon, even after the boys awoke from their nap, the little group sat there humming tunes, trying to decide which ones were best for the occasion. Granny Ivy was good. She forgot all about the smelly dishcloth over her shoulder as she reminisced about folksongs she used to sing, as a girl, before time.

When Bill Lamb came home at tea time, energy generated throughout the house. Every window was wide open, liver and onions sizzled in the kitchen, Beka was ironing her school uniform, the boys were dusting furniture under Granny Ivy's supervision and Granny Ivy wielded the broom about the hall and dining-room, singing at the top of her voice. When Lilla told her husband that Beka was returning to school, he didn't remove his hat. He fetched her shoes down from the attic, and spent half the evening cleaning and polishing them. And, in a rash moment of excessive high spirits, Beka promised to take the boys for a walk to see the shops on Albert Street the following day.

As they were eating liver, onions and fresh bread from Gordillo's, Daddy Bill said to Lilla,

'I suppose the next thing I'll hear is that you need cartloads of manure for new rose bushes, not to mention three dory loads of soil from upriver to nourish them, eh, Mam?'

'I'm turning over a new leaf, Bill. I'll keep the bushes that survived, but I'm not expending too much energy anymore cultivating rose bushes. But I'll still need manure and soil.'

'What will you plant, Mama?' Chuku asked.

'What should I plant, Beka?' Lilla asked.

Beka screwed up her face and holding her fist like a microphone before her nose, she growled,

'The magnificent poinciana soaring towards the sun-kissed skies, royal palm trees to stand like sentinels at the front gate, the lowly hibiscus to hedge our days with blossoms of scarlet . . . beautify your city, Belizeans, for it is yours!'

Everyone was in a happy mood and as they laughed at Beka's antics, Chuku said,

'Beka, gial, you sound just like the radio announcer!' and Beka replied in a perfect imitation of her mother's voice,

'Now, there's no need to make fun of Mr Trudell's elocution, Chuku. He trained in London, you know?' And the boys rolled on the floor in mirth. Granny Ivy rubbed her hand over Beka's hair plaited in neat corn-rows all over her head, and rising from the table, she grinned,

'I think you are missing your calling, Miss Beka. Bill, you should ask Mr Phillip to ask Mr Cain to allow Beka to act in his Christmas pantomime.'

'I might do just that, Ma,' Daddy Bill said. 'I might do just that,' and the dimples showed deeply in his cheeks as he smiled for a long, long, time.

CHAPTER 25

So it came about, that on a warm day in November, the freshman class stood out front on fresh green grass, in the shadow of the rainwater vat at school, waiting for the start of the programme to welcome the Mother Provincial to Belize. Beka rushed along the rows of freshmen handing out songsheets she'd thought of at the last minute, while Thomasita Ek neatened rows, sucking her teeth nastily at any freshman who refused to be bullied into a straight line. It was a lovely morning, and the clear soft blue of the sky, the sparseness of dazzlingly white clouds, and the lushness of every green growing bush, plant or tree, gave promise of cooler weather soon to come. Behind the freshmen, row after row, were seniors, juniors and sophomores. Promptly at nine o'clock, Sister Mary Virgil emerged from her office to introduce to them the Mother Provincial.

Beka expected to see a replica of Sister Virgil, but the Mother Provincial was squat and fat, with a sizable stomach. She smiled, mopping her swarthy face constantly, through the entire repertoire of the Glee Club, which included several boring tunes, and her wide brown eyes, which never seemed to blink, sparkled as she tapped one foot jauntily when the freshman class bounced into their rollocking medley of folksongs. She so infected the school with a sense of holiday that by the time the freshmen reached,

'Kean't work da mi plantaish, Kean't work deh at all,' the entire school was bellowing the chorus,

'Pinqwing juk me, pinqwing juk me, kean't work deh at all!'

At the end, clapping her chubby hands delightedly, she waddled over to the railing and said,

'Well, well, well! I can't remember the last time I've enjoyed myself this much. Thank you, thank you. You know, all this reminds me of a story, not an original one, I read it in a book about Asia. I forget which country it actually was, but it must have been Moslem, because the story was about a holy man called a mullah. Now this holy man made a pilgrimage to a holy place, and on returning to his own village, a great celebration was held in his honour. After the feasting was over, and the men were sitting around picking their teeth, one of his friends said to the holy man,

'Now tell me, mullah, did you learn the language of that country?'

'But, of course,' the mullah replied, 'how could I have spent six weeks there, and not know the country's language?'

'Well then, mullah,' another friend said, 'tell us the word for camel.'

'Why choose such an enormous animal?' asked the mullah.

'What is the word for flea?' a third man asked.

'Now you really are being silly,' the mullah said. 'Why choose such a small insect?'

'All right, then,' the first friend asked, 'what word did they use for sheep?'

'Ah,' the mullah said, as if deeply impressed by the sagacity of his friend, 'Good question. Unfortunately, I cannot say for I left the country just at the lambing season before they had time to name the sheep.'

After the giggles and hand-clapping died down, the Mother Provincial looked shrewdly about her for a while, then continued,

'When I return to Rhode Island, I shall feel a little bit like that mullah, of whom I read in high school; but due to the extremely interesting stories about Belize I read in the essay competition honouring the arrival of the Sisters of Charity to this country, I shall be in a *little* better position to give insightful, I hope, answers to the questions that will be put to me. I was interested to read of the conditions that prevailed in the latter half of the nineteenth century, of diseases like cholera, of the terrible hurricanes that continue to turn this town into shambles. I discovered that the cornerstone of this academy was laid in 1886, and many of the twists and turns that were taken to bring the school to what it is today. A tremendous amount of affection for the Sisters of Charity, past and present, was evident in those essays, and the thing that puzzles me now, as I recall all I read in those essays, is why more local women have not joined the order . . .'

There was a scattering of throat clearing which made the Mother Provincial pause before she said,

'I declare tomorrow a school holiday and would most sincerely urge any girl who feels she may have a religious vocation to visit me here at the convent before my visit ends on Sunday. I thank you.'

Amidst the roar of prolonged hand-clapping, Sister Gabriela hurried up the steps, a slip of paper in one hand, and three medals glittering on strips of sky blue ribbon, in the other. The Mother Provincial took the paper and mopping her forehead said,

'It gives me great pleasure to announce the winners of the essay contest honouring the seventy-fifth anniversary of the Sisters of Charity in this colony. Third prize goes to Antoinette de Freitas, senior; Second prize to Dolores Martinez Marin, sophomore; and the first place to Beka Lamb, freshman.'

Leading the way up the steps from the grass to the school verandah, Beka noticed in passing the stillness of the coconut trees spared by the storm, and along the verandah at the rear of the school, the sea, shimmering with deceptive innocence in the hot morning sunlight. She walked slowly along the verandah towards the Mother Provincial who dangled the three medals on her forefinger and smiled encouragingly at her. Sister Virgil, stony faced as ever, gave Beka a frosty smile that blighted the morning. As she stood before the three nuns, Sister Gabriela took the first place medal, a little larger than the others, and hunching over to pin it onto the right shoulder of Beka's uniform whispered,

'Well, Miss Lamb, not late this morning, I see!'

Tears burned Beka's eyes like the bite of fire ants, and the uniform belt, pinned too tightly around her waist, was cutting into her flesh. She looked into the ugly face of the nun, and saw behind the Cyrano nose and huge rimless glasses, empathy and a kind of affection. If Toycie had lived, if things had been different for Toycie, she would have been there on the verandah instead of Antoinette or Dolores or Beka herself. In Sister Gabriela's eyes was acknowledgement of that fact.

Beka walked through the wrought iron gate of the convent grounds later that day, the ribbons of the medal fluttering on her shoulder. She didn't bother to unpin her green bowtie now. She could wear it with renewed pride. Halfway down the street, a huge crowd was gathered outside the jail, and Beka joined the scores of convent girls running that way to see what had happened.

Members of the angry crowd held placards high above their heads, each card stating a grievance or praising the People's Independence Party and the General Workers' Union. Beka spied her Uncle Curo standing by the drainside, his bicycle leaning against the brick wall of the jail. Elbowing her way through the crowd, Beka hailed him saying,

'Hello, Uncle Curo, what is happening?'

'Afternoon, Beka,' Uncle Curo said. 'Prichad and Gladsen began serving time today for disloyalty to the British Government, such as I understand it. It's called sedition.'

'Is this the end of everything then, Uncle Curo?' Beka asked, thinking sadly of Granny Ivy's struggles.

Uncle Curo boomed his belly laugh and putting his ham hands across Beka's shoulders he said,

'The end, pet? Belize people are only just beginning! Soon we'll all be able to vote instead of only the big property owners, then we may get self-government and after that, who knows?'

Beka laughed with relief and in her heart she was suddenly excited for she had made a beginning too. She was about to rush homewards when she remembered the proof of her beginning and pointing to her shoulder said,

'Look, Uncle Curo! Look!'

'That looks so pretty, Beka! A medal, is it?'

'Yes, Uncle Curo, yes!'

After Beka had explained, Uncle Curo said,

'But this is impressive, Beka, yes, impressive. I have a little time before I must go to my duties. How about a little drink to celebrate?'

'Yes please!' Beka said.

Uncle Curo escorted Beka through the streets as if she had been awarded the highest honours in the land. He ushered her grandly into Escalante's Fresco and Ice Cream Parlour, drew a rickety chair for her to sit upon, and imperiously ordered two ice cold lemonades from the creole waitress who slouched over to ask them what they wanted.

CHAPTER 26

The sudden silence caused Beka to raise her head and examine the finger that had rested in the deep gouge on the arm of Granny Ivy's rocking chair. The finger felt slightly sore. She tilted her head listening to the last rush of water in the gutters and to the drip-dropping of raindrops off the roof close overhead. Easing up the sash of the window overlooking the street, she opened the shutters swallowing great gulps of freshened air and watching the silky smooth upper trunk of a palm tree glistening in the light of a lamp-post. Her tongue felt stale and her throat was parched, so Beka crept quietly downstairs to the kitchen.

Her family was asleep. The dining room floor was littered with strips of paper from the adding machine. She carried a tall tumbler of cool rain water out to the verandah and sat close to the stephanotis vine to wait for Granny Ivy. Small groups of people and individuals were hurrying home, some from the meeting at Battlefield Park, others from the cinema. Beka could guess who was coming from where by the clothes they wore. The people returning from the cinema were dressed up as if it were a Sunday evening.

When the yard gate creaked, Beka went to the top of the stairs and whispered,

'Shhhh,' so her Gran wouldn't waken the household with an exclamation of surprise.

'You still awake, Beka? It's nearly one in the morning!'

'Don't speak so loudly, Gran,' Beka whispered, listening to her Dad's snores on the other side of the wall. 'You'll wake Daddy and then he'll be vexed that I'm still up!'

'Let me sit here on the swing before we go to bed. My veins are killing me.'

'What went on at the meeting, Gran?'

'The Jamaican lawyer said there was little he could do to stop Gladsen and Pritchad from going to jail because anybody who criticizes the British Government can be prosecuted under the present law. There were a lot of speakers, but before we could get the full story, rain poured down and the meeting broke up. But, as I said to Eila, there'll be another.'

Granny Ivy eased off her shoes and said,

'Let me see that medal again, Beka, I didn't get a good look today.'

Beka went to her mother's glass-fronted cabinet and removed the medal from a tiny dish. Returning to the verandah, she dropped it into her grandmother's lap. Granny Ivy peered at it in the light of the lamp-post, weighing it up and down in the palm of her hand. Beka picked a small spray of bugle shaped flowers from the stephanotis vine.

'You know something, Beka?'

'What?' Beka asked inhaling the perfume of the waxy flowers.

'Before time this medal would certainly have been made of sterling silver. What kind of metal is this? Aluminium?'

Beka nearly choked trying to keep herself from screeching with laughter.

'Gran,' she gasped, 'you will never be done!'

'It's true enough, though,' her Gran said, leaning back against the swing, the ribbon of the medal wrapped around her thumb.'

'Remember that story about the polar bear you told me one time, Gran?'

'Which story?'

'Don't you remember you cried and said the polar bear died because the ice factory broke down?'

'Oh, that, sure, I remember.'

'I was sitting here trying to figure out what to do after I graduate, if and when.'

'Everybody deep inside have something special they really want to do, so it shouldn't take you long to fix on something.'

Miss Ivy looked at the medal balanced on her thumbnail and said,

'It'll be a struggle but that you've learnt to do. All going well, you'll graduate. I have no fear about that.'

'Are you fearing something then?' Beka asked, moving closer to her Gran.

'Not fearing exactly,' Miss Ivy said, 'just contemplating the day you fall in love and what that'll do to your high mind.'

Beka leaned forward, determination replacing the watermelon in her chest.

'Fall in love? Who? Me? I'll never fall in love. Just thinking about Toycie and Emilio hurts my stomach like after a good dose of senna leaves.'

Miss Ivy moved the medal back and forth before allowing it to drop with a hollow tinkle on the wide arms of the swing.

'In a sense you're right,' she said, 'when you care about someone the way you cared about Toycie, well, it's hard to imagine going through that kind of pain for anyone again. But, you'll get over it. The time will come.'

Beka knew that she'd never forget Toycie and all they'd been through together. Still, there was no use arguing with her Gran who always meant everything for the best. So she asked,

'Did you want to do something special when you were a girl, Granny Ivy?'

'Sure, I did, just like everybody else. I wasn't always an old husk.'

'What did you want to do?'

'I was hoping to get a job learning to train animals with a circus like that one that came to town.'

'Gran!' Beka exclaimed, and her Gran said,

'Shush, don't go telling the whole world!'

'Why didn't you get the job and go with the circus?'

'Well, for one thing, it wasn't a very practical idea and for another Toycie's first trouble caught me too, and I turned to rocking the cradle.'

Beka's silence was one of the worst things Miss Ivy had experienced in the longest while. She shifted her shoulder where Beka's head rested like an iron ball.

'But at least you didn't break down and die, Granny Ivy,' Beka said.

'There are ways and ways, Beka,' Miss Ivy responded, her voice low. 'But in Toycie's sense, no, you could say I didn't break down.'

'Tell me about it, Granny Ivy,' Beka said.

Miss Ivy glanced down at Beka drowsing on her shoulders and said,

'Shure, I'll tell you about it but not now. Go up and get some rest. It's Saturday and later you have the house to clean, errands to run and studying to do. But maybe tonight I'll tell you about it.'

'Aren't you coming to bed?'
'Not yet.'
'Sure?'
'Shure, I'm sure. Afraid to go up by yourself?'
'I'm not really afraid.'
'Well then.'
'Goodnight Gran.'
'Goodnight Beka.'

Giving her Gran a small wave of her hand, Beka stumbled into the living room and climbed the attic stairs. As she lay sprawled across her bed, staring across the rooftops of the town, Beka remembered the days spent swimming and diving with Toycie at St. George's Caye. Concentrating on the memory she relived the times they floated, fingers linked and spluttering with delight, upon the choppy aquamarine sea beneath the pier. Deliberately she spun her kaleidoscope of sunshine and seawater waiting for the twinges of pain she associated with these memories. There were none although the memories remained bright and clear. Settling the pillow more comfortably beneath her head, Beka smiled. Her watch-night for Toycie was over and she felt released — there was need no more for guilt or grief over a mourning postponed.

STUDY NOTES

BY DR EVELYN O'CALLAGHAN

UPDATED BY DR CAROL FONSECA

CWS

Heinemann

THESE STUDY NOTES will provide assistance and guidance to students and teachers studying *Beka Lamb* for the Caribbean Examination Council (CXC) examinations or at other levels. The author of the notes, Dr Evelyn O'Callaghan, carefully guides the reader to a clearer understanding of the novel's background and the author's stylistic techniques and thematic concerns. The critical sections highlight the main features and concerns and equip the reader to come to his/her own assessment. The study notes are not intended as a replacement for careful reading of *Beka Lamb*.

Dr Evelyn O'Callaghan was born in Nigeria and is of Irish and Jamaican parentage. Jamaica's first female Rhodes Scholar, she has taught at the University of the West Indies, Mona Campus in Jamaica and is currently Lecturer in English at the UWI's Cave Hill Campus in Barbados.

Dr Carol Fonseca gained her MA from the University of Leeds, England and received her doctorate from the University of the West Indies, Cave Hill, Barbados. Formerly Director of the Women's Department, Ministry of Human Development, Belize, she is presently an Adjunct Instructor in the Department of English at Florida International University in Miami.

CONTENTS

Section One
Brief Biography of Zee Edgell 176

Section Two
Setting and Historical Background 178
Literary Background 179

Section Three
Themes 181
Structure and Style 191
Characterisation 201

Section Four
Chapter Commentaries 207

Section Five
General Questions 224
Further Reading 226

SECTION ONE

BRIEF BIOGRAPHY OF ZEE EDGELL

Zee Edgell was born in Belize City on 21 October 1940 to Clive and Veronica Tucker, and grew up in a family of four sisters and three brothers. She was educated at Holy Redeemer School and St Catherine Academy in Belize and was the first Belizean woman to qualify as a journalist from the Regent Street Polytechnic (now the University of Westminster) in London. She holds a Masters Degree in Liberal Studies from Kent State University.

Her first job was as a trainee journalist on the Jamaican newspaper, the *Daily Gleaner*, from 1959–62. While studying for her Diploma in journalism, she worked on the clerical staff of *The Times* and *Woman's Own*, before returning to Belize. Back home, she taught at St Catherine Academy and also ran and edited a monthly newsletter, which she transformed into *The Reporter*, a small weekly paper.

Zee married Alvin George Edgell of Menominee, Michigan, who was then attached to the Cooperative for American Relief Everywhere (CARE) in Belize. They have lived in Nigeria, Afghanistan, Bangladesh, Belize and Somalia, and have two children, Holly and Randall, and three grandchildren. In addition to being a writer, Zee has served as Director of the Women's Bureau in Belize, assisting in upgrading the Bureau to the Department of Women Affairs in Belize. She also worked as a UNICEF Consultant to the Somali Women's Democratic Organization in Mogadishu, Somalia.

Her early influences were numerous and varied: teachers, poets, writers, journalists, oral story-tellers, song-writers and public servants of Belize as well as people in the community 'who seemed always to have something to relate that was interesting, hair-raising or revealing'. Her parents and grandmother were important influences, who 'believed in Belize and their place in it' and encouraged her to develop through education and political and social awareness.

Over the years Zee has read widely – Charles Dickens, William Shakespeare, Charlotte Brontë, Jean Rhys, Jane Austen, P.D. James, V.S. Naipaul, Harper Lee, Betty Smith, Toni Morrison, Alice Walker, Jamaica Kincaid, Edwidge Danticat, James Baldwin, Richard Wright, Ralph Ellison, Louise Bennett, C.L.R. James, Michael Ondaatje, Chinua Achebe and Matthew Kneale are only a few of the writers she admires. In addition, others like E.M. Forster and Virginia Woolf have helped to form her opinions on the craft of writing. Although acknowledging that she has been influenced by many authors, Zee tries to write in her own style rather than consciously imitating any of them.

SECTION TWO

SETTING AND HISTORICAL BACKGROUND

Beka Lamb is set against the political, social and cultural background of Belize in 1951–52, when the author herself was growing up in Belize City. The main autobiographical elements that the novel contains are sketched in from Edgell's own memories of what it was like to be a young girl in Belize during this period. The integration of these experiences is what gives the book a freshness and energy that allows the reader to become fully engrossed in the novel.

To fully appreciate the novel, the foreign reader may wish to know a little about Belize since the story tells of a country and its people in a time of change. Geographically, Belize lies on the Caribbean coast of Central America, with Mexico to the north and Guatemala to the west and south. Belize is the only English-speaking territory in Central America. Its unique cultural and political heritage in Central America is the result both of the failures of Spain to effectively occupy the area and three hundred years of English occupation. In the 1950s, Belize was still a British colony and was called British Honduras. Belize achieved independence on 21 September 1981. The country is divided into six districts, with Belize City the most populated area; in the 1950s it was the capital city. The present capital is Belmopan.

Although Belize covers 8,867 square miles, it is sparsely populated, with only 300,000 inhabitants (2007 estimate). Most people live on the coast, as dense forests occupy much of the interior of the country. The cultural and racial composition of Belize has made it the most ethnically diverse country in the region. In the 1950s the society was fairly divisive, despite tolerance and harmony in some areas. The largest groups were the Afro-Belizean 'Creoles' (usually in the professions and the civil service), and the Hispano-Belizean 'Mestizos' or 'Panias' (often in trade and commerce). The balance of the population consisted of Europeans ('bakras'), Black Caribs (a mixture of Africans and Caribbean Indians), Maya Amerindians, a few East Indians and Lebanese and, of course, intermixtures of all these groups.

Creoles tended to belong to Protestant churches and Spanish-speaking Belizeans to the Catholic Church, but it is the latter that exerted the most influence on the country's development, as is clear in the novel.

LITERARY BACKGROUND

Beka Lamb is the first English-language novel by a Belizean woman. It has been well-received in Belize, throughout the Caribbean and abroad. Edgell explains that although she wrote the story primarily for the people of Belize, she also wanted people everywhere to enjoy and learn from Beka's story. In 1982 the novel was joint winner of the Fawcett Society Book Prize.

The book, Heinemann's first original paperback in the Caribbean Writers Series, was first titled *A Wake for Toycie*. The change to *Beka Lamb* clearly reflects the focus on Beka herself, although her mental 'wake' for Toycie is an important part of the story. The novel deals with Beka's development towards maturity and independence – paralleled by her country's move in the same direction. Toycie's story and Beka's period of mourning for her friend are stages on the path to adulthood.

English, the official language of Belize, is used for the narration of *Beka Lamb*. However, most of the dialogue is in the Creole language, injected with Spanish and Amer-indian words and phrases to reflect the Belizeans' linguistic variety. Charles Hunter notes in his review of the novel that 'Here Belizean Creole has achieved the respected place of a full-fledged West Indian Dialect' and that it clearly demonstrates its literary potential.

The novel took Edgell ten years to complete, in between moving from the USA to Afghanistan to Bangladesh and raising two children. It was finally completed in Bangladesh, where the extreme heat and monsoon rains kept her indoors. She explains that from her desk where she wrote she was able to see the garden and since 'the vegetation there is so similar to my own home... I had no difficulty, as I sat there, remembering Belize and the people who walked its streets who had become so much a part of my being'.

In an interview with Ann Brill, Edgell comments on the difficulty women writers like herself face in finding time to write, but emphasises that it serves as a worthwhile outlet for addressing concerns. For Edgell, writing is not a hobby, but a way of life. She says 'I write like other people sing, or cook or bake or ride or run... I get extremely unhappy when I am not writing'.

SECTION THREE

THEMES

On the very first page of *Beka Lamb*, the word 'change' is used several times and the major themes developed in the novel all have to do with change in one way or another. In the following sections the main themes in the novel will be explored and examined.

Growing up

At the most literal level, *Beka Lamb* is the story of Beka's change, in about seven months, from an insecure, irresponsible child into a more serious, thinking, responsible young adult. The plot deals with the events of this period that effect this change within Beka, and the sometimes painful process of growing up.

Other West Indian writers have written about boys maturing to manhood, among these Michael Anthony, Ian McDonald, George Lamming, Geoffrey Drayton and V.S. Naipaul. Only a few have given the female viewpoint – Merle Hodge's *Crick Crack, Monkey* and Erna Brodber's *Jane and Louisa Will Soon Come Home* are interesting complements to *Beka Lamb* in the analysis of the theme of growing up.

At the beginning of the seven-month span of the story, Beka is seen to be unsure of herself – of who she is, what she wants and what she is to do with her life. Like many adolescents, she finds herself doing things she doesn't understand; 'What is wrong with me?' (p. 68). Ashamed of her failure to pass first form at secondary school, because she has not worked hard enough, she lies; 'I pass in truth, Daddy!' (p. 17). But lying is no solution, in fact, when she is found out Beka feels even more confused and lonely, isolated from her family who expected better of her.

Early in the novel it is made clear that Beka's family is very loving and supportive, and when Beka disappoints them with her laziness compounded by untruths, Beka feels guilty and wants 'to find a way to atone' (p. 30). The rest of the story shows how she goes about achieving atonement and makes her family proud by working hard and taking responsibility. Her winning of an essay prize and passing her term at school are proof of her efforts, although Beka also learns much out of school from the tragic events of her friend Toycie's life.

Toycie's mother went off to America when Toycie was two, and her father disappeared before she was born. Likewise, the prostitute National Vellor had 'No mother, no father, no school. What can I do?' (p. 128). In contrast, Beka is fortunate to have a caring family who support her through her difficult period growing up. This makes Beka seem irresponsible and lazy when she fails, while to a certain extent we are more able to understand Toycie's mistakes.

Yet Beka's desire to 'atone', to mature, involves a time of withdrawal from the family. This too is natural. As the adolescent grows up, she takes more responsibility for her own life, discovers her own merits, and thus finds that 'she was growing less dependent on the family's praise to make her feel whole' (p. 151). Beka feels 'detached' from family concerns to a certain extent, as she is becoming a person in her own right with ideas of her own. This does not involve a loss of familial affection, merely an increase in self-awareness as an independent young adult.

Some chapters deal more fully with the theme of growing up than others. In chapters 13, 15 and 16 we note Beka's increasingly supportive role in her relationship with the older and supposedly wiser Toycie. Growing up involves assuming responsibility for others, offering help, advice and strength when called upon to do so. Clearly it is part of Beka's maturation process that she is able to be this type of friend to Toycie. After Toycie's expulsion, however, she is beyond help – from Beka, or anyone else. Interestingly, Toycie lives out the remainder of her short life in a schoolroom fantasy: *her growing up process cannot continue.*

Women

Related to the theme of growing up is the question of women. What kind of woman is Beka to become, faced with a bewildering variety of role models? Father Nunez lectures Beka's classmates on the choice between the model of Eve and that of the Virgin Mary (p. 90). The example of Eve is actualised in many of the women in Beka's extended family and in the Creole neighbourhood, including her own grandmother, who engage in pre-marital sex and often raise children out of wedlock. This is not considered abnormal among the Creole community.

But the nuns of St Cecilia's, who epitomise the model of the Virgin Mary, consider such behaviour immoral. Hence Toycie, vomiting on the clean chapel floor, is seen as a source of contamination to be removed from the school before her sin infects others. Since the nuns control education, and education provides an alternative to the 'washing bowl underneath the house bottom' (p. 2), girls like Beka and Toycie must break with Creole culture and morality, 'shedding the lives they led at home the minute they reached the convent gates' (p. 112).

At school, they must 'leap through the hoops of quality purposely held high by the nuns' (p. 112), like animals being trained to perform difficult tricks. Torn between the culture that frowns upon the 'brown skin gial' and her illegitimate baby, and the pressure to achieve a different life through education (see pp. 24, 64 and 116), they end up acting out a part, pretending to be what the nuns require.

But the cultural and moral conflict takes its toll. Beka covers up her confusion and insecurity by telling lies and putting on airs, and this is why her father calls her a 'phoney'. It seems unfair of him since Beka is being taught at school to imitate the ways of another culture – how can she be anything other than a 'fake'? Toycie, seeking love and affection, falls short of the nuns' ideal and is expelled, though as Roger Bromley puts it in his review of the novel in *New Society*: 'Toycie is destroyed, not by her pregnancy, but because, like Hardy's Tess, the woman always pays'. Emilio, on the other hand, escapes unharmed.

Bromley points out in his article 'Reaching a Clearing: Gender and Politics in *Beka Lamb*' that most of the models of women in Creole society are devalued. Nurse Palacio is overworked and abused; National Vellor is mocked and exploited; Miss Eila depreciates herself as ugly and unmarriageable. Like many Belizean women, they judge themselves from an external standard, in this case a male standard. Even the strong Granny Ivy cannot vote, so her power is very limited. The women who *do* have power, like Sister Virgil, use it to tell the girls that they are weak and must learn to deny themselves.

Beka is faced with a choice between all these models of womanhood – even at home, there is her modern, conservative mother and her subversive grandmother with her roots in the older culture. As Bromley explains, Beka must learn to negotiate a 'middle passage' between woman as fallen Eve and woman as impossibly pure saint. Beka's mother notes that 'there are more opportunities nowadays' (p. 18), and with Beka's schooling and her grandmother's teaching she can reach a 'clearing', an open space of her own in the midst of all the contradictory role models. The novel deals with the difficulties involved in this pursuit.

Madness

Linked to the confusion and distress resulting from facing choices of role models is the recurring theme of madness as escape. In my review of *Beka Lamb* in the Institute of Jamaica's *Jamaica Journal* I mention some other West Indian novels that focus on the woman driven 'mad' by conflicting pressures.

In *Beka Lamb* we are told of 'that half-crazy coolie woman' (p. 5), National Vellor, alone in the world and trying to be financially independent, yet snubbed and abused for selling her body – no wonder she becomes 'half-crazy'. Then there is Sister Mary Bernadette, prevented from pursuing her teaching career because of her political beliefs; she feels that 'not teaching, I may go mad in truth' (p. 88). Then, of course, there is Toycie, wishing to please the nuns *and* Emilio, but finding herself deserted by both. Since reality is too painful to cope with, Toycie withdraws into a fantasy world in her mind, a world of school from which she cannot be expelled.

It is easy to think that only those with terrible problems become mentally ill. However, the exploration of this theme in *Beka Lamb* seeks to show how thin the line between reality and fantasy really is. At the novel's beginning, Beka is finding it difficult to deal with reality and has been lying outrageously, rather than accept the unpleasant truths of her situation.

Certain forms of imaginative fantasy are necessary – Beka withdraws from the pain of Toycie's madness and death for a time, until the pain is partially healed. It is fantasy that makes a Sunday stroll into an adventure (p. 15), imagination that transforms squalid poverty into something bearable (p. 98). Indeed, when Beka's mother encourages her to turn her lies into stories, it is suggested that imaginative fantasy can be turned into creative excellence. And for those who have no creative release from the pressures of reality, fantasy may turn into an escape, a withdrawal from which there is no return.

The tragic events in Toycie's life force Beka to face the reality of a society that judges Toycie according to the standards and 'ideal' stereotypes of a colonial culture. Realising that Toycie's downfall is intrinsically tied up with her being a Creole, Beka becomes even more determined to ensure that her own life does not break down.

Death

The ultimate escape is, of course, death, and the novel deals with the problem of death for those who lose someone close. Death is also a change, but a sudden and shocking change.

Toycie's death comes as no surprise to the reader, since the first chapter clearly states that many months have passed since 'Toycie gone' (p. 3). In addition, there are many details foreshadowing death as the novel builds toward the crisis: the wreath mentioned on the first page; Beka's little sister and brother who passed away years ago; and the graveyard where Toycie and Emilio meet on the caye. Great-grandmother Straker, old and with a full life behind her, passes away. Beka feels sad, but is soon able to find comfort in her memories.

Toycie's tragic death, in contrast, far away in the dangerous Sibun bush, is far more distressing. Beka reacts with hysterical grief, and retreats into herself like a wounded puppy, not having the heart to face the world.

But the point is that although death may take away the physical body, spiritually Toycie remains a part of Beka, who loved her, just as Granny Straker's spirit 'will live with Beka here' (p. 73). Friendship is strong in Beka's heart and she honours Toycie in her memory and in her life. As Sue Greene explains in the *New West Indian Guide*, the life Beka chooses for herself 'is both the result of her understanding of Toycie's fate and the means by which she would thwart its repetition'. Toycie's life is continued in Beka's, when Beka accepts the essay prize that Toycie would have won had she lived. Beka carries on Toycie's pursuit of excellence.

The novel's development suggests that in time, our acceptance of a loved one's death can help us to move on from pain to fulfilment of dreams and plans we shared with that friend. Thus a part of that friend lives within, helping to make us stronger and, in Beka's case, wiser.

Social change

The thematic changes discussed so far relate to the lives of individuals; the theme of social change through education applies to the whole society, indeed to the entire West Indian region. Another writer, Earl Lovelace, tackles the theme of social change and erosion of the old, traditional culture in *The Schoolmaster* and *The Wine of Astonishment*.

For young, black, working-class West Indians in the 1950s, education was a means toward social and economic betterment. After Beka passes first form her family sees her transformed from a 'flat-rate Belize Creole' into someone with 'high mind'. Hence education in a good school is seen as a 'treasure', and those lucky enough to get this chance are urged to make the most of the opportunities and advantages that such schooling will open up.

At the same time we have already noted that the demands of the educators, the American nuns, sometimes put severe pressure on Caribbean students to become imitators, 'fakes' and 'phonies', pretending to be better than their own families – this is how Belizeans view Father Nunez. In addition, a foreign dominated education will teach students little of their own history and culture – Sister Gabriella admits this (p. 94), and Zee Edgell focuses in *Beka Lamb* on filling this gap.

So when Granny Ivy complains that 'these schools around here teach children to... look outside instead of in' (p. 147), she speaks correctly for the period. The world of school had little to do with the world of home, little to do with traditional culture, 'the old ways', so Miss Winny notes that 'nowadays everybody so genteel with all this education... that they shame to do the old things' (p. 76). Under colonial rule, people were encouraged to break with the traditional culture, to move away from their roots.

The novel shows that while education for progress is a good thing, this should not mean a total and alienating break with the older ways, but rather a compromise, grafting 'the best of the old onto the best of the new' (p. 90). Beka's Carib teacher seems to be moving in this direction, and when Beka organises a programme of Belizean folk songs as well as classical tunes for the visiting American nun we are meant to see this as a positive change.

Political change

The last important thematic change to be analysed is political change, from colonial dependence to national independence. In the 1950s, nearly every West Indian territory began to demand more of a say in the running of its government. *Beka Lamb* contains a fictional account of the political stirrings in Belize at this period, as the author has acknowledged in several interviews.

The political information is given to the reader mainly through the discussions of Granny Ivy and Mr Lamb. Resentful of the unfair exploitation of Belizean labour and resources by the British government and the economic hardships brought about by the arbitrary devaluation of the Belizean dollar, certain Belizeans had formed a new party. This is called the People's Independence Party – in fact, the title was the People's United Party, which was supported by the General Workers Union. Opposition to the party comes chiefly from those Belizeans who believe that the P.I.P. are accepting funds from Guatemala, a neighbouring country that claims Belize as part of its territory. Mr Lamb warns that 'Our politicians are new to politics, and they'd better watch which countries they accept aid from including Guatemala' (p. 7).

Issues are further complicated by Belize's divided stand on West Indian federation. The British Government and its followers support the linking of the British territories, but the P.I.P. oppose this move until Belize is independent. As Granny Ivy, loyal to the P.I.P., explains: 'The British Government, and the British Lumber Company want federation because they would get more cheap labour' (p. 55). Since the British Lumber Company and the government own most of the land (p. 54) and only landowners can vote (p. 167), Belizeans have little choice but to work for the 'starvation wages' offered, while 'colonial exploitation took and is taking abroad the little wealth we possess, leaving us impoverished and destitute' (p. 107).

In protest, the party has sent a petition to the king of England requesting more self-government by Belizeans, economic improvements and an end to federation plans. For this they are accused by the British Governor and his followers of disloyal, anti-British and communist sympathies. As the novel ends, the party-dominated City Council is dissolved and leaders Prichad and Gladsen (in reality, Leigh Richardson and Philip Goldson) are imprisoned for sedition.

Anti-British sentiments (pp. 54, 107, 108 and 167) signal the beginnings of a strong nationalist movement in Belize, which have since resulted in universal suffrage, increased self-government and, in 1981, independence. *Beka Lamb* records some of these early political changes and is thus, as Roger Bromley points out in his article 'Reaching a Clearing: Gender and Politics in *Beka Lamb*' as much about the growing up of Belize as it is about growing up in Belize.

Colonialism has resulted in economic underdevelopment, but

also a feeling that everything in Belize is second-rate and any improvements must be made by outsiders like 'the Company' (p. 3). The depressing description of the state hospital where Toycie is taken (chapter 20) reinforces the negative effects of colonial rule: money made from the lumber industry is sent out of Belize, while the city's main hospital is falling apart from lack of funds, and no one seems to be able to do anything to rectify the situation.

However, the political changes hint at a change in Belizean thinking – a desire to move from passive acceptance towards active patriotism that will make improvements. It seems that Beka is one of the new young nationalists – certainly her pride in her country is evident when she changes the label on Toycie's guitar from 'Made in Spain' to 'Made in Belize'. The novel's ending is optimistic for Belize's future despite the party's problems. As Uncle Curo says, 'Belize people are only just beginning' (p. 167).

When Beka feels that she too has made a beginning (p. 167), she is being linked with her young nation. Some critics, like Charles Hunter, in his review of *Beka Lamb*, feel that the 'political undercurrent is at most peripheral to the plot of the novel.' Others, like Roger Bromley, claim that the personal and the political are inextricably linked, and that the novel deals as much with the decolonisation of women as with the decolonisation of Belize.

While the political events and crises do coincide with Beka's own growing pains, it is with Beka that we are primarily concerned. On occasion, however, Beka speaks for Belize. When she feels pity and disrespect in the look of the American nun, she is moved to defiance: 'If you think all Belize people break down so easily you are mistaken!' (p. 161). Here, she is the voice of her nation, determined to stand up and move forward into a new era, to claim the respect and the wealth they have worked for over generations. On the political, cultural, social and the personal levels, the theme of change is fully explored.

STRUCTURE AND STYLE

Time

Beka Lamb is structured fairly simply along chronological lines. Chapters 1 to 3 establish the central characters and set the scene in terms of the physical, social, cultural and political environment. Chapters 4 to 25 follow in flashback the earlier events that have wrought a change in Beka's life. Chapter 26 completes the day in Beka's life that began in chapters 1–3 and continued in chapter 25.

What is completed in the flashback is an episodic reconstruction of a critical period in Belizean history, and in the lives of Beka and her closest friend. But it is also the completion of an imaginary wake for Toycie. Hence, midway through this mourning period (chapter 12) is a *real* wake, another death; after this, Beka's fortunes improve while Toycie goes down deeper and deeper into depression.

The neat structural patterning makes for a balanced and symmetrical work. For example, the novel begins with the end (Beka's story ends with her winning of the essay-prize), and ends with a reference to her 'watch night for Toycie' (which marked the beginning of the flashback). Again, *Beka Lamb* begins and ends with the paralleling of Beka's joy at her achievement and her memory of Toycie; this complements an important resolution in the work – the fact that she achieves partly through Toycie, partly because of what she has learned from Toycie's failure.

Several critics have commented on these techniques of balance, parallel and contrast. Heidi Ganner, in her article 'Growing up in Belize: Zee Edgell's novel *Beka Lamb*', points out that 'impartiality is a key feature in the novel', and that the author always establishes a balance between opposing views and attitudes. Charles Hunter comments on the balance and contrast in mood and atmosphere: 'the magic of it all and the tragic of it all: Sunday walks and 'Nancy stories on the one hand, on the other hand, drab hospital, depressing mental home and hurricane'.

Narrative perspective

The narrative perspective, or point-of-view, moves between objective authorial reportage (including dialogue) and Beka's own consciousness. On the very first page of the novel, we can see the transition from one to the other. The first paragraph is clear, simple reportage of facts – on such and such a day, in such and such a place, this happened. We are then told what 'her Gran said' – incidentally, note the immediate link between Granny Ivy and political debate.

The narrative returns to what seems to be objective description ('The front veranda was in its evening gloom...'), but moves unnoticed into Beka's mind, for the flowering vine 'reminded Beka of the wreaths at her great granny's funeral'. The greater part of the narrative follows this pattern, and it is to the author's credit that we rarely notice a clash between the two perspectives.

Heidi Ganner thinks there is some inconsistency at times, and notes several episodes in the flashback section that are supposed to be seen through Beka's consciousness, but which in fact move out of her mind and are described in the third-person by the author, thus acquiring a sense of dramatic independence but interfering with the pretence at Beka's intimate reminiscing – see, for example, the authorial intrusion 'In those days...' (p. 112). Roger Bromley, in contrast, claims that the apparent disjointedness is not inconsistency, rather a kind of fluid, exploratory narrative style that is fragmented yet connected, as are consciousness and experience in real life.

Perhaps these varying opinions result from the different time frames within which the narrative functions. On one level, we have the author, in the 1980s, writing about Belize in the 1950s; on another, there is Beka in the 'present' (November) remembering events in the 'past' (April); and at other times, she recalls events in the more distanced past (her little brother's death, her Sunday walks with Toycie and so on). Confusion and overlapping of these time-frames may cause confusion about narrative perspective.

Beka's consciousness

Generally, Beka's thoughts and feelings are not explicitly articulated but suggested. In chapter 7, Mr Gordillo asks if she has passed first form. Rather than answer, she shakes her head; rather than look at him, she fidgets with the display case in front of her. She becomes aware of the noise and the smell in the shop, and that Mr Gordillo's face has gone red with disappointment. She feels hot, itchy with prickly heat. She politely refuses Mr Gordillo's sympathetic gift of chocolate, leaves as fast as she can, and 'ran all the way home' (p. 40). Nowhere in this episode are we told that Beka feels ashamed and embarrassed; nevertheless, her actions and the uncomfortable sensations she experiences convey this information quite clearly.

The narrative style of Beka's point-of-view tends to follow the leisurely, roundabout pattern of a sensitive consciousness, filled with distractions, explanations, memories, overheard conversations and worries. At the same time, many of these details, memories or distractions are not there simply to imitate the workings of her mind; they may have some important connection with the story's development. For example, as Beka runs home from Mr Gordillo's shop, she recalls an earlier lunchtime when she returned home to find her mother's father on a rare visit. All the information we gather from her memory is that Beka didn't like her grandfather much, and Mrs Lamb seems tense in his presence.

At the same time, the memory is related to Beka's present

shame and embarrassment, since this grandfather stopped her mother's education (as Beka's father may stop hers); and because this grandfather (who's illegitimate, as Toycie's baby will be) has no loyalty to Belize and would rather invest his money in England – in other words, he is related to those who hold the colonial attitude that nothing local is valued, respected or successful. Beka has been determined to fight such opinions, although by her failure she seems to be supporting the pattern of 'breaking down'.

We should note the subtle links, associations and connections that lie beneath the narrative surface and have to be searched out. This applies equally to Beka's growing-up process: her knowledge of life's meanings will only come through reflection on its complex and hidden secrets that she must work out for herself. Understatement is a feature of the deceptively simple narrative style.

Language

The language in which Beka's thoughts, feelings and observations are expressed is the language of objective narrative too: simple, standard West Indian English. The language used to represent the speech of nearly every character in the book, excepting the American sisters, is a modified form of Belizean Creole. However, perhaps due to the natural colloquial tone in which Beka's thoughts are couched, there is little obtrusive contrast with the Creole language that she uses in dialogue. Compare, for example, Beka's fears for Toycie spoken aloud in her great-granny's room (p.77), with her thoughts on Toycie's pregnancy and expulsion (p.121). The first is in a form of Creole, the other in informal Standard English; *both* sound perfectly realistic for the consciousness of a troubled young girl.

Authorial explanation and comment

A great deal of information about Belize is casually inserted into authorial reportage. Chapter 1, just over five pages, conveys many of the institutions (school, jail, 'Government House') and the economic deprivation (Miss Eila has no running water; little to eat; can't afford a wake for Toycie) that characterised British rule in the 1950s. A specific society is being described, and as the details accumulate rapidly – place names (p. 4); popular music (p. 4); the custom of beating children (p. 19); popular dishes (p. 26); the importance of a funeral and a wake (pp. 62 and 72); and so on – this society becomes more and more concrete and real for us. Using the device of the girls' Sunday walk, we are given a virtual guided tour of the city. Certainly a Belizean critic such as Dean Barrow, in his review of the novel, praises the rich textural evocation 'of the sights and sounds of old Belize'.

By and large, necessary information is assimilated into the narrative. The word 'sampata' may be unfamiliar, so the author uses a pair of alternative phrases to ensure we understand the meaning: 'hook your sampata' / 'buckled her... sandal' (p. 30). The explanation is contained effortlessly in the flow of action. The same technique is used to clarify 'chicharron' (p. 79) and 'fresco' (p. 98). Even where no specific definition is given, the, general meaning becomes obvious in context – the 'punta' (p. 76) is plainly an energetic dance (in fact, a Carib dance).

Occasionally authorial explanation is intrusive, not assimilated into action or dialogue. This applies to the complex issue of Belize's racial composition. In the 'maskman' reference that opens chapter 6, we learn about the racial makeup of 'Creoles' and 'Caribs'; we also gather that there's little intermarriage between the groups. Here, the explanation is contained in an episode that is thematically relevant, reinforcing the idea that racial prejudice can lead to tragedy (as in Toycie and Emilio's case). But elsewhere, authorial explanation is more noticeable and seems like social commentary rather than part of Beka's consciousness: 'But, as is often the case, wealth, class, colour and mutual shyness, kept the children of the two families apart' (p. 51). Would the young Beka be likely to articulate the situation this clearly and concisely?' We become aware of the author's voice providing elaboration of class and colour relations.

Generally, however, information on Belize's pot pourri that is necessary to the plot is provided without distracting from the story. Perhaps to make sure there is no bias in Beka's opinions and perceptions, she is right in the middle of the class and colour hierarchy – product of a dark father and a fair mother, and from a family that is neither rich nor poor, she is a perfect 'in-between', representative Belizean Creole.

Foreshadowing

Other stylistic techniques contribute to the novel's meaning in less obvious ways. There are several instances of foreshadowing – suggestions or predictions of events that later come to pass. When Beka reflects on Toycie's involvement with Emilio she is afraid for her friend, because Granny Ivy had predicted that she 'would wind up with a baby instead of a diploma, if she wasn't careful' (p. 47). Of course, this is what happens, with tragic results.

Again, the picture of Toycie and Emilio walking together 'in the direction of the old cemetery' (p. 48) also hints that her connection with Emilio will in some way lead to death – and indeed this proves to be the case. Strictly speaking, since we know from the first chapters the outcome of the story, such foreshadowing seems unnecessary. Stylistically, however, the technique serves to remind us of how the final state of events is dependent on previous episodes, and to create an impression of inexorable movement towards crisis and resolution. It also serves to provide a certain amount of pathos, in that we can interpret hints and pick up predictions long before the young protagonists, who are unaware of the forthcoming tragedy.

The natural environment

A less direct method of conveying information is through the treatment of the natural environment. In the novel, the natural world is more than a background for characters – it often reflects their moods, or mirrors a change in their fortunes. At the caye, Beka is depressed and anxious, and feels deserted by Toycie. All the fun has gone out of her seaside holiday and this is reflected in the landscape: 'grey clouds, grey island, and empty, grey sea all around' (p. 49). The scene looks the way Beka feels: lonely, overcast and grey. And when Toycie turns her back on Beka to join Emilio, Beka feels that the whole island, the scene of childhood happiness, has 'turned away, turned away from old friends who needed the splendour of its healing' (p. 49). The caye is personified, given human qualities, and Beka feels that everyone has turned his/her back on her, including the island.

In the flashback chapters, the weather often suggests the state of human affairs. On the day Toycie vomits in the chapel, it is hot, sticky, overcast, which contributes to the atmosphere of tension; a crisis is coming. When Beka finally faces the painful memories of the past in her 'wake', the rain symbolises spiritual release and renewal. And the external hurricane the Lambs experience prefigures the 'tidal wave' of grief that 'crashed in Beka's brain' at the news of Toycie's death (p. 158). At the end of the novel, the natural images of 'sunshine and seawater' reflect the healing of Beka's hurt – now her memories are 'bright and clear' (p. 171).

Sometimes, the environment may embody a more universal meaning. The Sibun bush where Beka and Toycie spend childhood holidays is described as a kind of Eden, beautiful and tempting, but with hidden dangers. This is evident in the mango grove, where the sweetest fruit come from a tree that grows right over 'a deep sloping hole in which house garbage was thrown and burned' (p. 136). A general truth is implicit here – the most tempting pleasure is often accompanied by dangerous consequences. Both Toycie and Beka learn this lesson in the course of the story.

Other natural symbols

Other natural symbols in *Beka Lamb* include certain flowers that are linked with aspects of character. The bougainvillea vine symbolises Beka's personality – at first wild, undisciplined, 'all flash and no substance', in need of radical pruning. But it is strong, and after her time of testing Beka determines to live again, just as the bougainvillea stump, cut right down, decides to put out new shoots (p. 158). Beka's hardy spirit is compared with Toycie's, which is linked to the delicate, shy plant (the mimosa, which Jamaicans call 'shame a-lady') that closes all its leaves at a touch. Toycie, without the protection and support of a family, is terribly vulnerable and after her betrayal by Emilio can only close herself off from life's touch.

The stephanotis vine that is stripped from the Lamb's verandah by the hurricane leaves the house naked and vulnerable; so is Beka, after the emotional 'hurricane' that ravages her at the news of Toycie's death. In time, she builds up protective defences against such pain, like the vine that grows once more, to shade and protect the privacy of the verandah.

Lilla Lamb struggles to cultivate English roses, unsuited to tropical climate and soil, in preference to local flowers. This symbolises her desire for improved social mobility, for modernity, for 'culture' that is non-Belizean, or at least, of a 'higher' social class than the world of Cashew Street. By the end of the novel, Beka has taught her to value local blooms – that is, to be proud of her Creole traditions, to acknowledge the value of the 'old ways' too.

Finally, flowers in general symbolise hope: so Toycie's hopes ('gay, bright flowers', p. 32) transform the poor, dingy reality of her life in poverty-stricken surroundings. Similarly, the vines and flowers that are re-planted after the hurricane's destruction, symbolise the hope of the Lamb family, and of human nature generally, that after death and despair, life will once more be renewed and, in fact, blossom.

Imagery

Images add meaning in the novel by suggesting important aspects of character, mood or incident that are not stated explicitly. Sometimes images occur in clusters, recurring in the text and sharing some similarity. Taken all together, such a strand of imagery may point to meaning not immediately apparent.

One such strand centres around the idea of safe, secure, enclosed space – the 'private place' of the verandah (p. 1); the snug rocking chair (p. 16): the protection of a family wrapped around you (p. 27); the comfort of Greatgran Straker's bedroom (p. 77); the 'sanctuary' of the Institute (p. 108) and the refuge of the house during the hurricane (p. 156). Yet sometimes the enclosure-images become restrictive and claustrophobic. Toycie's withdrawal into herself, her refusal to leave the house (p. 125), leads to her imprisonment in the asylum (p. 160). And the home that offers Beka security becomes a refuge, then a hiding place, run-down, dusty and gloomy (p. 160). The ambivalence of this image cluster suggests that although Beka, the insecure adolescent, often wishes to return to the safe protection of childhood, she cannot hide away from life, no matter how difficult it may be. Maturity means venturing out, perhaps nervous and alone, but with the courage to meet life head on.

Another strand of imagery has to do with immersion in water – water enveloping, drowning and obliterating a person. From Beka's initial dream of falling into the filthy river (p. 7), to Toycie's actual fall (or leap) into the creek (p. 127), such images are implicit threats that life's mistakes can overwhelm the young women and sweep away their dreams and hopes. Note Toycie's attraction to the sea (p. 15), which is beautiful, but dangerous – and it is by the seaside that she yields to Emilo. The sea-image as negative is also seen in the chapel where Toycie, in trouble, is separated from her friend by 'an ocean of polished floor' (p. 85).

For Beka, this image cluster suggests impending loss of control; even her sanity threatens to be swept away. Examine the occasions on which she experiences 'the roar of seawater in her head' (p. 91); the 'tidal-wave' in her mind (p. 43); the roar of crashing water in her head (pp. 128 and 158), and note how the image of engulfing water recurs in times of emotional stress. Luckily, Beka does not allow herself to be swept away, and it is significant that her final memories of the sea are benign and unthreatening (p. 171).

Incidentally, the creek of Beka's dream is full of 'excrement' and 'filth'; the canal Toycie falls into is the same water into which Miss Eila empties her stinking slop-bucket (p. 1); and when Beka thinks of washing clothes for a living, it's in a 'swampy yard' with 'the stink from the outside latrine' (p. 22). The smell of latrines, excrement and waste emptied into creeks and canals is associated with the poorer side of town, and indeed with poverty – the fate of Toycie and others like her when life sweeps away their opportunities. This 'life' is more like death, a living death, and thus the unpleasant smells later in the novel are linked with 'the odour of death' (p. 130), 'a muddy stench' of decay (p. 157), preparing for Toycie's own end, which, in some ways, we feel to be preferable to the life of dirt and stinking poverty that would have been her fate.

Finally, there are a number of references to thick woods or forest, through which Beka and Toycie must find a way, an open space, a clearing (see pp. 10, 136 and 137). These images convey once more the threat of life's misfortunes overwhelming the individual, who must struggle bravely to make her own 'clearing', her own safe space in the midst of confusion. Of course there are other recurring images (for example, the 'watermelon' Beka feels weighing down her chest) all of which add further levels of meaning to what seems at first the simple story of two young girls.

CHARACTERISATION

A careful study of the novel's themes supplies information about the roles played by various characters in the development of the work. The main point to remember is that Beka is at the core of the book, and other characters are only important in that they affect her in some way.

As Roger Bromley points out, individuals assume representative functions, identified with specific ideology orientations that impinge on Beka's developing consciousness. Thus other characters represent aspects of her own personality that she must somehow come to terms with and integrate – Toycie represents Beka's vulnerable, insecure side; Granny Ivy her nationalistic tendencies and so on. And again we note the technique of balance, since the novel sides with no one viewpoint but gives a balanced picture of the people and the motives that are at work in the community.

Beka herself has been dealt with at length; we can look briefly now at the other important characters.

Toycie

Toycie's mother went off to America when she was two years old and her father disappeared before she was born. A senior attending St Cecilia's Academy, she is Beka's dearest friend and, in many ways, is everything Beka would like to be. Slim, brown-skinned, attractive, she is poised on the brink of adulthood. Aware of the value of education, she is clever and hardworking, and gifted musically. Toycie is a loyal friend to Beka and her family, and is grateful to her own aunt, hoping to improve Miss Eila's life once she graduates.

But Toycie isn't unbelievably perfect. She and Beka are close 'because Toycie remembered what it was like to be fourteen' (p. 34); she's able to dream and make-believe like any youngster, and to enter into Beka's games without seeming condescending (see pp. 44–45). Indeed, at times Toycie is the more childlike of the girls, more innocent and trusting, and more unwilling to face the truth of her pregnancy. Toycie is, in fact, more vulnerable than the stronger Beka, and quicker to collapse under pressure. Toycie and Beka are balanced against each other in the way they respond to the difficulties of growing up.

The social stigma of being an unwed mother is clearly illustrated through Toycie's character. Rejected by her parents, the nuns at her convent school, her Mestizo boyfriend and his family, Toycie's life falls apart.

Beka's Family

To a certain extent the three adults in Beka's family represent different aspects and attitudes of Beka herself. This is natural as she has obviously been shaped by them, and her opinions formed by them.

Bill Lamb is a 'self-made man', who has worked his way out of poverty to a position of financial security; he is a dedicated, hard-working employee. He loves his family, has a temper when provoked, but is fair and proud of Beka's achievements. He's also very responsible and always ready to help in a crisis, not just in his own family, but also the Qualos.

However, what's important in the presentation of 'Daddy Bill' is his socio-political position. Socially, he wants 'to progress in the business world of the town, but he was quite satisfied to remain in the class where he was comfortable. He had no use for 'artificiality and sham' (p. 21). Thus he criticises Beka for pretending to be something she is not when she puts on airs or tells lies. Bill Lamb doesn't wish to be like the Hartleys, the Creole elite, and reminds Beka that the Lambs are 'humble people'. At the same time, he demands respect for his class, as is evident in the argument with Sister Virgil (pp. 119 and 120).

Politically, he represents the view that supports neither recriminations over past injustices in Belize (p. 37) nor a dramatic break with the British in the near future. He advocates progress through economic self-sufficiency and moderate change, as practised in his own life, along with gaining international support for Belize.

Granny Ivy represents the opposite perspective in the contemporary political debate. As a nationalist, Granny Ivy is an active member of the new political party, which is fighting for Belize's independence. For her, the treatment of Belizeans by their foreign rulers has been disgraceful, on a national as well as an individual scale (see her reference to Mistress Tate-Sims on p. 56). She constantly reminds Beka of the injustices perpetrated 'before time' and because of her distrust of British rule, Granny Ivy wants complete national independence for Belize. Since the new party upholds these aims, she is a loyal and devoted member; in the long run, it is her patriotism that inspires her and she is furious with what she sees as Beka's lack of commitment to Belize (p. 147).

Granny Ivy is also important as a source of information in the novel, and functions as the link between Beka and 'the old ways' of her ancestors. Granny Ivy best demonstrates the figure of the Creole matriarch who transmits values, beliefs, customs and traditions. She's a kind of 'cultural memory' and Beka's interest in her country's political history shown in her essay, for example, is the result of her grandmother's influence. Granny Ivy is strong-willed, outspoken, strict and quite violent in her threats, but ultimately devoted to her son and his family. She's energetic, always bustling around in the kitchen or off to political meetings with her dear friend, Miss Eila. Her character provides an alternative reading of Belize's colonial history from a female perspective.

Lilla Lamb complements her husband in several ways. He is dark-skinned; she is light. He doesn't wish to climb the social ladder; she wishes to move to a 'nicer' area. He dislikes pretension or putting on airs; she wants Beka to wear her hair in the latest fashion, and to rid herself of any 'low down' habits or associations with the wrong people, like National Vellor.

Lilla is overly concerned about the 'old' ways poisoning the 'new'. Her own unfinished education makes her desire all the more her family's progress towards modernity and 'cultivation' – note that she defends the British-trained radio announcer's 'cultivated voice' (p. 163). For this reason, she wants Beka to keep away from the old ways ('a bunch of superstition') that might 'poison' the new society. This contempt for traditional culture is a bone of contention between her and Granny Ivy. She repeatedly warns Granny Ivy to stop filling Beka's head with old-time stories. Lilla also exhibits her own insecurities about Caribs and Creoles sharing a similar history. But it is patriotism that motivates Mrs Lamb's desire for social and economic progress, not wishing her class or country to appear in a bad light. Beka shows something of this attitude when she is ashamed of Miss Arguelles's behaviour, who she sees as 'letting creoles down' (p. 104).

Lilla Lamb is rather fragile, subject to headaches that force her to rest often. She's pretty, well-spoken and, despite her constant correction of Beka, loves her daughter and hates to see her unhappy. She learns from Beka not to distrust the 'old ways' so much, and to value Belizean natural beauty as much as imported British flowers.

Other characters

The other characters in the novel are less important and generally serve as stereotypes – undeveloped personalities who represent certain generalised social 'types' of people.

Miss Eila is the poor, hardworking and longsuffering guardian, who has worked all her life for Toycie and is cruelly disappointed. But rather than blame her niece, she fights with Granny Ivy for a fairer society where they'd have more rights. In her life, we see all the ills of underdevelopment and poverty that Toycie and Beka have a chance to escape and that the Lambs, in their different ways, hope to end through social and political change.

Emilio Villanueva is the spoilt son of a fairly well-off family, who have sold their caye property to finance his education. Handsome, athletic and popular, he is nevertheless a callous manipulator, a hypocrite and finally a coward. His belated offer to marry Toycie – when he graduates, that is – strikes no one as sincere after his pompous moral condemnation of her (p. 109). We never get a glimpse of Emilio's thoughts or feelings, and so he remains for us a type of the selfish Casanova who uses, and then deserts, women.

Mrs Villanueva appears in only one light, that of an affected, snobbish social climber. We gather this from little details such as her impressing her friends by mentioning the full name of the agency her husband works for, and in the contrast between her gushing protestation of love for Toycie (p. 65) and the hostile, contemptuous attitude with which she regards Toycie's association with her precious son (p. 103). Toycie is acceptable until she presumes to become more intimate with the family; at this point, Mrs Villanueva reveals her true opinion, and it is very like the opinion about Miss Arguelles: 'Only the creole, no culture.'

The nuns are the Sisters at St Cecilia's, Beka's and Toycie's school. Sister Virgil represents the negative and Sister Gabriella the positive side of the nuns. Sister Virgil's personality is reflected in her physical appearance and bearing – cold, sharp, strict, unfeeling and uncompromising in her moral and social judgements. Sister Virgil's lessons are based on her belief that sex is associated with sin. She preaches that women must learn to control their emotions and her sole objective is to ensure that in keeping with Victorian principles, her school produces women who are good wives and mothers. Sister Gabriella who approaches Beka about entering the essay contest being held to commemorate the 75th anniversary of the Sisters of Charity, is large, plump, kind and smiling, the exact opposite of the headmistress in appearance and character. As Charles Hunter says in *The Christian Herald*, a Catholic Belizean newspaper, Sister Virgil is more concerned 'with the immaculate floor, the spotless reputation of St Cecilia's Academy and her own inviolable conscience, than the tainted soul of poor Toycie'. But she is balanced by the atoning Sister Gabriella whose understanding and encouragement help develop Beka's potential, and who represents the positive application of foreign education.

Father Nunez is balanced by Father Rau in the same way as the two nuns. Father Nunez, whose family history is detailed in chapter 14, is not important as a character but as a test case of how foreign and local values interact. His orthodox Catholic doctrine, especially on morality, takes no account of the way most people live in Belize.

Other characters, like Greatgran Straker, Mr Gordillo and Beka's classmates, have very little part in the novel's action and thematic development, and will not be discussed here.

SECTION FOUR

COMMENTARIES

Chapter 1

In this chapter we learn about Beka's family and the city in which they live. On the one hand there are the shops, bars, lights, noises and people of the street; on the other, we hear of His Majesty's Prison, Government House and the British soldiers at Airport Camp. One set has to do with the life of the Creole inhabitants; the other refers to the forces of authority who rule the people. We are meant to note the differences between them. We also note the juxtaposition of the school and the prison, both designed to educate Belizeans to conformity and to eliminate any dissident voices.

The mood of the chapter is quite solemn, even sad – there's a mention of 'wreath' and 'funeral' on the very first page – despite the pleasure at Beka's success. Miss Eila still grieves for Toycie, and Beka, hidden on her sheltered verandah, has been too frightened and upset to think about death until now. The rest of the novel will relive the girls' friendship and its tragic end.

Chapter 2

This chapter continues to fill in details of the current political situation in Belize. There seems to be change and unrest everywhere; trouble may come from Guatemala, from those who are tired of British rule or from the new party. Since Mr Lamb thinks the Caribbean is in a 'mess', it is suggested that such problems existed throughout the West Indies at that time, as people began to claim control of their own country's resources. Belize's unrest is representative of increasing demands for autonomy in the Caribbean during the 1940s and 1950s.

We also learn a little more about where the members of Beka's family stand in the social hierarchy – they're not rich, but they are better off than Miss Eila, and Mrs Lamb wants to see Beka progress even further.

Beka's dream at the beginning of the chapter is symbolic. She dreads falling into the filthy creek water, as Toycie 'fell' morally, was degraded and disgraced. Beka feels in the dream, as Toycie felt in her time of trouble, that people around were only looking and laughing, without really trying to help. The fear that Beka wakes with (note the heavy rhythm of alliteration in the description of her breathing 'like a pestle pounding plantains'), is the same panic that she has been feeling for some time, as noted at the end of chapter 1.

Chapter 3

Much background information is supplied about Belize and Belizeans in this chapter. Some details are not particularly relevant to the story, but help us to understand the way the society works and thus prepare us for attitudes and behaviour patterns we shall encounter in later chapters. For example, casual mention is made of different clubs for the different racial groups in the city. This helps us to note that these groups did not mix socially, so that we are prepared for the opposition the Toycie–Emilio relationship will meet.

The incident of the circus bear dying at Barracks Green reinforces the theme of death, which is built up as the novel progresses. It sets the tone for the wake that Beka is keeping for her friend Toycie, whose death was also sad and unnecessary.

Chapter 4

We see in this chapter that being a 'phoney' is not limited to telling lies. Beka judges herself and her family as superior because of appearances – how she looks, the airs she puts on, the size and colour of her house – what Mr Lamb calls 'artificiality and sham'. He thinks such concerns signify her shame at what she and her family really are.

The author is by no means suggesting that self-improvement is wrong: merely that it should not involve becoming a 'phoney', pretending to be better than others, looking down on one's origins. Beka seems to be learning this lesson, for the chapter ends with her admitting her failure, and trying not to lie again, even if the truth about herself is less impressive than the 'phoney' facade she has been presenting.

Chapter 5

The theme of change is carried on from the previous chapter, as social changes are coming. In her great-grandmother's time, the working class could not even protest their unfair treatment; now trade unions have been formed to protect workers' rights, and soon many people will have a vote.

Beka too is changing. Mr Lamb had compared her to the bougainvillea vine, 'all flash and no substance' (p. 24). When the bright, strong plant is cut down by her father, this suggests a cutting away of Beka's 'flash', her 'phoney-ness', her lies and superior airs. Now she will have to prove her real worth instead of hiding behind pretended achievements.

Chapter 6

The incident of changing labels reveals the growing patriotism of Belizeans at the time. As Beka explains, Guatemala's claim to Belize came through Spain originally and so, accordingly, all connection with Spain must be avoided. Claiming that the beautiful guitar was made in Belize shows faith in Belize's potential; perhaps one day their nation really will produce such excellence.

There is irony, however, in the fact that Creole Toycie is so fond of a young 'pania' with a Spanish name. We see how different threads are being woven together as the novel develops – social, cultural, political, racial and personal factors all influence each other.

Chapter 7

Flower symbolism is further developed in this chapter, as Beka is again associated with the hardy bougainvillea that her grandmother hopes will grow anew. Mrs Lamb is linked with the delicate rose, which needs 'richer soil' than this poor neighbourhood can provide.

However, both Beka's parents are loyal Belizeans, not hoping to move away to England (like Mrs Lamb's 'half-bakra' father) or to America (like Toycie's mother). The episode of the guitar labels in the previous chapter, with its implications of national pride, is reinforced here when Mrs Lamb says that her husband has 'got faith in this country'.

Once again, we note a darkening mood in Granny Ivy's pessimistic view of life, where 'peace and happiness only visit in spells', and in the reference to death and the cemetery. These are used to build up a gloomy atmosphere, foreshadowing Toycie's death.

Chapter 8

In literature, natural imagery is commonly used to tell us of the inner feelings of characters, as with Beka's tension at the start of the chapter. So when the beach front is described as 'deserted' with 'grey clouds, grey island, and empty, grey sea all around', the author is portraying Beka's feelings of loneliness, deserted by her friend, with nothing to look forward to but grey, empty days. The emphasis placed on this desolate landscape suggests further unhappiness to come for the two girls.

Chapter 9

In this chapter, we note Beka's growing determination to do well at school and her maturing awareness of her good luck in having a loving, stable family. We also learn about the growing unrest in Belizean society that, like Beka, wants to grow up and take responsibility for itself. Note Beka's memories of the parade honouring the English Governor and his wife, and recall that the predominant colours were the red, white and blue of the British flag; yet the Belizean Beka sees these colours in terms of her own tropical landscape – white of sea foam, blue of the sea and red of hibiscus. Long after the British flag is gone, these natural colours will remain.

The most important development in the chapter is the growing intimacy between Emilio and Toycie. Although not explicit, the description of Toycie's 'shamefaced' appearance and Emilio's dishevelled clothing suggests that their relationship is now a sexual one. The setting of this development – the cemetery with its broken gravestones – and the news of Greatgran Straker's death are devices that cast a pall of doom over the lovers.

Toycie's recognition of how alone and unprotected by family she is only serves to heighten the dangerous situation she is in if she should become pregnant. For, as Beka has pointed out, Emilio is unlikely to marry her and without finishing school, Toycie could hardly support herself, much less a child. Although we can work out these facts, Beka and Toycie feel only a confused sense of something being wrong – we know more than they do, and this heightens the story's pathos.

Chapter 10

When a character says or does something in a novel that we, the readers, know to be false or spoken in ignorance, the literary term for the contrast is irony. Mrs Villanueva, socially superior and snobbish, could never love Toycie as a daughter; neither does she know that Emilio has told Toycie he'll marry her after graduation, and make her a real daughter-in-law to Mrs Villanueva. Thus her statement is ironic, and although Beka says nothing, the suggestion is that she's aware of Mrs Villanueva's true feelings hidden behind her forced politeness.

Note that Beka clearly represents a new era in her family's history. Greatgran Straker had commented on Beka's distanced relationship with the land; she's expected rather to excel in the area of education, and to represent her family there.

Chapter 11

We learn about Mrs Lamb's character in this chapter, which needs careful reading. Although light-skinned, and therefore 'superior' in the old, racially stratified Belizean society, she was poor, and knows what it was like to be looked down upon. In order to progress, she wants to cut ties with the past.

Many West Indians feel that because their ancestors were

slaves or indentured servants, this is something to be ashamed of. But, the author implies through Beka's teacher, there is no need for this shame; in fact, keeping the old traditions is a good thing, for you cannot know yourself if you don't know where you come from. Hence Beka is able to teach her mother something new, and when she shouts that she would marry a Carib man when she grows up, she is saying that she is not inhibited by the prejudices and fears of the older generation.

Her wish to keep a record of her family's racial and cultural history is a sign of her pride in that ancestry, complicated as it may be. It will help her to find her true identity, unadorned by lies or pretensions.

In this way, Beka can make something creative out of her tendency towards untruth. Art, therefore, can be seen as therapeutic for the individual who is trying to come to terms with the difference between fantasy and reality.

Chapter 12

In terms of social observation, the chapter provides an accurate record of some West Indian customs and practices. The dishes and beverages that are popular are named, as are the folk-stories that are common, and the dancing and spirit possession that may occur on semi-religious occasions. These are some of the actual traditional practices that were referred to in previous chapters. As long as communal events continue to take place, the old ways will live on, just as Miss Eila claims Granny Straker's spirit will live on in Beka.

For Beka, the atmosphere is clouded by her fears for Toycie. The continuity of patterns of irresponsible male behaviour, from slavery days down to the present, is taken for granted by the older women. Miss Flo is in no way ashamed of her illegitimate great-grandchildren. But Beka and Toycie are of a different generation, and because of the sacrifices made for their education, a different type of behaviour is expected of them.

Again, implicitly the repetition of references to extra-marital relationships, unwanted pregnancies and illegitimate children, suggests to us that Toycie is in trouble.

Chapter 13

The dominant mood in this chapter is one of increasing tension. The weather is oppressive – the sky overcast, the day hot and sticky. The effect of the weather on people is also detailed – tempers will be short as it is 'the kind of day that fries the brain making a person dull of eye, heavy of tongue and unable to concentrate' (p. 80).

Beka's clothes are uncomfortable and constricting, aggravating her prickly heat. Her mother is anxious, her grandmother impatient, her little brother troublesome. Even her friendship with Toycie seems strained. All these details achieve an atmosphere of impending doom – the day promises nothing but trouble.

Confronted by a statue of the Virgin Mary, symbol of the nun's purity and perfection, Toycie nearly faints. Note that the school is a modern one, and there will be no toleration here for the old Creole behavioural patterns – like Miss Flo's grand-daughter's childbearing.

Ironically, it is in the beautiful chapel, light and airy, that the crisis occurs. In this holy place, before the eyes of the whole school, Toycie vomits. We're made to focus on the 'slimy mess splattered on the sunlit splendour of the chapel floor' – note the alliteration and onomatopoeia, as the hissing 's' sounds conjure up horrified gasps from the girls, and the low, angry voice of Sister Virgil spitting out her disgusted order to Beka to 'clean this up'.

The last image of Toycie is her following the headmistress, as a prisoner to trial. Some chapters rely for effect on rapid action, others on dialogue; here it's the detail which captures mood that is most important.

Chapter 14

Many West Indian writers have criticised colonial education in the pre-independence Caribbean. No matter how well intentioned, foreign educators caused problems while instilling their values and priorities into youths of a different culture. And since the schools prepared students for 'the London examinations', little local history was taught – nor, indeed, anything else that told of West Indian life.

As Mrs Lamb told Beka, the church – here, through schooling – had the power to improve the lives of black people. The trouble is that Father Nunez's orthodox Catholic doctrine, especially on morality, takes no account of the way most people live in Belize. It is the conflict between foreign and local values that makes Beka frustrated and causes her dislike of Father Nunez, not realising that he, too, is an unhappy product of this very conflict.

The introduction of Sister Bernadette reminds us of other references to insanity – crazy National Vellor, the 'crazy house', the climate testing everyone's sanity. Sister Bernadette is Irish (and therefore, presumably, anti-British) and has been accused of 'talking politics' to the students, so Sister Virgil forbade her to teach. Because she is denied her job, she feels she is going mad. Denied an opportunity to fulfil themselves, women may indeed withdraw from reality. The point is that such 'madness' is less their own fault than that of a rigid system, which tries to force them into unfamiliar, unfulfilling ways of life.

This prepares us for Toycie's predicament. We also see that Sister Virgil's cruelty to Sister Bernadette makes it unlikely that she'll be kind to Toycie, whose Creole world she is totally ignorant of.

Chapter 15

In this chapter, we are given further details of conflicting political opinion in Belize, and see that people can become emotional in their arguments. Miss Arguelles's display of anger is thus set in context. Note that although Beka feels shame at Miss Arguelles's vulgarity, she is implicitly showing a connection with her – they are both Creoles.

The news of Toycie's pregnancy has stripped the girls' childhood world of all joy and beauty. The words used to describe the 'magic' that Toycie brought to her humble surroundings at home (p. 98) or in the streets (p. 101), are 'enchanted', 'sparkles', 'blazing', 'adventures', 'fairytale', 'delighted', 'transform', and 'painted mansions'. But now these positive images of light, happiness, magic are darkened by 'the erosion of Toycie's spirits and confidence' (p. 94).

A clear comparison is made between Mrs Villanueva's immaculate appearance and Toycie, who looked 'a trifle scruffy'. Although Toycie is the one in need, Emilio (also described in terms of superiority, as a 'prince') is far more attentive to and supportive of his mother. We may be reminded of the two visions of woman in Father Nunez's sermon – the pure, superior Mary and the fallen Eve, degraded by the 'sins of the flesh'. Like so many men, Emilio pays homage to the former while using and discarding the latter.

Chapter 16

The juxtaposition of Belize's exploitation by the wealthy and the foreign, with Toycie's exploitation by the richer, socially accepted Emilio, brings together the political and personal threads running through the novel. We are meant to see that a human compromise in both situations could have averted chaos and tragedy.

There is irony, however, in the speaker's call for national unity, when we see that even at the level of personal relationships between Creole and 'pania', such terrible difficulties arise.

Once again, in Emilio's cowardly excuses for discarding Toycie, we see the double-standard by which men and women are judged. It seems fine for a 'modest Catholic boy' to 'fool around' before marriage; but this makes the girl immoral and unfit for marriage, even though he has been partly responsible for the transformation. There seems to be a flaw in Catholic teachings used here to justify such unfair reasoning.

Beka has realised the value of education 'so that her life does not break down that way', and the chapter ends with her studying hard. Toycie also knows this – her only wish now is to graduate. But we know that with a baby, her wish will not be fulfilled.

Chapter 17

The description of Toycie's gradual disintegration – in body, in spirit, and now in mind, 'as if every sensible thought had left her' – recalls other references to madness in the novel, particularly that of Sister Bernadette, going crazy because she's denied her job, her main purpose in life. Again, we are led to expect Toycie's final breakdown and to understand the reasons for it.

The expectations that lead the convent school students to play certain roles, 'to leap through the hoops of quality purposely held high by the nuns' (p. 112), are also responsible for mental breakdown and confusion. They find themselves acting a part, putting on airs, living a lie at school; their own Belizean culture is seen as vulgar, undisciplined or morally degraded, and so they confess their guilt every day – 'through my fault, through my most grievous fault' (p. 113). The purpose of Sister Gabriella's talk with Beka is to explain that it is not her fault, but the fault of two cultures, the old, native one and the new, foreign one, in conflict. Beka's generation must try to make a useful pattern for life from these clashes.

Chapter 18

This chapter clarifies the moral and social conflicts between Catholic and Creole values. The values of sacrifice and hard work on Miss Eila's part to achieve a precious education for her niece are unimportant to Sister Virgil. She is linked with the stone-eyed statue of the Virgin Mary, and with the hardness of reflecting glass. As Mr Lamb says, she uses religious teaching as a stick to beat Toycie, rather than, as Christ advocated, to offer her mercy and hope. For Sister Virgil, there can be no compromise with the Creole culture, which she judges as harshly as she does Toycie.

Note that while Toycie is to be punished by losing all opportunities, Emilio Villanueva will give up nothing; again, we see the double-standard for male and female.

The change in Toycie is signalled in physical appearance, and in symbolism. Her eyes are dull, her uniform unbelted, she can hardly stand upright. She's too 'disoriented' to appreciate her friends' concern; in fact, they appear as nightmare strangers to her. Toycie is withdrawing from reality, as the little plant with the purple-white flowers shrinks from Beka's touch. No one can help now. Too hurt and shocked to bear any more, Toycie is cut off from life, hope and friendship. Beka realises her friend's child-like vulnerability, and knows she won't have the strength to cope with her misfortune.

The only note of hope in this chapter is the potential friendship of Beka and Thomasita Ek, who is Mayan.

Chapter 19

We can contrast the beginning and the end of this chapter. Beka realises the beauty of her school environment at the moment she may lose it all, if she should fail. Her classroom is described in detail – breezy, clean, lit by sunlight, surrounded by blue sea and sky; the glossy desks, the neat row of books are lovingly grouped to make an ideal picture. In fact, the picture represents the 'treasure' of education, which generations of Belizeans have worked for so that Beka and Toycie might reap the benefits.

Compare this scene with National Vellor's humble room – poor, smelly, with a rough bed, a fly-stained calendar and the bedraggled, half-crazy woman who lives there, reduced to a life of prostitution because, as she explains to Beka, she had no opportunities. The lesson is clear. Without school, Toycie also has nothing and no hopes of achieving a life beyond poverty and degradation. No wonder she has given up hope.

References to impending madness begin to accumulate. Toycie's withdrawal and inability to understand what is happening, clearly demonstrate, as Miss Eila explains, that 'she's gone someplace so far inside herself that she forget us back here' (p. 125). Even Emilio's belated offer to marry her after he graduates (which no one believes, anyway) has failed to make her respond. Again, there's the strange National Vellor with her 'luminous, glowing black eyes' and her eccentric dress. Finally, Beka's own mind becomes disturbed by these awful events. Note the description of her vision blurring; the crashing flapping noise in her ears; the scream that she wants to bay at the moon; her heart beating too rapidly – all of her senses are stretched to the limit as hysteria 'threatened to engulf her'. However, we know Beka is strong and has grown up in the last few months. She will survive and learn from the experience.

Chapter 20

Although short, this chapter is fairly horrifying. Details of dirt, blood, medical instruments, pain, screams and fear are deliberately piled one upon the other. It seems too much to bear and Beka fears for Toycie's life, convinced that she smells the odour of death. Few of the institutions in this novel have helped or sheltered Toycie, whether it be school, church, hospital, or – in the next chapter – mental asylum.

The physical suffering at the hospital seems less frightening than the indignities to come at the 'crazy house'. The unkempt Toycie has to be forcibly held down, screaming and fighting, so as to be given sedation. In a way, Toycie, as Beka knew her, is dead; she has gone for ever.

Chapter 21

The description of the asylum is not as horrifying as that of the hospital, despite Beka's fear – conveyed in a building up of associated words like 'drugs', 'medicinal smell', 'dangerous', 'heart beating', 'gripping the bars', 'painful', 'concentration camp' (p. 133). The truly disturbing sight is poor Toycie, totally out of touch with the present.

We see the changes in Miss Eila too. She is thinner, greyer, dressed in black, with sunken eyes. She feels she has failed Toycie, and only the thought of returning to the safety of their ancestral home keeps her spirits up.

Look carefully at the description of the Sibun forest. Although it seems at first like a paradise, full of perfumed plants and abundant, sweet fruits; we are also aware that danger lurks within – snakes, getting lost, Tataduhende. In paradise innocence was corrupted by evil and death came into the world; Toycie, whose innocence has been corrupted, is in danger in the earthly paradise of the Sibun.

The matron's words on the treatment of women by some men in the West Indies sums up this thematic topic. Instead of respect and care, the sexual relationship leads to men's revenge and the humiliation of women. The author is clearly implying that something is wrong with certain male–female relationships in our region.

Finally, the reference to Beka's changing, although she's not sure if it's for better or worse, harks back to Sister Gabriella's words at the end of chapter 17. Perhaps out of all this suffering, Beka will gain in some way.

Chapter 22

In this chapter we see Beka, vulnerable and afraid of being hurt, finding refuge in her schoolwork; this echoes the description in chapter 1 of her sheltering behind the stephanotis vine on the verandah, sorting out her thoughts about Toycie's tragedy before facing the world again. In fact, it is through her research, her attempts to understand Belize's past and present, that she will finally understand and accept the complexity of events.

Granny Ivy warns that this foreign education is teaching young Belizeans to look outside, to look abroad for fulfilment, instead of seeing the value of their own culture. Although this is an important comment on colonial education, Granny Ivy doesn't understand that Beka's wish is inspired by fear lest she be caught in the trap that ruined Toycie.

Chapter 23

As tension builds and disaster threatens, we see changes taking place within Beka. Her growing academic competence, and the resultant independence and self-respect this gives her, is linked with the political maturity of a Belize now ready for independence and self-government. Throughout the novel, we have seen comparisons of Beka with her country. Now, as we see Belize moving towards autonomy, we are prepared for Beka's growth into adulthood.

However, the author reminds us that these are early days in Belizean political development, by using the metaphor of stilt men to describe the new political leaders. Although raised above the ordinary by their power, their positions and policies are yet tentative and uncertain.

The ominous approach of the hurricane is linked with stories of death and destruction from the previous storm of 1931. And death is linked with Toycie in the comment about the 'crazy house' blowing out to sea 'with all the patients in it'. Although no longer at the asylum, Toycie is associated with it, and her destruction hinted at in this reference.

Chapter 24

The chapter is full of balances and contrasts. Although the actual hurricane is over, news of Toycie's physical death (her social and mental destruction have already occurred) assaults Beka like a fresh storm. The images of wind and rain crashing in her mind are used to suggest a crisis of grief; they have signalled moments of fear and anxiety in the past. Yet at the very moment when everything seems to be breaking down, there is a breakthrough: the bougainvillea vine puts out new shoots. So Beka too has a spirit that will survive and grow, remembering Toycie but not desolated by grief for her.

Again, the stephanotis vine, representing Beka's sanctuary as her emotional scars heal, is blown away; this suggests Beka is exposed and vulnerable to pain. Yet it too will root again, this time anchored to a more secure trellis; life will renew itself after the most severe misfortunes. Hence the chapter ends on a note of happy optimism.

Note Beka's defiant mental reply to Sister Gabriella; 'If you think all Belize people break down so easily you are mistaken!'

(p. 161). Again, she is identified with her country's resilience. The image of a new garden to be planted by Mrs Lamb – this time of tropical flowers – is evidence of Belizeans' faith in the future of their country.

Chapter 25

The story is coming to an end – or rather, returning to the start, just as Beka's time of testing is coming to an end, with a new beginning. She's a different girl now, more sensible and responsible, confident of her own worth without needing to embellish her achievements with lies. Again her development is linked with that of Belize – both new, young, full of hope and ambition.

Beka has learned from Toycie – to follow her good example, and not to repeat her mistakes. Thus she'll transcend Toycie's life, unconsciously obeying Sister Gabriella's injunction to 'go as far as the limitations of your life will allow' (p. 116). The mood of the chapter is generally that of an energetic holiday spirit. Even the angry crowds are somehow infused with an excitement that is optimistic.

Chapter 26

The day that began in chapter 1 is now over, and a new day has begun. The rain has stopped, the stephanotis vine has not only grown back after the hurricane, but is blooming sweetly. An atmosphere of optimism prevails, looking forward to new possibilities and at peace with the past. Although it's clear that Beka will 'never forget Toycie and all they'd been through together', the pain associated with her memory has been assuaged by her 'wake'. And in a sense, this wake has clarified the lessons Beka has learned from it all; so that, at the end, she is a better and wiser young woman.

SECTION FIVE

GENERAL QUESTIONS

1. Examine the characters of Mr Lamb, Mrs Lamb and Granny Ivy as representing different perspectives and different aspects of Beka herself.

2. Choose three minor characters and say how each contributes to the novel.

3. Evan X Hyde claims that 'The tragedy of Toycie is a compound of race and class politics, small town ignorance, and the rigid rule of the Conservative Church in the 1950s.' Discuss this view.

4. Roger Bromley states that 'Women in Belizean society are doubly devalued: as colonials, they are disenfranchised and as females, they are second class citizens.' Discuss this view of women in the novel.

5. How far does the Catholic Church influence events and affect people in the novel?

6. Discuss several ways in which Beka's development is paralleled by that of her country.

7. 'Lying is a way of denying Beka's true identity.' Analyse the theme of self-acceptance in the text.

8. Write an essay on the use of imagery in *Beka Lamb*.

9. Balance is one of the features of *Beka Lamb*. Explore how this is achieved in relation to characterisation, structure and style.

10. Would you agree that alienation and love are the two main themes in *Beka Lamb*?

11. Discuss the importance of race, class and colour in *Beka Lamb*.

12. Discuss the role of education and its effects on character in the novel.
13. Discuss the treatment of political events in *Beka Lamb*.
14. Do you agree that Beka has changed from a 'flat-rate creole' into a person with 'high mind'?
15. Discuss Mr Lamb's opinions regarding Mr Ulric's business and why it is doing badly in light of Beka's tendency to put on airs and lie.
16. 'Sometimes I feel bruk down just like my country.' Explain how Beka's comment is linked with Belize.
17. Why are Granny Ivy and Mr Lamb in disagreement over the decorations for National Day?

FURTHER READING

Brodber, E. (1981). *Jane and Louisa Will Soon Come Home*. London: New Beacon Books.

Bromley, R. (1985). Reaching a Clearing: Gender and Politics in *Beka Lamb*. *Wasafiri* 1 (2), pp.10–14.

Ganner, H. (1984). Growing Up in Belize: Zee Edgell's Beka Lamb. In: MacDermott, D., (ed.) *Autobiographical and Biographical Writing in the Commonwealth*. Barcelona: Editorial AUSA, pp.89–93.

Greene, S. (1984). Six Caribbean novels by women. *New West Indian Guide* 58 (1.2), pp.61–74.

Hodge, M. (2000). *Crick Crack, Monkey*. Oxford: Heinemann, 2000.

Hunter, C. (1982). Beka Lamb: Belize's First Novel. *Belizean Studies* 10, pp.14–21.

O'Callaghan, E. (1983). Driving Women Mad. *Jamaica Journal* 16, pp.70–71.

THE CARIBBEAN WRITERS SERIES

The book you have been reading is part of Heinemann's long-established Caribbean Writers Series (www.caribbeanwriters.com). Details of some of the other titles available in this series are given below, but for a catalogue giving information on all the titles and the African Writers Series write to:
Heinemann Educational Publishers,
Halley Court, Jordan Hill, Oxford OX2 8EJ;
United States customers should write to:
Greenwood Heinemann, 361 Hanover Street,
Portsmouth, NH 03801-3912, USA.

MICHAEL ANTHONY

Green Days by the River

In *Green Days by the River*, Michael Anthony conveys the confusion of a teenager growing to maturity and the difficult choices that have to be made. The novel explores the complexity of human relationships and the need to come to terms with our discoveries about those around us. A perceptive novel about a boy on the edge of adult responsibilities.

The Year in San Fernando

Francis has spent his first twelve years in his 1940s Trinidad village. Leaving behind family and childhood, Francis is sent to the city as servant-companion to old Mrs Chandles. In San Fernando he must meet the demands of the ailing old lady and her imposing son. As the sugar cane ripens and the seasons change, Francis's loneliness gives way to awakening sexual interest and growing self-confidence. Michael Anthony's semi-autobiographical novel delicately portrays a young man's rite of passage into the adult world.

The Tide of Intrigue

This is both a thriller and an exploration of the corrupting power of the drug peddler's get-rich-quick ethos. Once an individual is drawn in, a life of deceit begins, and all relationships become tainted with the hidden crime.

Cricket in the Road

In his introduction to the collection of short stories, Michael Anthony says that he started writing stories as the result of a competition in a Trinidad newspaper. 'What was new and refreshing to me was the treatment of local themes and the use of the local idiom. It made the literature look 'real' to me... My main desire was always to write about something I actually knew and experienced...'

ZEE EDGELL

Time and the River

Time and the River is about freedom and slavery, hope and betrayal. It tells the story of people who don't own their own land or time, or even their own bodies. Leah Lawson is the daughter of a slave owner and a slave woman in Belize. In dreaming of a better future, Leah must make some difficult choices. Her life takes drastic turns, changing her from slave into mistress, and forcing her to take the lives of her family and best friend into her own hands.

Beka Lamb

Set in Belize, *Beka Lamb* is the record of a few months in the life of Beka and her family. The story of Beka's victory over her habit of lying, which she conquers after deceiving her father about a disgrace at school, is told in flashback. Her recollections begin when she wins an essay prize at her convent school. Beka's reminiscences stand in lieu of a wake for her friend Toycie. The politics of the small colony, the influence of the matriarchal society and the dominating presence of the Catholic church are woven into the fabric of the story to provide a compelling portrait of ordinary life in Belize.

MERLE HODGE

Crick Crack Monkey

A revealing novel of childhood about Tee, who must leave her home with all its warmth and spontaneity for the pretentious middle-class society of Aunt Beatrice to be made socially acceptable so that she can cope with the caste system of Trinidad. Alone and alienated, Tee struggles to understand the world she now inhabits. Her acceptance of Aunt Beatrice's values would mean rejection of the people that she knows and loves.

EARL LOVELACE

The Schoolmaster

Earl Lovelace's novel tells the story of an isolated rural community coming into contact with the wider world. The villagers learn, only too cruelly, that 'progress' can mean the destruction of cherished values. Paulaine Dandrade wants to see progress, and helps to persuade the other villagers to build a school. But he never imagines that the arrival of the schoolmaster will bring violence and tragedy to his own family. *The Schoolmaster* is a story of love, hope and betrayal, and the nature and inevitability of change.

The Wine of Astonishment

Bolo is a champion stickfighter – tall, good-looking, the bravest of all the young men in Bonasse. When, time and time again, he sees his people humiliated by change and American troops, his instincts as a leader come to the fore. The stand he makes, however, takes on bizarre and tragic forms.

BERYL GILROY

Frangipani House

Set in Guyana, this is a beautifully written protest at institutions which isolate and a way of life which denies respect and responsibility for the weak.

VICTOR S. REID

The Leopard

Set in Kenya during the Mau Mau rebellion, this is the story of Nebu, a simple Kikuyu who was once a houseboy for an English plantation owner. Now he is a Mau Mau who takes pleasure in witnessing the deaths of his former white masters. After a raid one day, Nebu leaves his Mau Mau gang and embarks on a journey of self-discovery that *Time Magazine* described as 'an imaginative masterpiece'.

CURDELLA FORBES

Songs of Silence

Songs of Silence is a colourful patchwork of observations of life in 1960s rural Jamaica, as seen though the eyes of a young girl. Held together by the sure and simple voice of a child, this powerful narrative is interspersed with the whisper of adult reflection, rendering the accounts at once sensuous and disarmingly honest.

GWYNETH HAROLD

Bad Girls in School

The atrocious behaviour of Taj, Cally and Katty has disrupted the school. The principal, determined to bring back order, has isolated them for expulsion. However, the soft-hearted chairman of the school board, with the help of the naïve young librarian, thwarts her plans. A special programme is set up for the rehabilitation of the girls. Will the bad girls reform, or simply continue to tear down all that is good around them?

V.S. NAIPAUL

Miguel Street

The vibrant community of Miguel Street is brought to life through the eyes of a child. The growing boy delights in their humour and eccentricity, but he gradually becomes aware that no-one can run from reality forever. *Miguel Street* is both a nostalgic view of childhood recalled in exile and a study of the limitations of life in 1940s Trinidad.

MARLENE NOURBESE PHILIPS

Harriet's Daughter

Set in Toronto, two girls, Margaret – a second generation West Indian immigrant, and Zulma – coming from a joyous life with her grandmother in Tobago to a tense and unhappy relationship with her mother and step-father, become friends and comrades in various adventures.

PAULETTE RAMSAY

Aunt Jen

Sunshine, a young Jamaican girl, is desperate to know and understand her identity. Written as a series of letters to her absent mother, *Aunt Jen* traces the changing attitudes of a child entering adulthood as she begins to realise and accept the truth behind her mother's departure.

MARIA ROBERTS-SQUIRES

October All Over

Set in the aftermath of the Grenadian revolution, this novel tracks the parallel lives of two generations of Grenadians. Racial and personal prejudices join political differences in a climax that threatens both the individual characters and the country as a whole.

NAILAH FOLAMI IMOJA

Pick of the Crop

A varied cast of characters support Leroi in his quest to be Calypso King in the Pick of the Crop competition. But he also has to learn to handle popularity and success, impress his girlfriend's friends, and stop those who are keen to sabotage his achievements.